IMAGES of America

SOUTH NASHVILLE

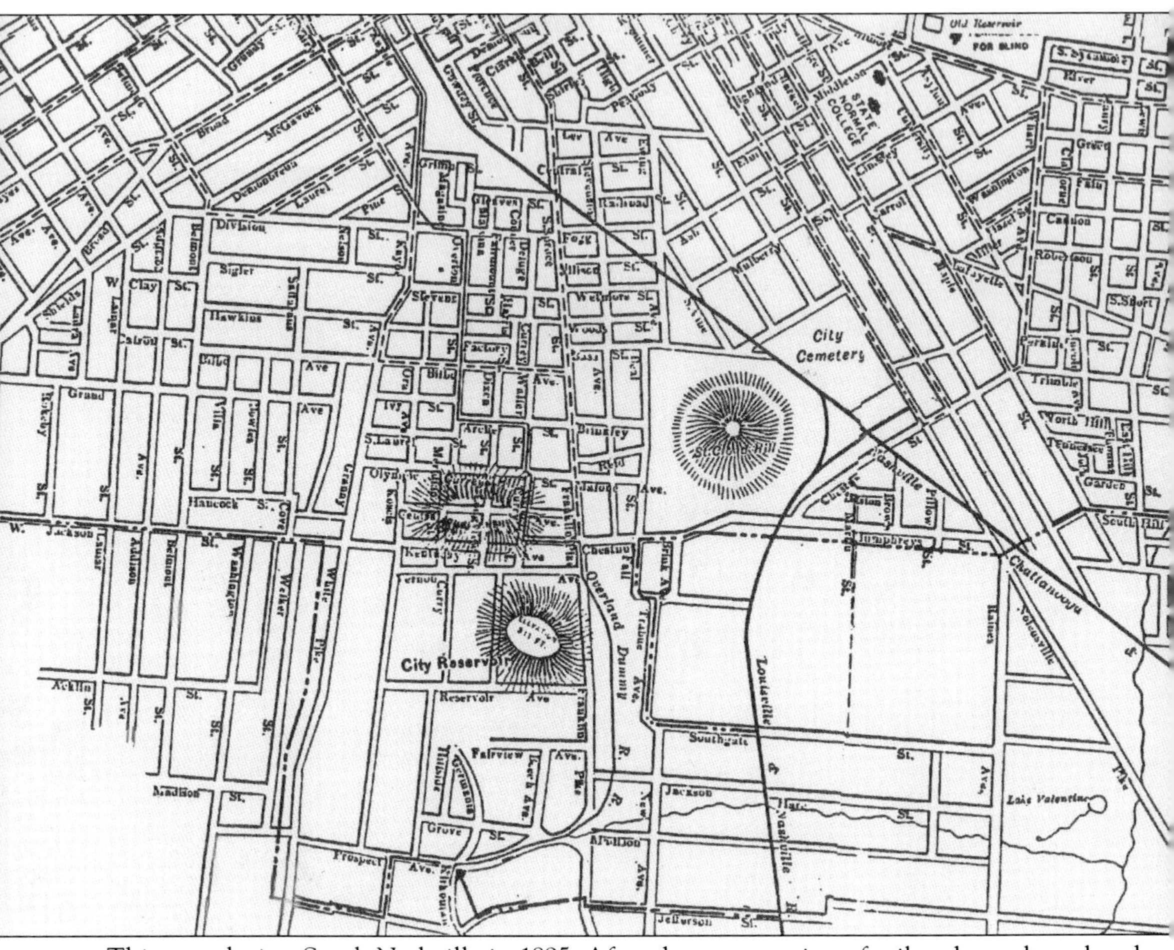

This map depicts South Nashville in 1895. After the construction of railroads southward and during the years following the Civil War, the city expanded rapidly toward the south, attracting mills, factories, and other industries. As a result, the construction of residential neighborhoods soon followed. From the beginning, this district has attracted a culturally diverse population due to the availability of blue-collar jobs. During the next 150 years, the area considered South Nashville would eventually expand to the county line after the creation of metropolitan government consolidating the city of Nashville and Davidson County in 1963. (Metro Nashville Archives.)

ON THE COVER: For more than half a century, Cascade Plunge, located at the Tennessee State Fairgrounds in South Nashville, was a favorite attraction during an era when air conditioners were not available to most folks. The large swimming pool offered something for every age group, including a diving board, water slides, a snack bar, and other concessions. The attraction evokes great memories for baby boomers who remember spending enjoyable times with friends during hot summers. The swimmers in this scene take time to pose for the photographer in this scene from the mid-1950s. (Nashville Public Library, Special Collections.)

IMAGES
of America

SOUTH NASHVILLE

Ralcon Wagner

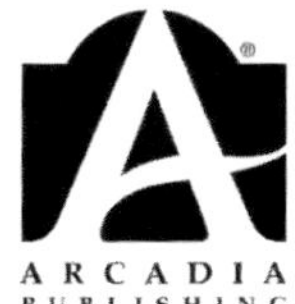

ISBN 978-1-4671-2807-0

Published by Arcadia Publishing
Charleston, South Carolina

Printed in the United States of America

Library of Congress Control Number: 2017948495

For all general information, please contact Arcadia Publishing:
Telephone 843-853-2070
Fax 843-853-0044
E-mail sales@arcadiapublishing.com
For customer service and orders:
Toll-Free 1-888-313-2665

Visit us on the Internet at www.arcadiapublishing.com

To my mother, Bernadine "Bunny" Wagner, who taught me at a young age to appreciate and respect history

Contents

Acknowledgments		6
Introduction		7
1.	The Early Years	9
2.	Transportation	17
3.	Life in South Nashville	23
4.	Churches and Schools	39
5.	Notable Buildings and Landmarks	49
6.	The Tennessee State Fair	61
7.	Municipal Airport and Berry Field	85
8.	Interstates and Urban Renewal	105
Bibliography		127

Acknowledgments

Behind any successful project, there are always dedicated and talented people with a passion for keeping history alive, instrumental in helping to put all the pieces together. I gratefully acknowledge the many great folks that helped to bring this history to printed form. First and foremost, my gratitude goes out to the professional staff at the Nashville Public Library, my initial contact for getting the photographs and information needed. This includes the staff of the Metro Nashville Archives: Ken Fieth, Drew Mahan, Kelley Sirko, Leanne Garland, and Sarah Arntz. Also equally important was the support from Andrea Blackman and Elizabeth Odle of the Nashville Public Library, Special Collections Division. This project would not have been possible without the assistance of Megan Spainhour of the Tennessee State Library and Archives, the National Archives, Pamela Yeager and Marcy Rae Werner with the Archives & Special Collections, University of Louisville, and Dr. W.O. Greene III, Frank Holt, Fannie Fischer Jones, Hank Sherwood Jr., Mary Beth Walton, and many others that contributed materials. Thanks and appreciation goes to Angel Hisnanick of Arcadia Publishing for her continued encouragement and patience from the beginning. I would like to recognize Gene Hawkins and James D. LeCroy, historians who spent much of their lives in South Nashville. Both shared their memories and spent hours assisting the author with proofing and fact-checking the captions. I would like to thank my wife, Rita, for her continued patience and willingness to assist with proofing the copy and providing fresh ideas.

Introduction

During the past 150 years, the district of what has commonly been referred to as South Nashville has changed dramatically over the course of time, with its boundaries and makeup continuously evolving and expanding. From the city's earliest beginnings, the development south of the business district has always played an important role in the city's growth. As new industries and neighborhoods were built, the city rapidly grew southward. Until the 1850s, there was primarily farmland south of the corporate boundary, with the exception of Nashville's public cemetery and the University of Nashville.

The earliest ground transportation heading south of Nashville business district consisted of privately owned turnpikes that diverged in all directions from Nashville. Turnpikes were built by landowners who collected tolls from those on horseback or animal-drawn wagons. The more prominent roads included Franklin, Nolensville, and Murfreesboro Pikes. In time, the turnpikes were taken over by local governments and improved with gravel and, decades later, with pavement. These later became primary corridors for long-distance travelers. During the 1920s, the primary highways would become part of the federal highway system.

The Nashville & Chattanooga Railroad was chartered in 1845. Just six years later, the railroad operated the first train between Nashville and Antioch, representing the first operational railroad to operate in Tennessee. In 1860, a second railroad, the Tennessee & Alabama Railroad, would begin operating trains between Nashville and Columbia, Tennessee. With two railroads slicing through South Nashville, lumberyards, mills, and other industries grew along the rights-of-way.

The following year, the city was in the middle of the Civil War, with much of the fighting battles taking place to the south of the city including the Battle of Nashville. In 1862, a star-shaped barricade, Fort Negley, was built by the Union army atop St. Cloud Hill, roughly two miles south of downtown. Named for Union army commander general James Negley, it was the biggest inland fort constructed in the United States during the battle.

Universities have had a presence in South Nashville beginning with the opening of Davidson Academy in 1785. During the next four decades, the college evolved through several name changes, becoming the University of Nashville in 1826. The George Peabody State Normal School opens as part of the University of Nashville in 1875. This was ultimately incorporated as the George Peabody College for Teachers in 1909. During this same time, colleges catering to young women were being established across Nashville, with many of these located south of the city. In 1890, the Belmont College for Young Women was established at the former Acklen estate. In 1906, another girls' preparatory school, Radnor College, opened in the Grandview Heights community on Nolensville Pike several miles south of the city.

During much of the late 19th century, entertainment was limited to the populace of South Nashville. Two popular attractions would open during 1890s that would become the biggest attractions for both Nashville natives and tourists alike. Glendale Park would attract people of all ages seeking a respite from the city. For more than 50 years, Cumberland Park provided enthusiasts of thoroughbred horse racing a grand place to enjoy the sport.

The 1930s and 1940s brought many changes to South Nashville. The city's new municipal airport located five miles southeast of the city on Murfreesboro Road opened on November 1, 1936, bringing the region into the age of commercial aviation. The facility, renamed Berry Field in 1939, was served by two airlines operating dozens of new routes.

As automobiles became more affordable, the highways were soon widened to accommodate the additional traffic. By the late 1950s, these roads and frequent traffic jams could not adequately handle the throngs of motorists. In 1956, the national Interstate Highway Act was passed during the Eisenhower administration.

New construction began on the new superhighways, but also with a cost—established neighborhoods would be demolished as buildings and even entire streets would be removed to make room for the new interstates displacing thousands of residents and businesses. South Nashville would be hit hard—blocks of dense population were leveled for the new right-of-way that would eventually carry Interstates 65, 24, and 40. In many cases, inner-city neighborhoods to the south of downtown Nashville were destroyed and soon began to deteriorate. Many structures in the chopped-up districts were deemed by city leaders as substandard housing.

During the 1950s and 1960s, hundreds of structures thought to be an urban blight were torn down to make way for new public housing developments, city parks, and widened streets. The stark contrast changed the landscape abruptly. As a result, many residents, moved out of the city to more modern suburbs.

On June 28, 1962, the voters of both Nashville and Davidson County voted in favor of creating a true consolidated government, the first of its type in the nation. Later that year, county judge Beverly Briley was elected as first mayor of the new metropolitan government. Effective April 1, 1963, Nashville and the county became a single entity, resulting in a myriad of small towns outside of the old city limits being absorbed into the enlarged metro area. Several incorporated cities within the county opted to remain independent, retaining their zoning regulations, existing police departments, and other government offices, but would still be included in the new Metropolitan Nashville–Davidson County. Outlying cities in southern Davidson County making this decision included Berry Hill, Oak Hill, and Forest Hills.

After the 1963 consolidation, it was now common to hear people refer to anything in southern Davidson County as South Nashville since the southern city limit and county line were now the same. South Nashville continued to grow rapidly throughout the 1960s. The city was propelled into the jet age with the opening of a new terminal at Berry Field in 1961. The construction of new shopping developments in suburban areas made shopping more convenient than ever. In late 1967, a shopping center, Hundred Oaks Shopping Center, opened on Thompson Lane and became one of the largest retail centers in the South. While it was not the first enclosed mall in the region, it was certainly the largest and most impressive.

In recent years, South Nashville has experienced growing pains and challenges as older established neighborhoods undergo widespread gentrification, attracting younger families and demographics.

One

The Early Years

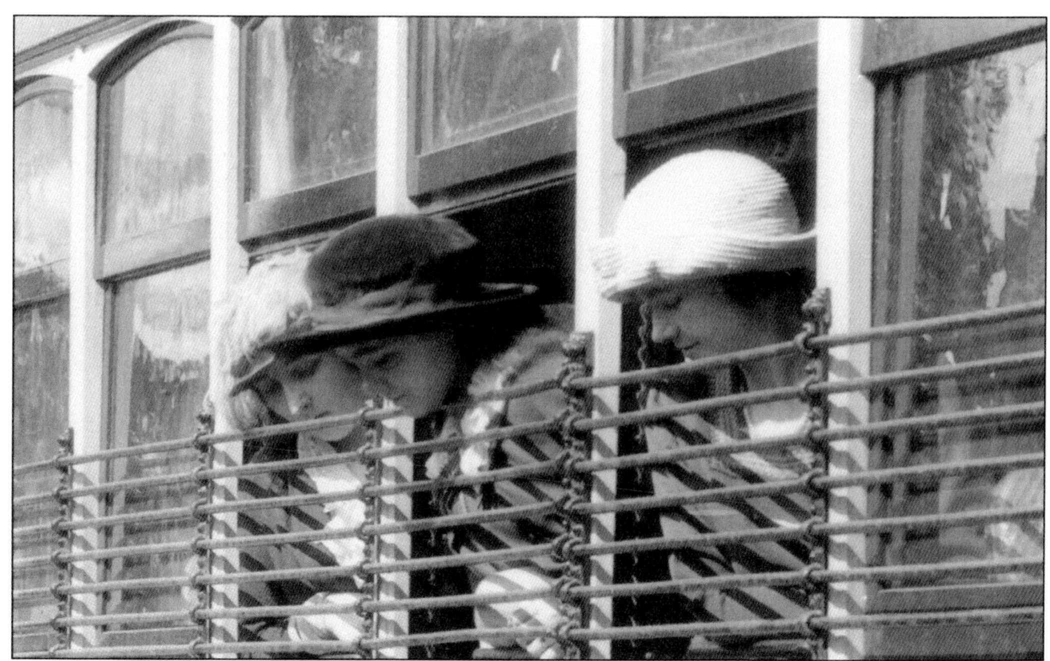

Between the mid-1860s and 1920s, South Nashville experienced many changes. Following the Reconstruction Era, the area witnessed industrialization and accessibility to higher education. New electric streetcars and affordable automobiles made mobility easier than ever to visit destinations such as Cumberland Park or the Glendale Zoo. Here, three young ladies enjoy themselves on a Glendale streetcar in the early 1920s on just such an outing. (Ralcon Wagner collection.)

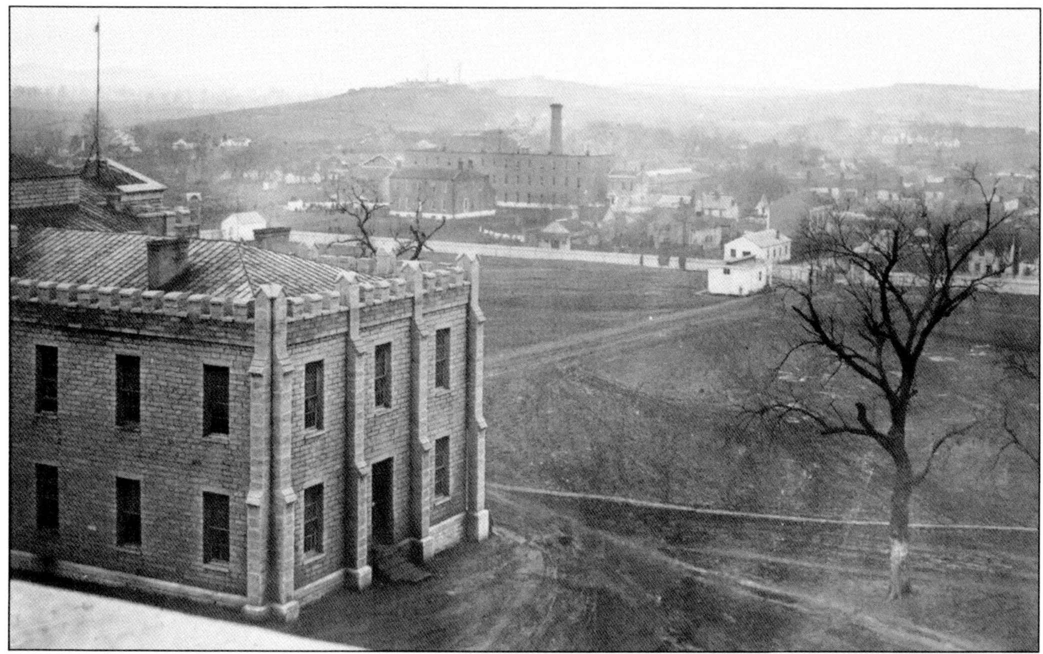

In one of the earliest images of South Nashville, looking southeast from the roof of Lindsley Hall, the University of Nashville can be seen in the foreground in this December 1864 view. In the distance, the newly constructed Fort Negley can be seen. (Tennessee State Library and Archives.)

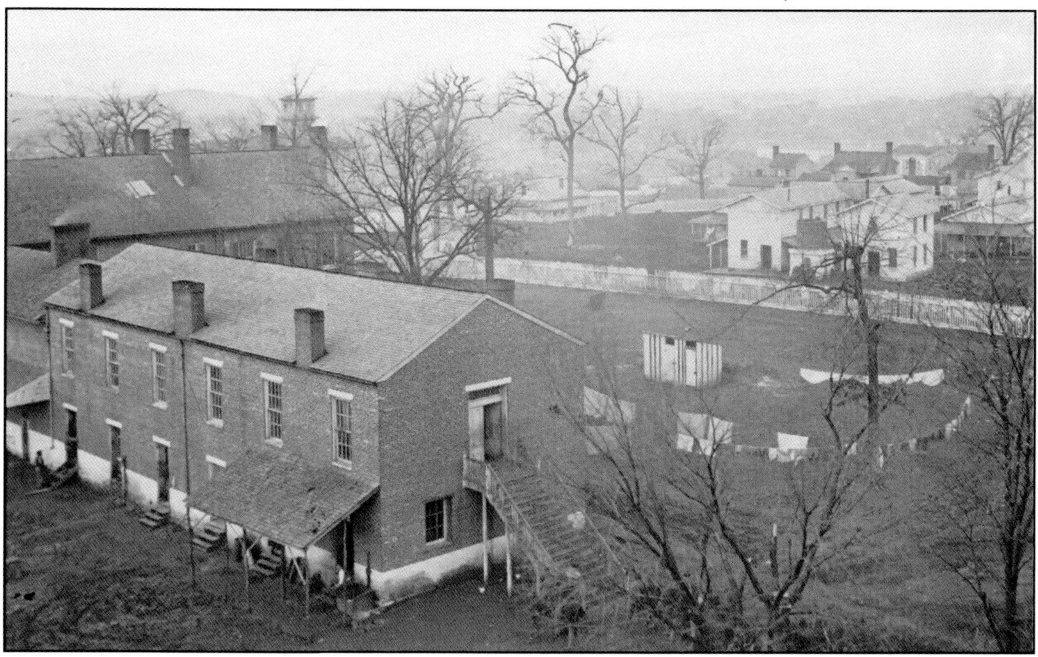

This composition, recorded by Civil War photographer George Bernard, was probably made at the same location and date as the previous image but facing south depicting additional structures on the University of Nashville campus. The day this photograph was recorded was probably a cold one, judging from smoke emerging from the numerous chimneys and hazy sky. (Library of Congress, Civil War Collection.)

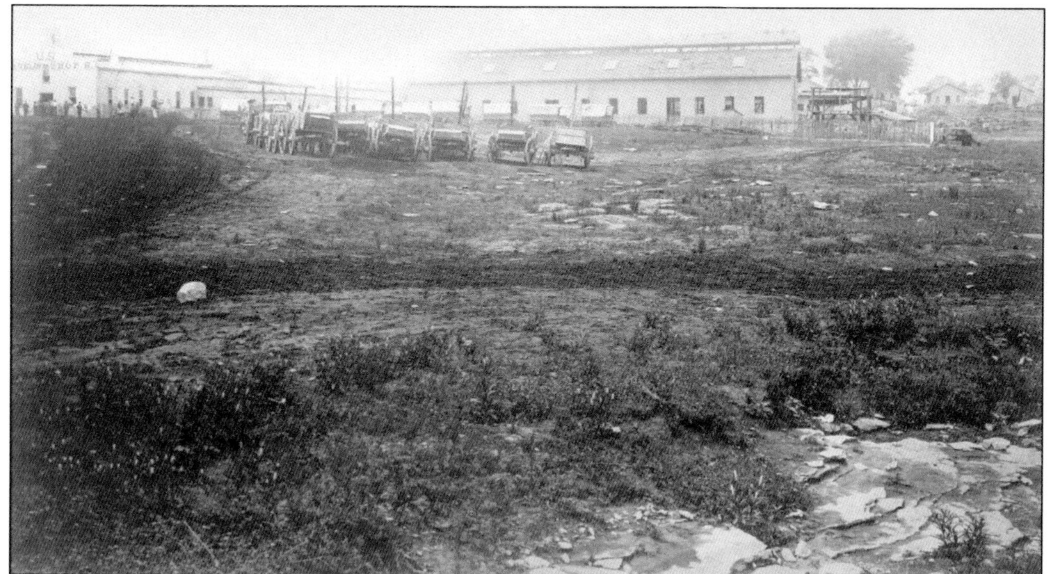

Much of the Civil War took place in South Nashville for several years. The landscape reflected this; numerous buildings were constructed or seized by Union soldiers. This is the US quartermaster's repair shops on Franklin Pike on the outskirts of Nashville during March 1864. (Library of Congress, Civil War Collection.)

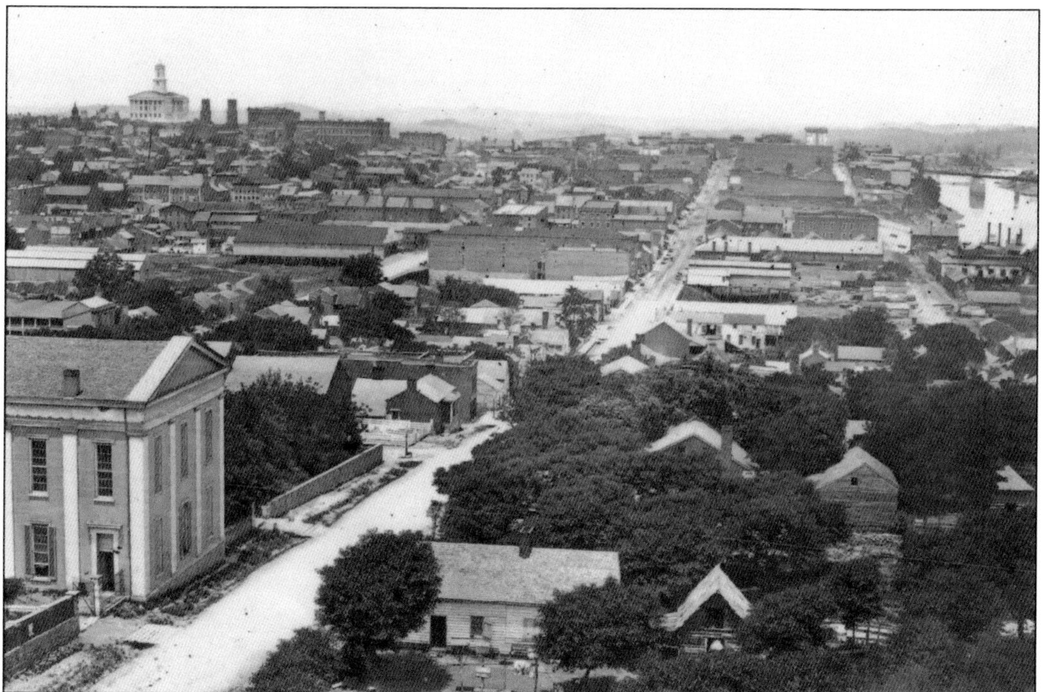

This early-1880s view looks north from the roof of the old Howard School. Downtown Nashville and several landmarks are visible in the distance. The Tennessee State Capitol, the twin spires of the First Presbyterian Church, and the Maxwell House Hotel dominate the skyline. The prominent street going through the middle of the scene is Market Street, today's Second Avenue. (Tennessee State Library and Archives.)

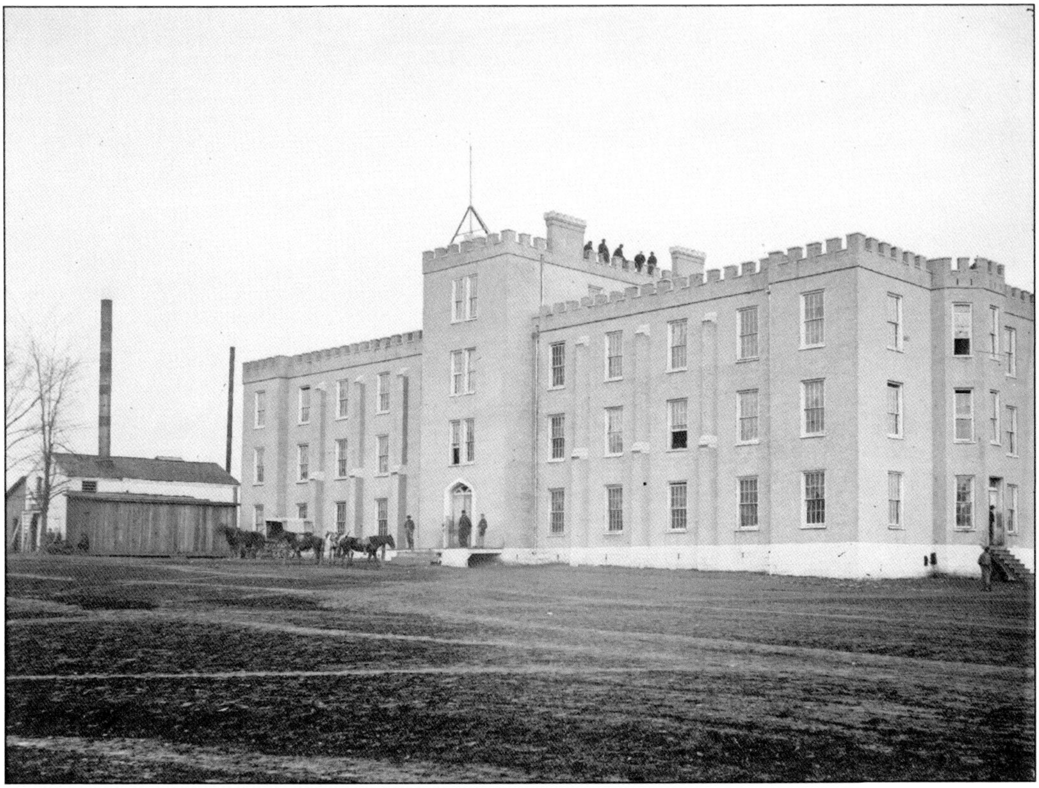

A heavily guarded federal military hospital is seen in 1864. Before wartime, the brick and stone building was known as Lindsley Hall, part of the University of Nashville. After the conflict it served as part of Peabody Normal College and later as the Children's Museum of Nashville. Today, the structure is used for city offices. Below, the US quartermaster's warehouse, located near Lindsley Hall, was recorded around the same time. Looking north toward downtown Nashville, the cupola of the state capitol, the twin towers of the First Presbyterian Church and the Maxwell House Hotel are faintly visible above the roofline. Both compositions were recorded by noted Civil War photographer George Barnard. (Both, Library of Congress, Civil War Collection.)

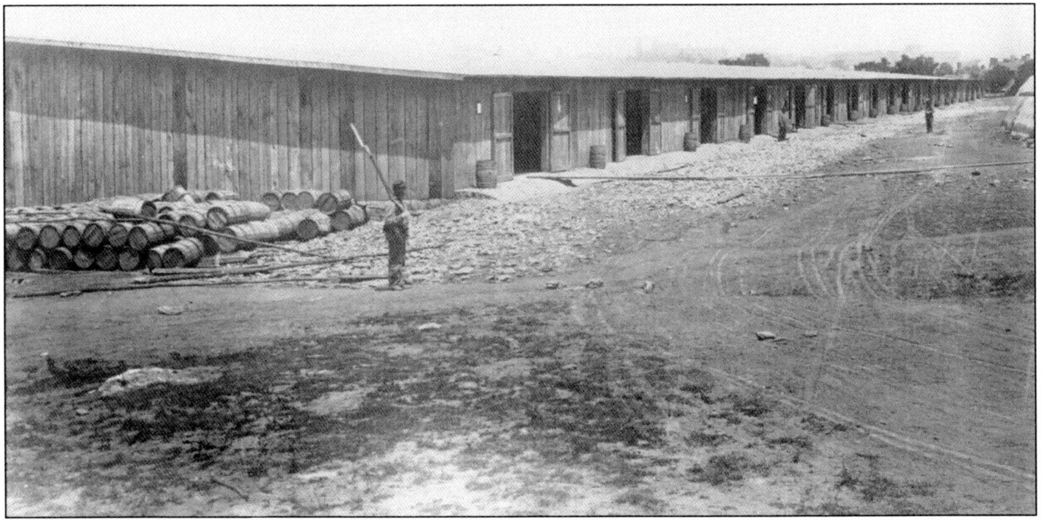

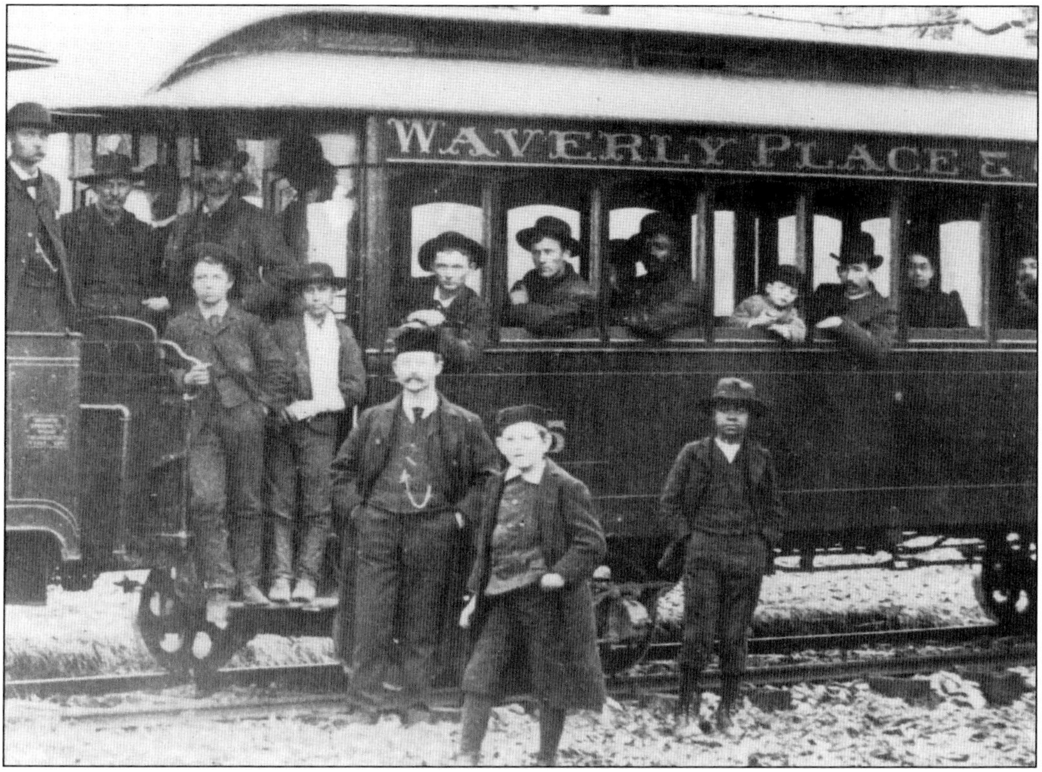

The crew and passengers aboard the Overland Dummy Railway pose for this composition at Glendale Park. The line opened around 1887 between downtown Nashville and the popular attraction. The wood car says, "Waverly Place and Glendale Park" on the side. The Overland was the first of three steam dummy lines to operate in the area. This operation was converted to electric power during the 1890s. (Ralcon Wagner collection.)

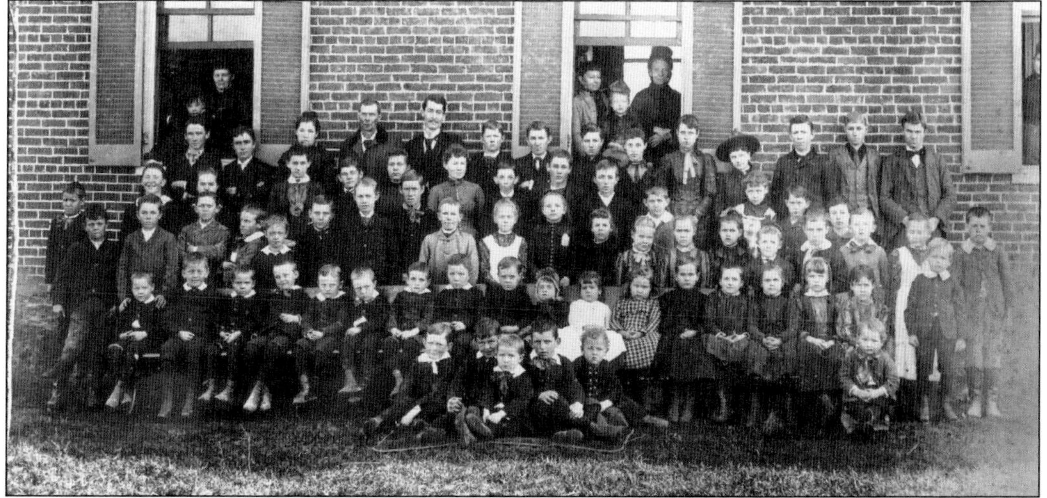

Before the creation of Nashville's metropolitan government in 1963, the county school system was made up of dozens of school houses in small communities. One of these was Flat Rock Elementary School, located in the town of the same name. In 1895, faculty and students pose for a school photograph. (Tennessee State Library and Archives.)

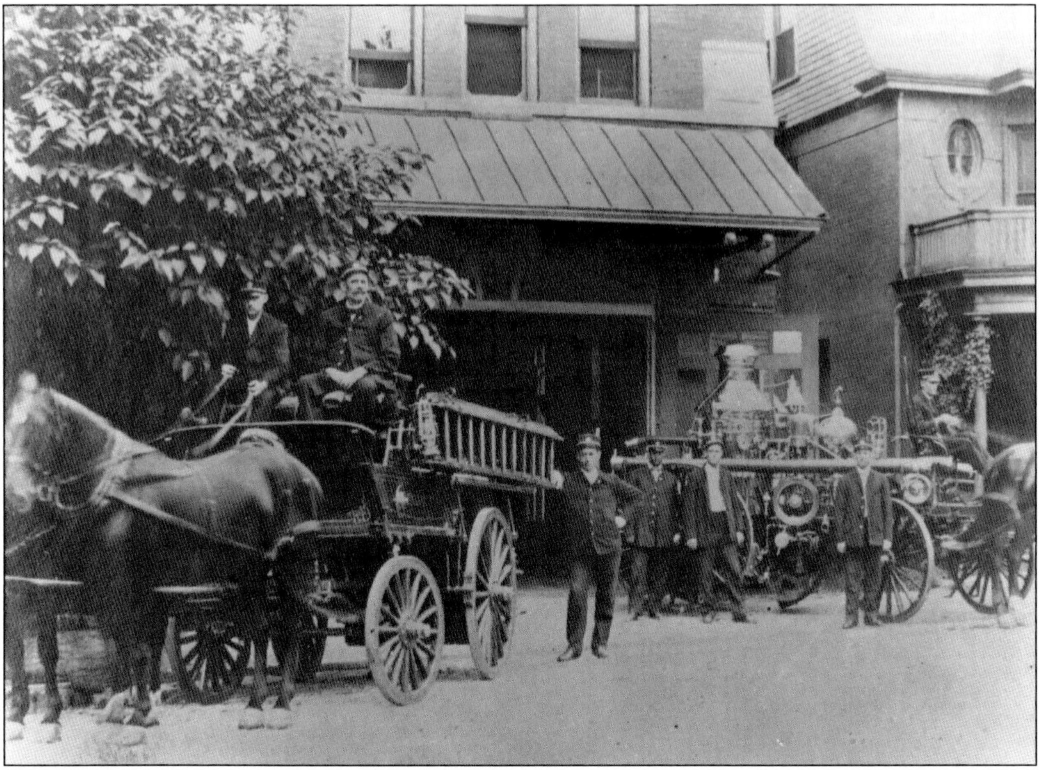

The firefighters of Engine Company No. 6 proudly pose with their two horse-drawn fire wagons in front of the firehouse on South Market Street around 1895. Market Street was later renamed Fourth Avenue South. (Tennessee State Library and Archives.)

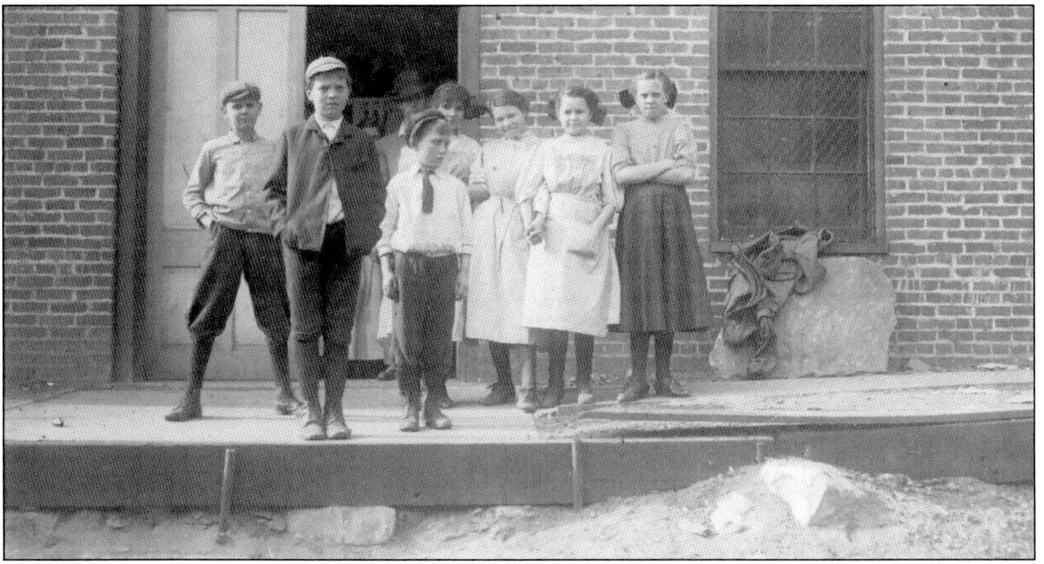

The use of child labor in textile mills was commonplace during the late 19th century and into the early 1920s. A group of children are seen during their break at the May Hosiery Mills in South Nashville in November 1910. New federal regulations passed during the 1930s restricted child labor. (Library of Congress, National Child Labor Committee Collection.)

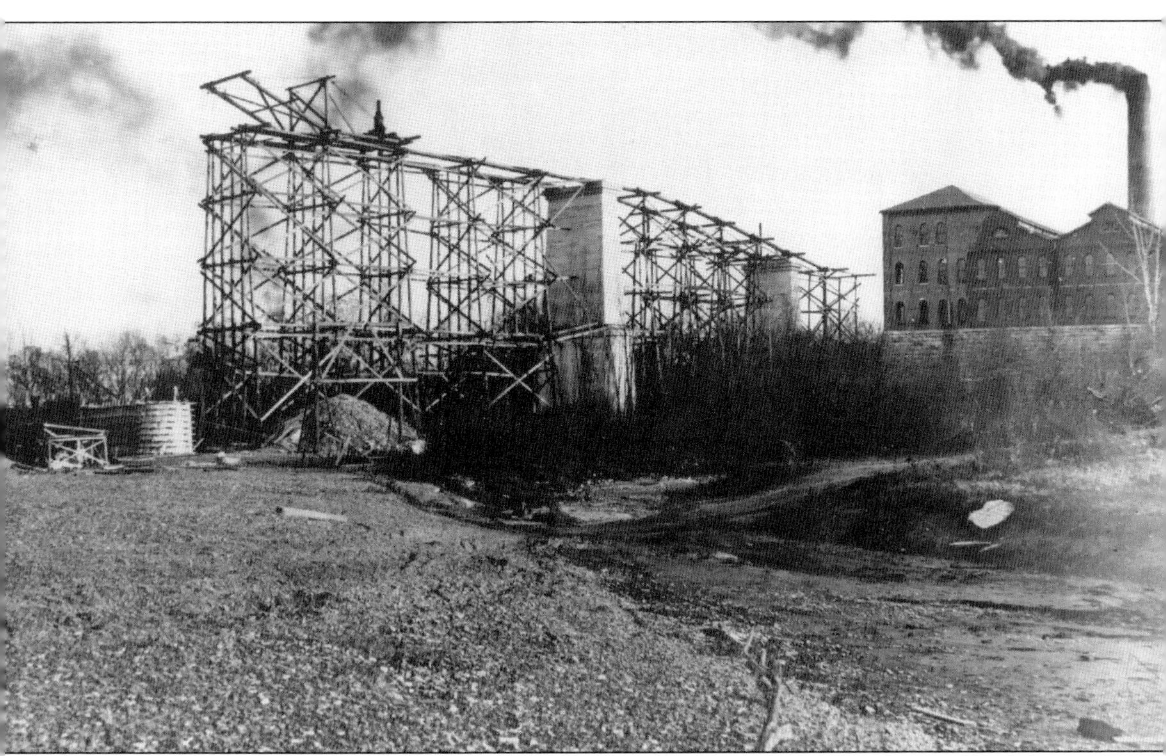

Construction is well underway on the Lewisburg & Northern Railroad bridge over the Cumberland River in 1907. When completed, the span linked the east and south sections of Nashville, diverting trains away from congested rail yards downtown. The 1889-built George Reyer Pumping Station, part of Nashville's waterworks, can be seen at right. Today, both the rail bridge and the water plant remain in operation. (Metro Nashville Archives.)

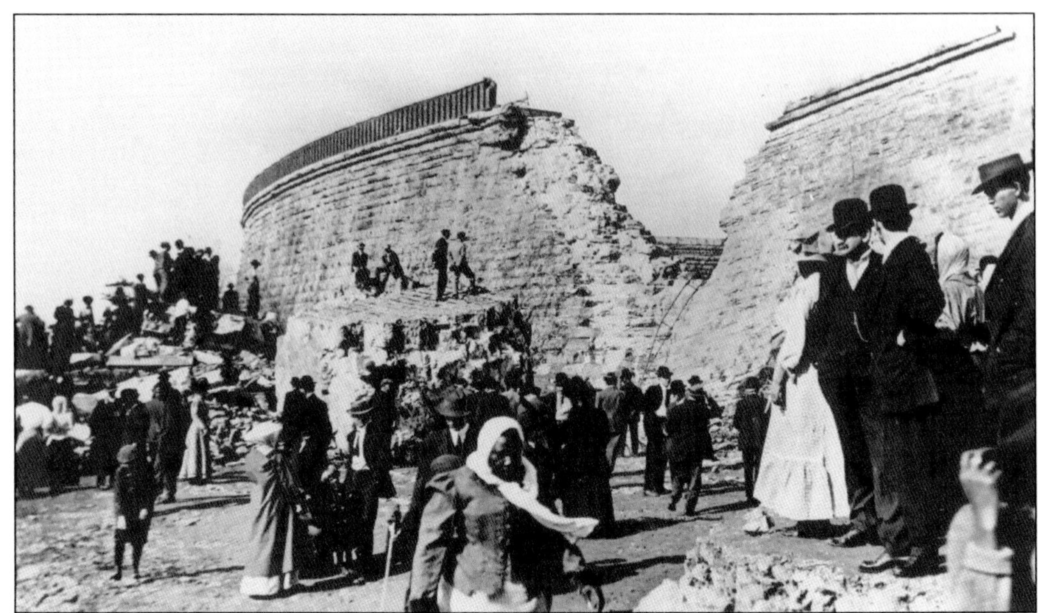

One of Nashville's most historic landmarks is the City Reservoir, situated in the Edgehill neighborhood along Eighth Avenue. The granite structure, completed in 1889, was built on Kirkpatrick Hill, the highest point in South Nashville. Just past midnight on November 5, 1912, the east wall of the reservoir burst, sending 25 million gallons of water downhill, wiping out many homes and causing more than $100,000 in damage. Surprisingly, there were no serious injuries. Fortunately, the 33-foot-high reservoir is divided into two sections by a core of concrete, and the western portion was not damaged. The reservoir remains in daily use today. (Both, Tennessee State Library and Archives.)

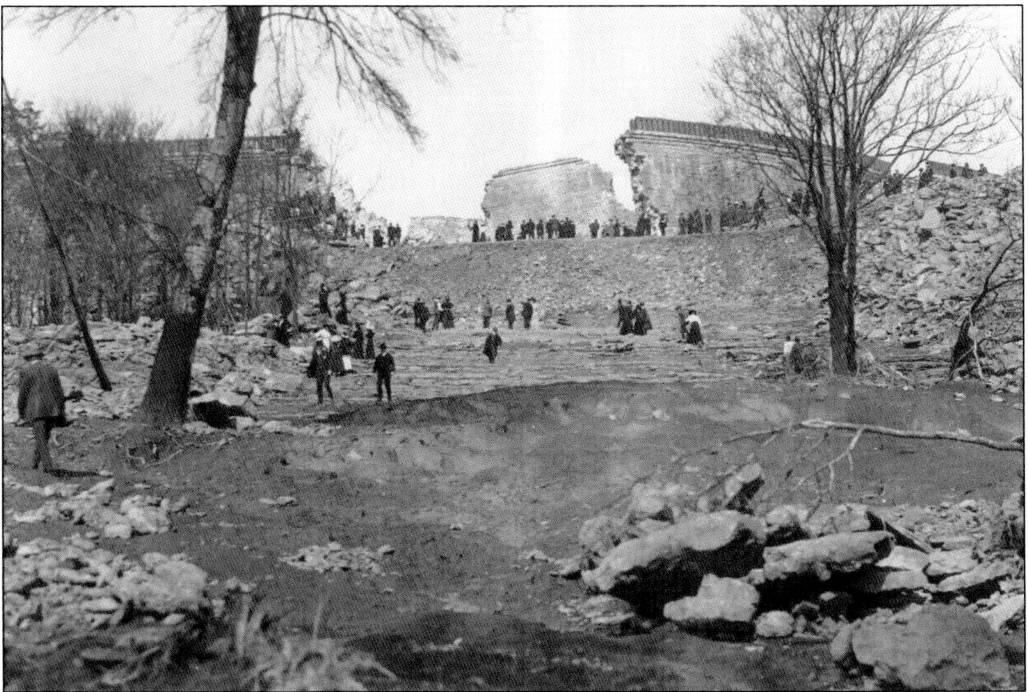

Two

TRANSPORTATION

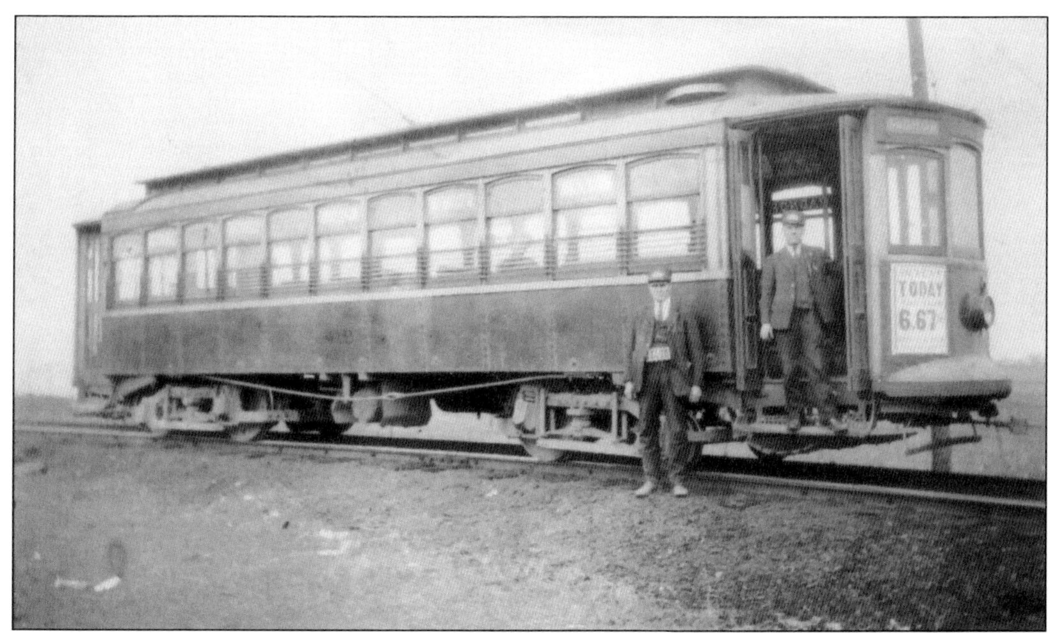

Transportation always played an important role in Nashville's growth. Public transportation in South Nashville began with streetcars during the 1860s. The Radnor line has provided a vital link to South Nashville since the turn of the century. In this view, two car men stand with their trolley near the line's terminus at the Louisville & Nashville Railroad Radnor Yard. (Kathy Bottoms collection.)

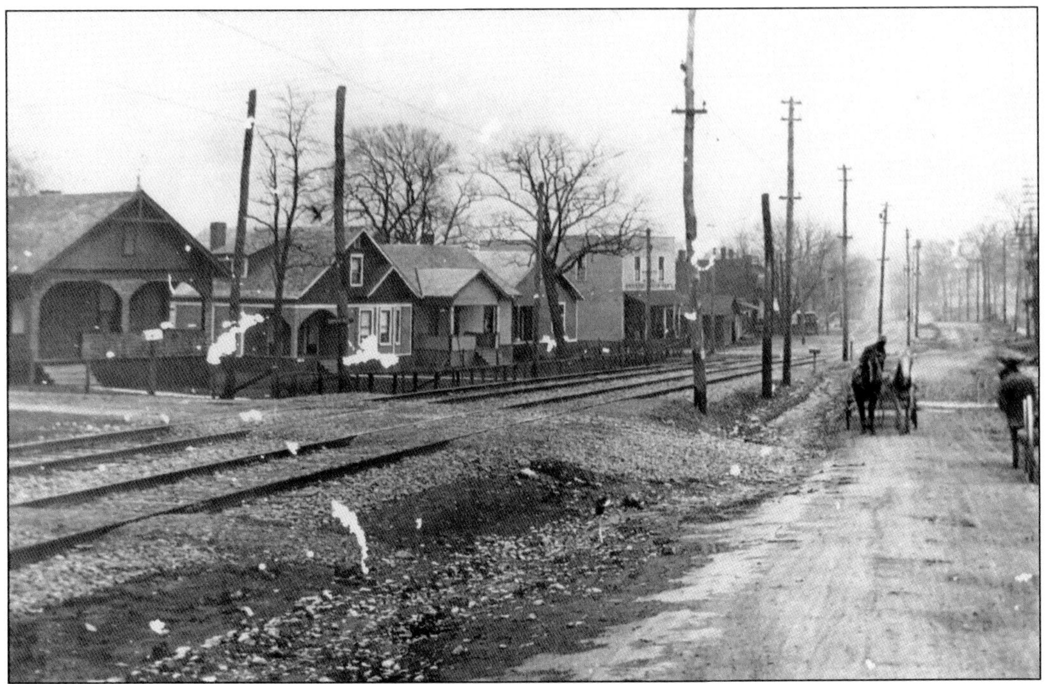

Public transportation played a vital role in the growth of South Nashville. From the 1880s to 1941 streetcars were the primary means of getting around. In this scene, the tracks of the Nashville Railway and Light Company are shown along the east side of Nolensville Pike in the Flat Rock community in 1910. (Tennessee State Library and Archives.)

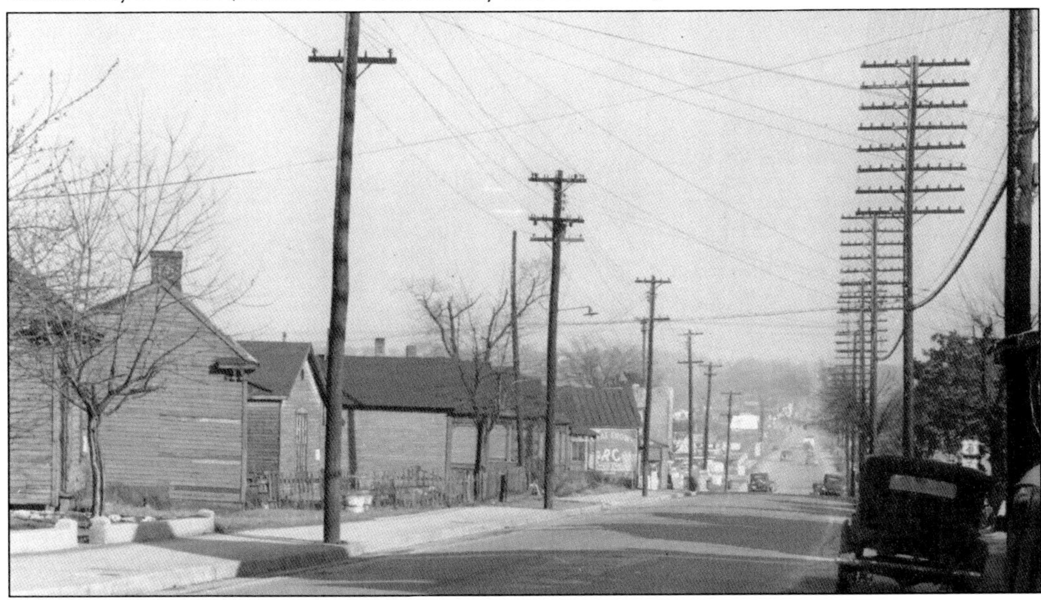

Lafayette Street is a primary street traveling southeast from downtown Nashville. Also known as US Route 41, this highway connected the Midwest and Florida. During the 1940s, the highway was widened to four lanes, and new motels and restaurants replaced aging clapboard buildings. This view shows Lafayette Street at Maury Street looking south during the 1930s. (Metro Nashville Archives, MDHA Collection.)

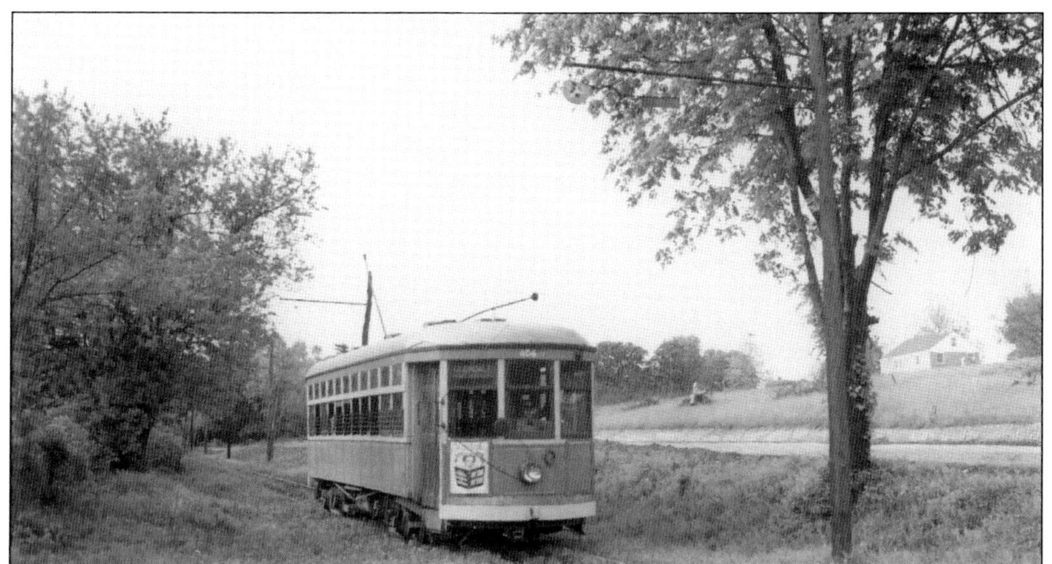

For many years the Glendale streetcar line connected downtown with the privately owned Glendale Park and Zoo, traveling over a picturesque route though South Nashville. This view shows a Tennessee Electric Power Company car traveling north near Lealand Lane and Kirkwood Avenue around 1940. (David H. Steinberg collection.)

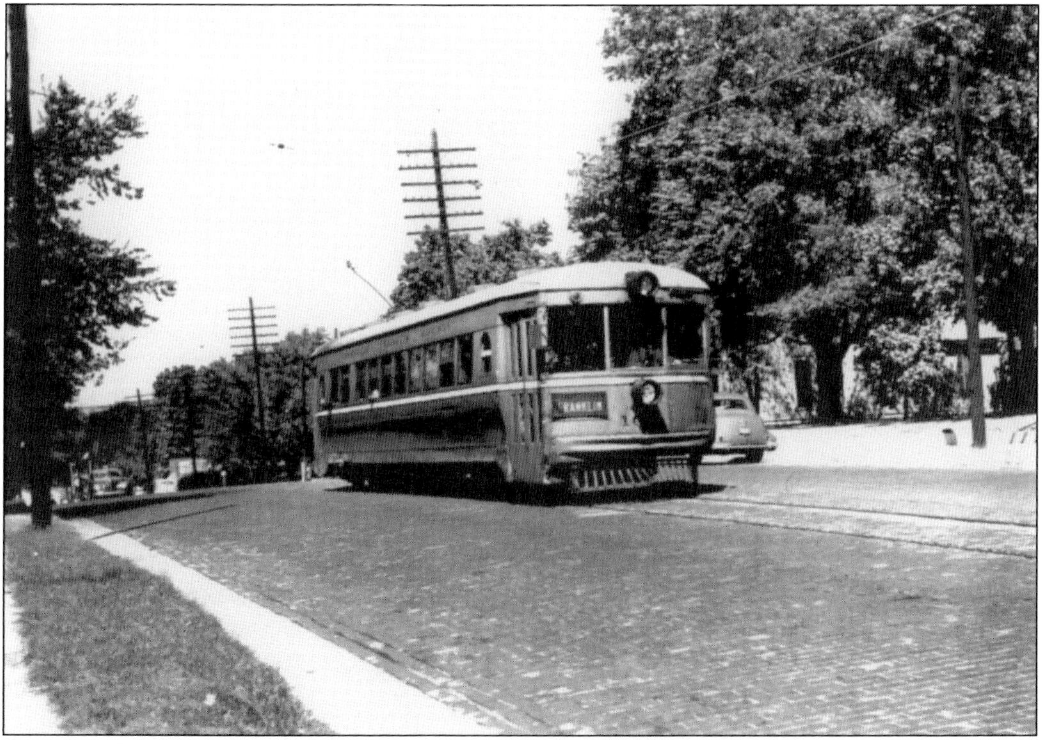

A Nashville-Franklin Railway car trundles south down Franklin Pike near Bradford Avenue in 1940. The interurban line provided a reliable transit option for South Nashville residents traveling between the city and the communities of Brentwood and Franklin, Tennessee. The electric cars were replaced by buses in 1941. (Hank Sherwood collection.)

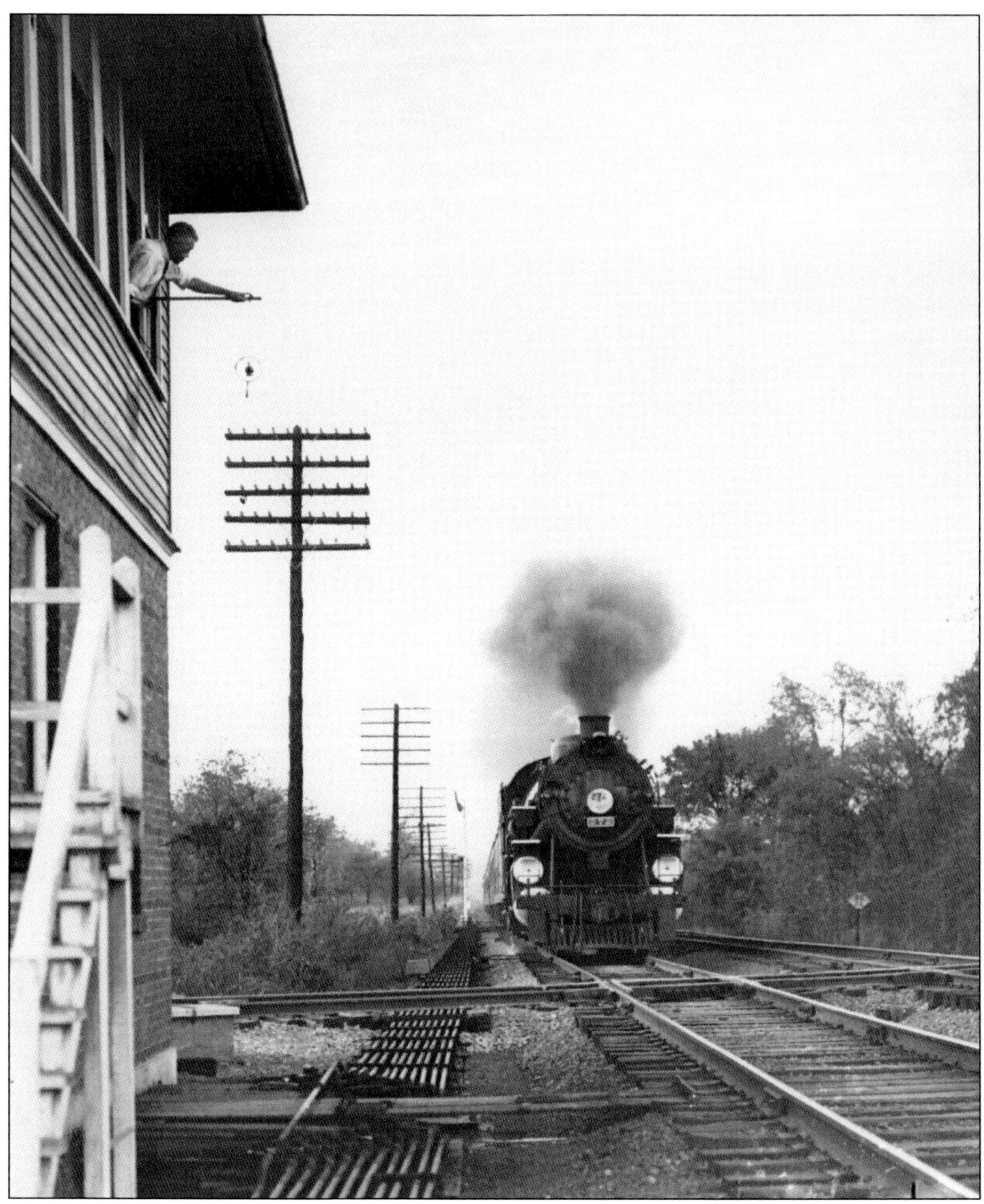

For many years, Nashville radio station WSM regularly broadcast the Louisville & Nashville Railroad's Pan American leaving town. This view shows a radio sound engineer holding a microphone out the window of the Vine Hill interlocking tower in South Nashville capturing the sounds of the Louisville & Nashville Railroad's crack train as it passes by in 1939. The clear channel radio station regularly broadcast the famous train roaring by as it headed south, bound for New Orleans. (Louisville & Nashville Railroad Company Records, University of Louisville Archives.)

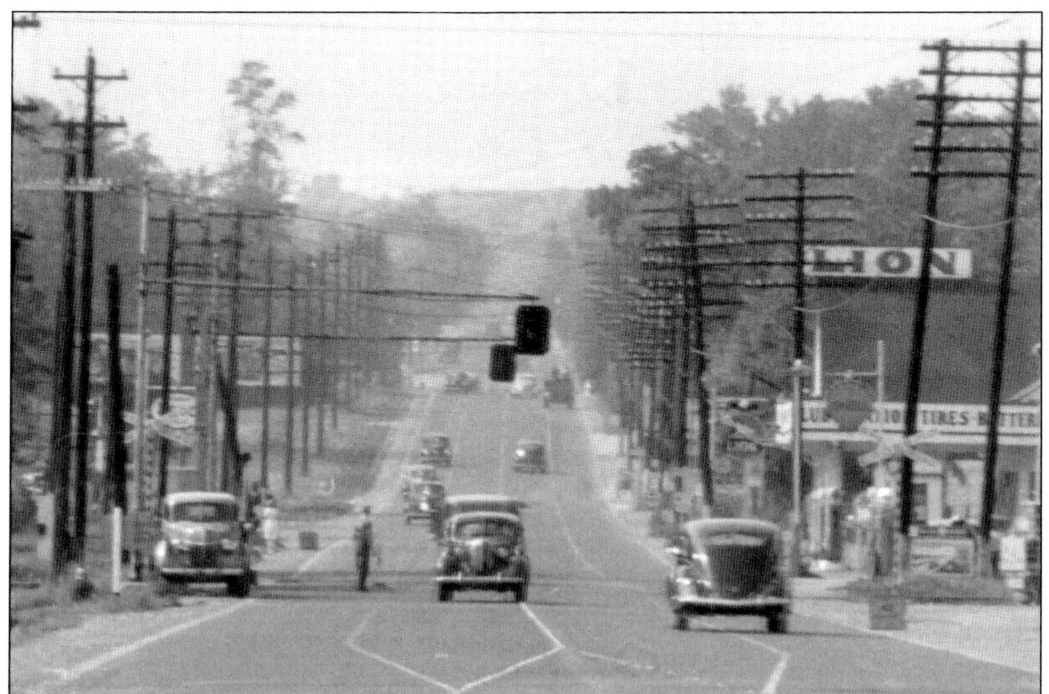

Nashville's population spread to suburbs in all directions during the 1940s. The Franklin Road corridor experienced growth as well, especially in the Melrose and Berry Hill communities, south of the city. This highway, also known as US Route 31, linked Nashville to Birmingham, Alabama, and points south. This view faces north on Franklin Road near Berry Road during the mid-1940s. (Metro Nashville Archives, MDHA Collection.)

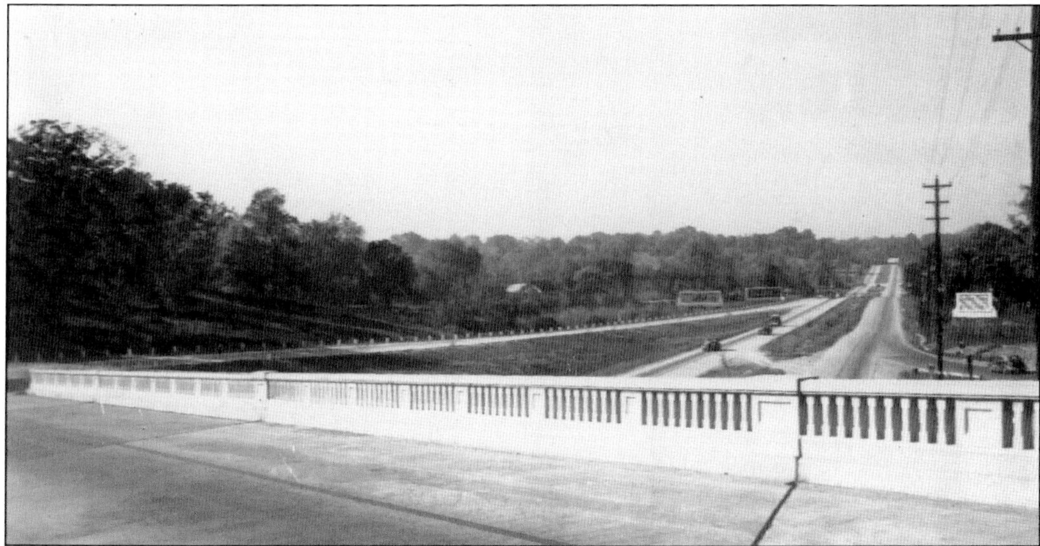

Murfreesboro Road was the first highway in middle Tennessee to be widened to a four-lane road. As part of the project, a grade-separated interchange was constructed where Vultee Boulevard diverted from the highway in the Glencliff community. The junction was designed to alleviate traffic congestion for defense workers at the Vultee Aircraft plant, and travelers headed to Nashville's airport. (MDHA Collection, Metro Nashville Archives, MDHA Collection.)

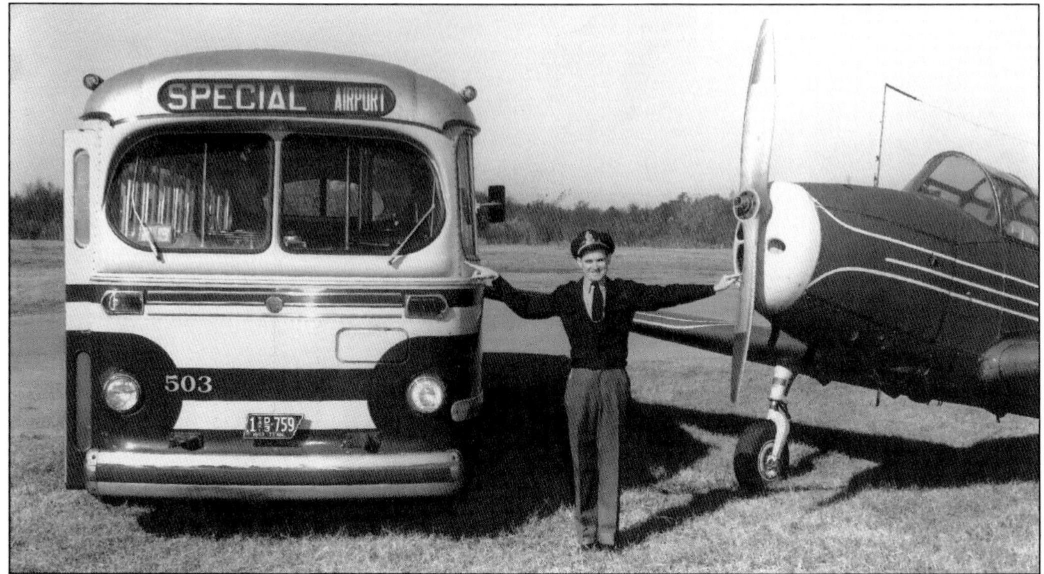

To better serve Nashville's Berry Field Airport, the Vultee Aircraft plant and the Murfreesboro Road corridor, the Nashville Coach Company instituted a new bus route in 1941. During this time, bus lines were extended in all directions to better serve those living in the suburbs. This publicity photograph was made to promote the service. (Metro Nashville Archives, MTA Collection.)

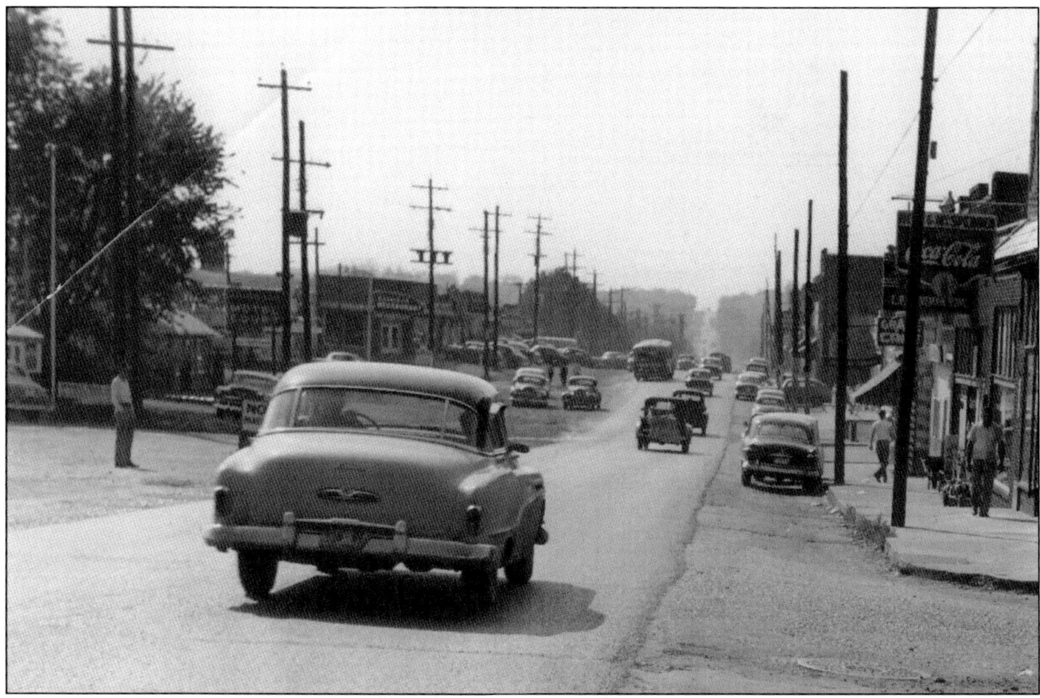

During the years following World War II, vehicular traffic between Nashville and the suburbs increased dramatically due to all the people now commuting from outlying areas. Widening of major roads became a priority for highway officials. This 1954 image of Nolensville Road, looking south from Newsome Street in Woodbine, illustrates the widening of a busy arterial street. (Metro Nashville Archives, MTA Collection.)

Three

LIFE IN SOUTH NASHVILLE

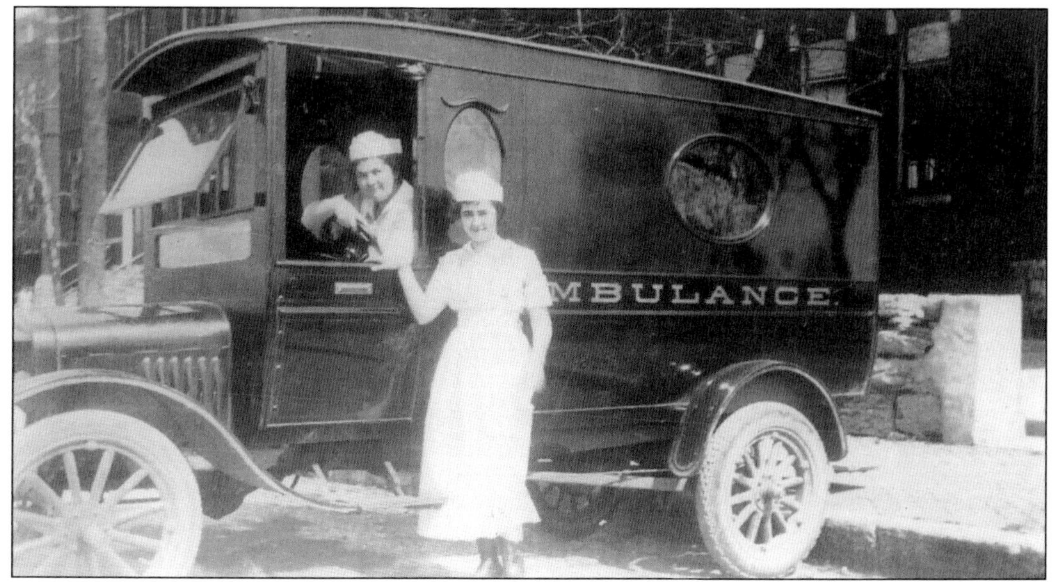

During much of the 20th century, life in South Nashville was simpler; people worked longer hours but took pride in their families and in their jobs. Since World War I, women have played a vital role in volunteering wherever they were needed, including in previously nontraditional roles. Two American Red Cross volunteers stand by their ambulance, believed to be in front of Nashville's General Hospital, around 1919. (Metro Nashville Archives.)

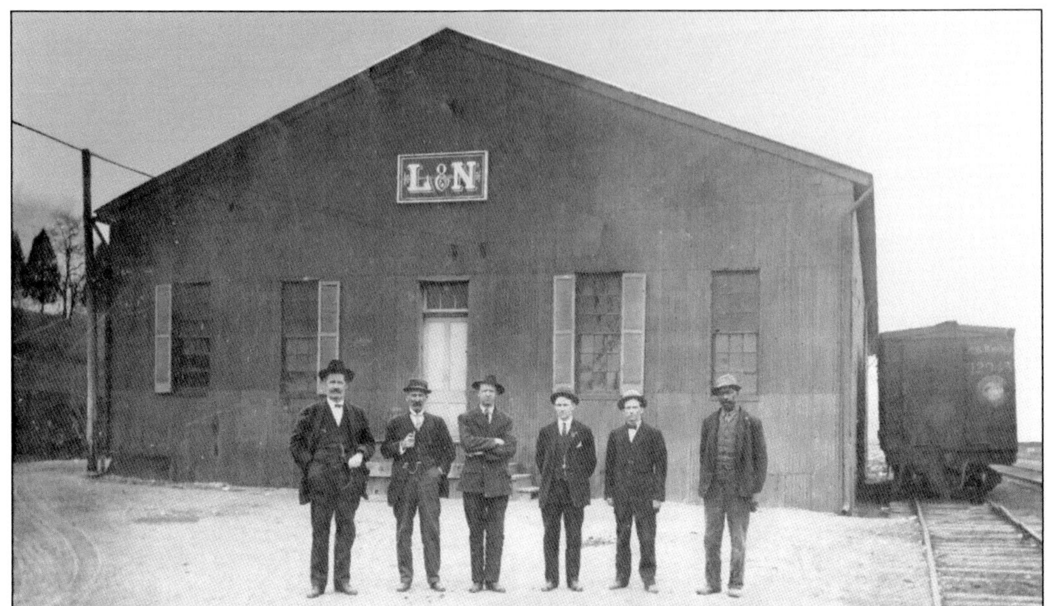

Employees of the Louisville & Nashville Railroad are seen at the railroad's South Nashville yard near Chestnut Street around 1918. The base of St. Cloud hill can be seen at far left. About this time, L&N had opened its sprawling Radnor Yard several miles south, ultimately consolidating this and several smaller facilities. (Ralcon Wagner collection.)

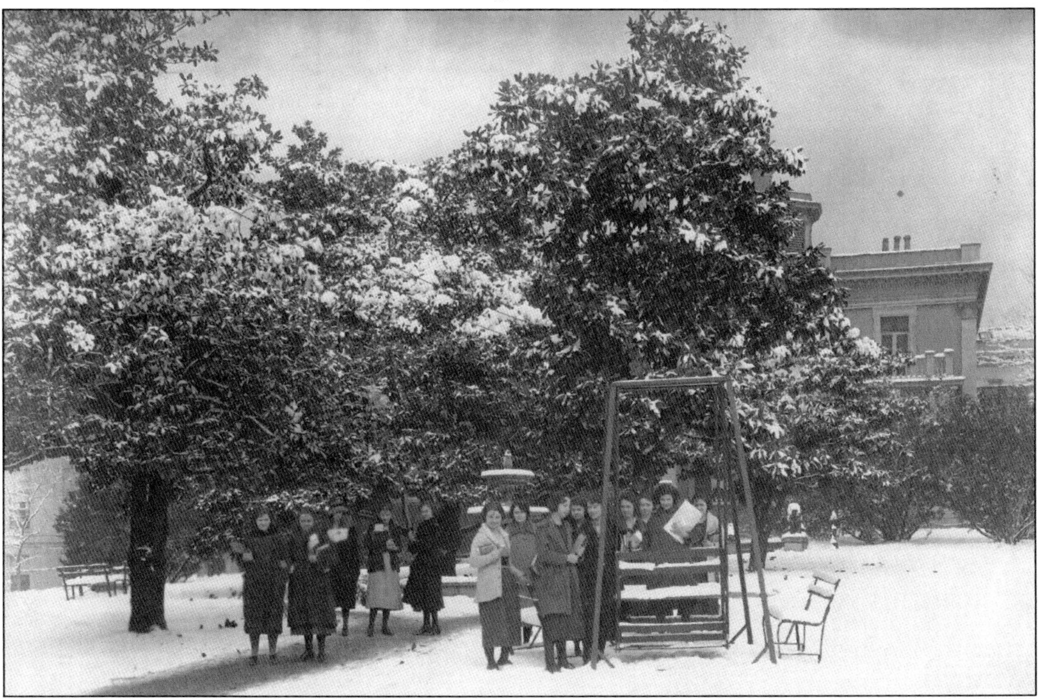

Several students from Ward-Belmont College pose during a break between classes on a winter day in the early 1920s. The prestigious girl's college had a major presence in South Nashville for 38 years. In 1951, the facility was purchased by the Tennessee Baptist Convention, becoming a coeducational, four-year institution. (Tennessee State Library and Archives.)

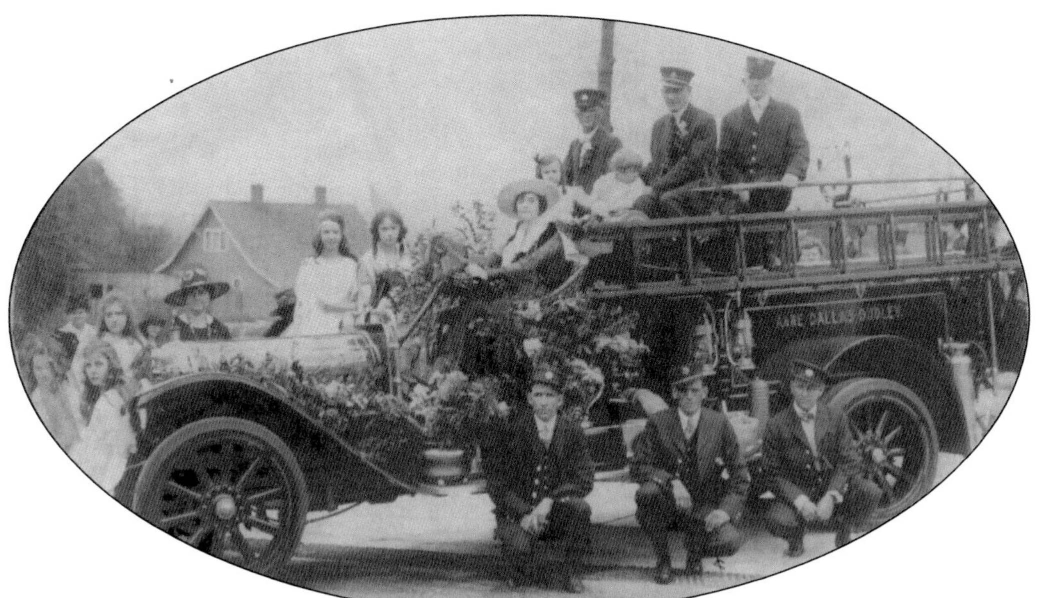

In a show of support, the firemen of the Waverly-Belmont fire station christened their new fire truck after Nashville suffragist Anne Dallas Dudley. During the ceremony on May 10, 1919, the firemen proudly pose in front of their truck with the guest of honor, Mrs. Dudley, seated at the wheel. The young girls are daughters of local suffragettes. Arthur A. Fischer is at center of first row. (Fannie Fischer Jones collection.)

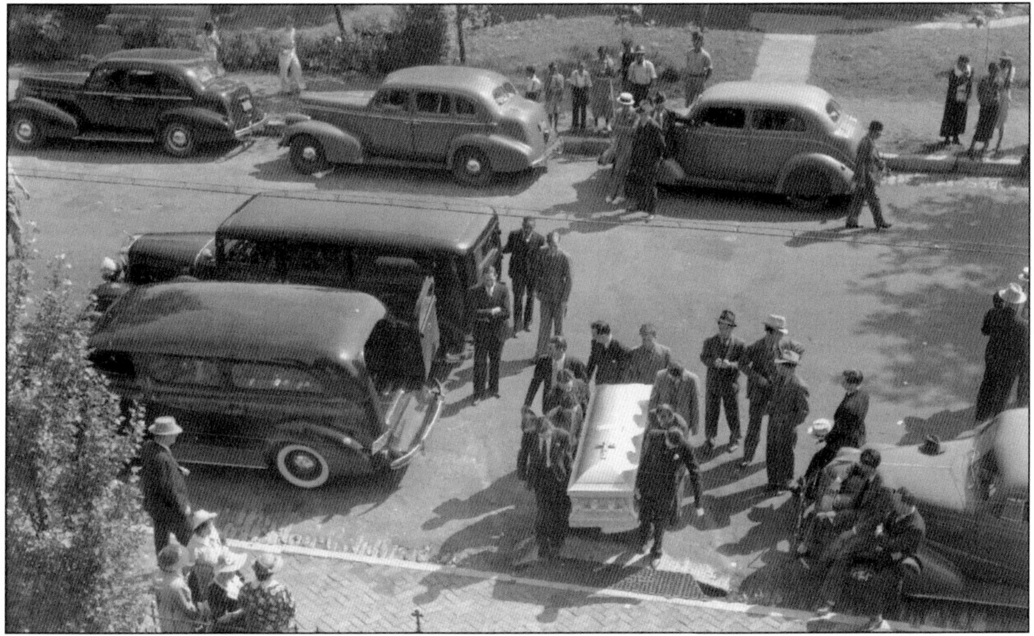

For decades, families of traveling horse traders, calling themselves Irish Nomads, descended on Nashville annually each May to attend the last rites of relatives who had died during the year, attracting thousands from the region. During this traditional pilgrimage, a mass funeral was held, business exchanged followed by a dance. In 1938, a casket is carried into St. Patrick's church as bystanders watch. (Metro Nashville Archives, Banner Collection.)

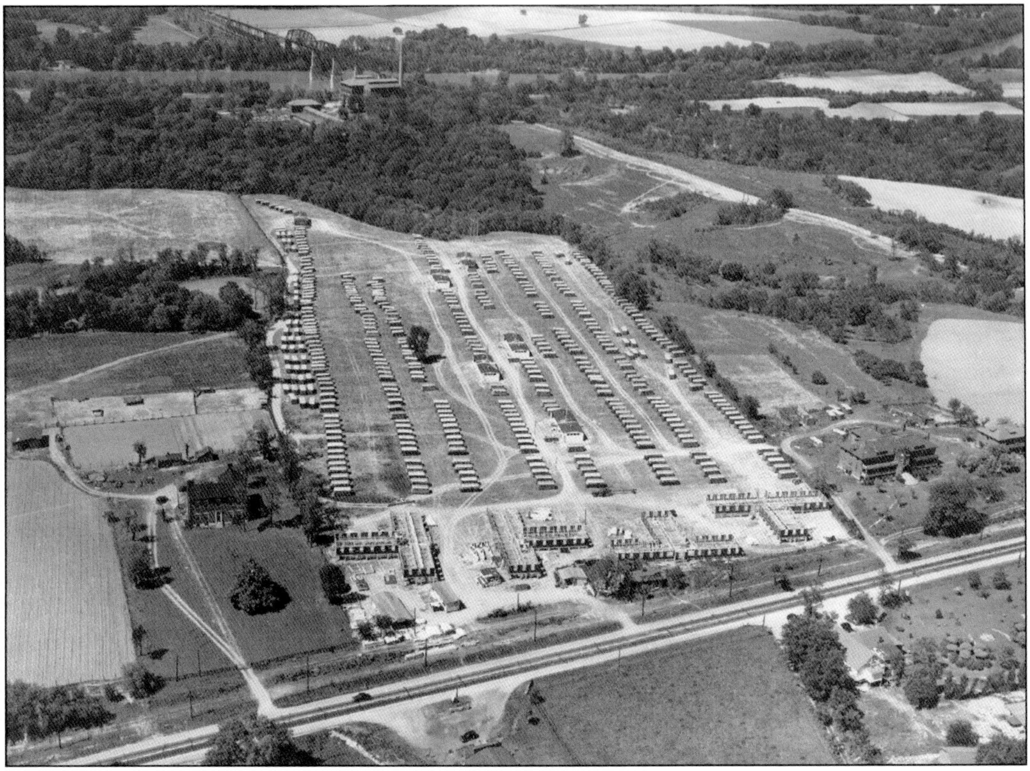

After the 1941 opening of the Vultee Aircraft plant at the Berry Field airport, months before the start of World War II, Nashville experienced a critical housing shortage for hundreds of defense workers throughout the region. In order to relieve the situation, the federal government leased a 100-acre site east of the city near Lebanon Road and Spence Lane for use as a trailer camp for temporary emergency housing for aircraft workers. The camp, located three miles from the Vultee plant, housed 450 trailers, four dormitories and six utility buildings. The above aerial image looks north with the Omohundro Water Treatment Plant in the background, and Lebanon Road is below. The second view, recorded around the same time, faces west. (Both, Tennessee State Library and Archives.)

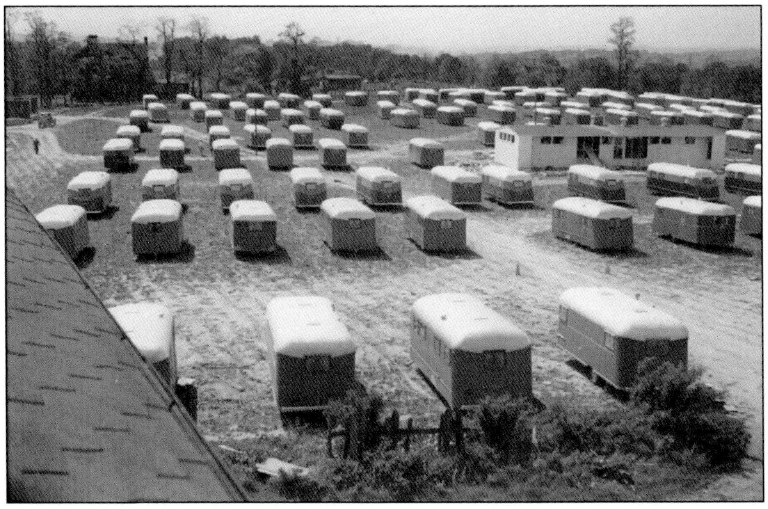

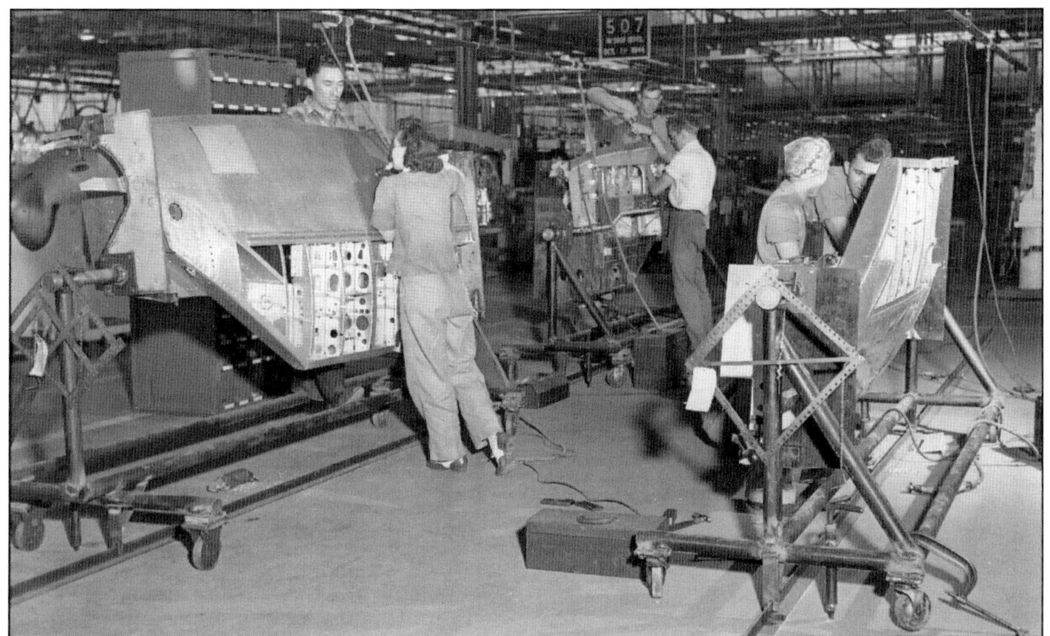

Commencing in 1941, the Vultee Aircraft Corporation began production of military aircraft near Nashville's Berry Field. The facility produced several models that included the A-31/A-35 Vengeance dive bomber and the P-38 Lightning fighter. During the World War II era, Vultee was the first company to build aircraft on a powered assembly line and to use women in production-line positions. The image above shows men and women building parts for P-38 Lightning fighter aircraft. Below, workers in the foreground are making installations in the forward boom, while in the background, the final assembly conveyor line for the wing and center sections can be seen. Both images were recorded around 1941. (Both, Tennessee State Library and Archives.)

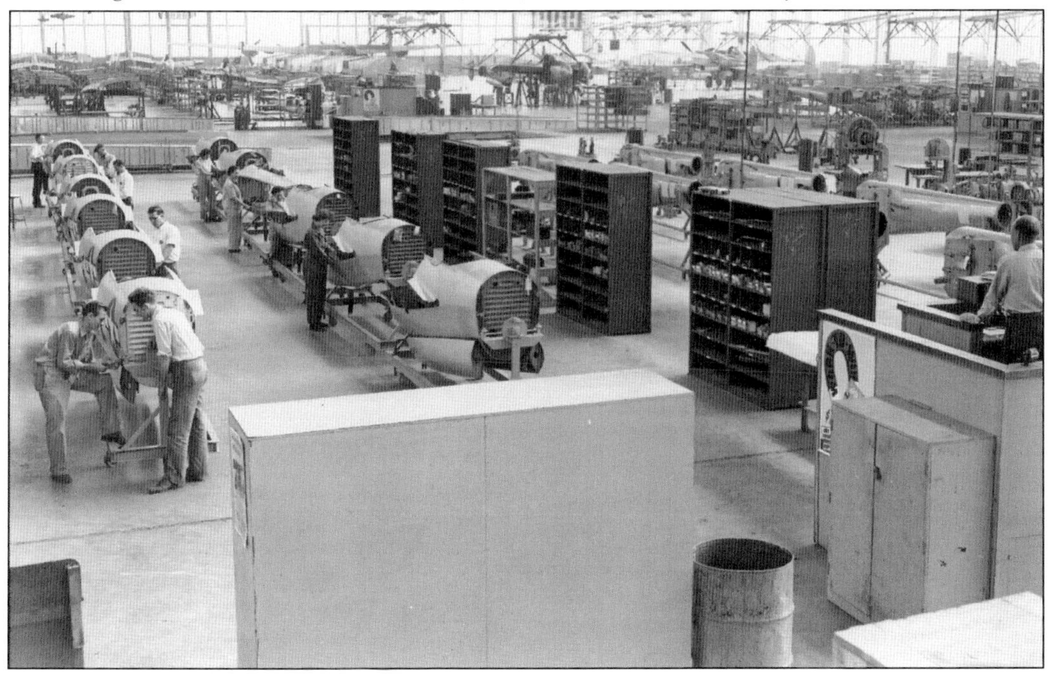

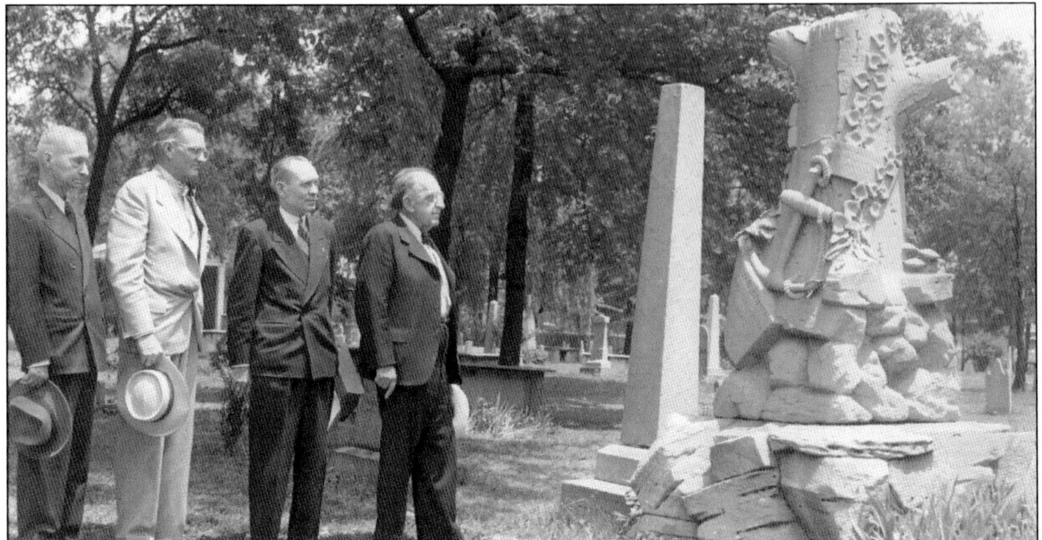

Members of the Nashville Elks lodge gather at the tomb of Capt. William Driver during a wreath laying ceremony at the Nashville City Cemetery during Flag Day 1948. Driver was the first to call the American Flag "Old Glory" during the 1860s. Those shown, from left to right, are William Beard, Dr. Walter R. Courtenay, Stanley Horn, and Frank Barth. (Tennessee State Library and Archives.)

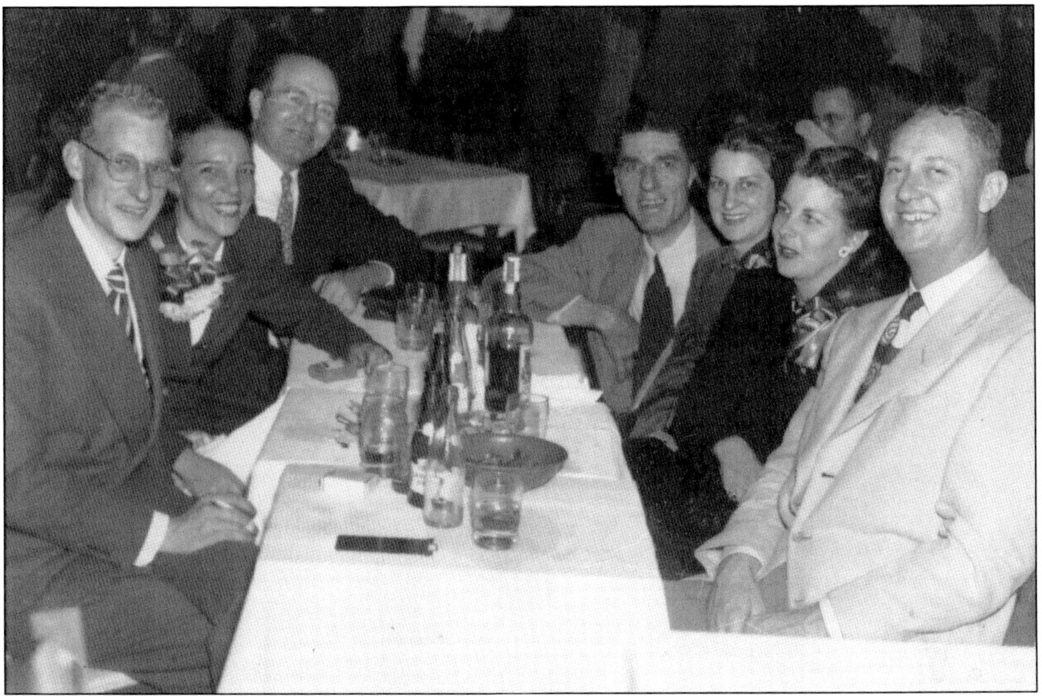

The Club Plantation was an upscale supper club located just outside Nashville city limits on Murfreesboro Road during the 1940s and 1950s. The establishment featured popular orchestras and entertainers. Seated at the table in this scene from the late 1940s are, from left to right, Jack Sibley, Ruth Lewis, Burton Brooks, Buford Lewis, Alene Brooks, Vonceil Greene, and Dr. William O. Greene Jr. (Dr. W.O. Greene III collection.)

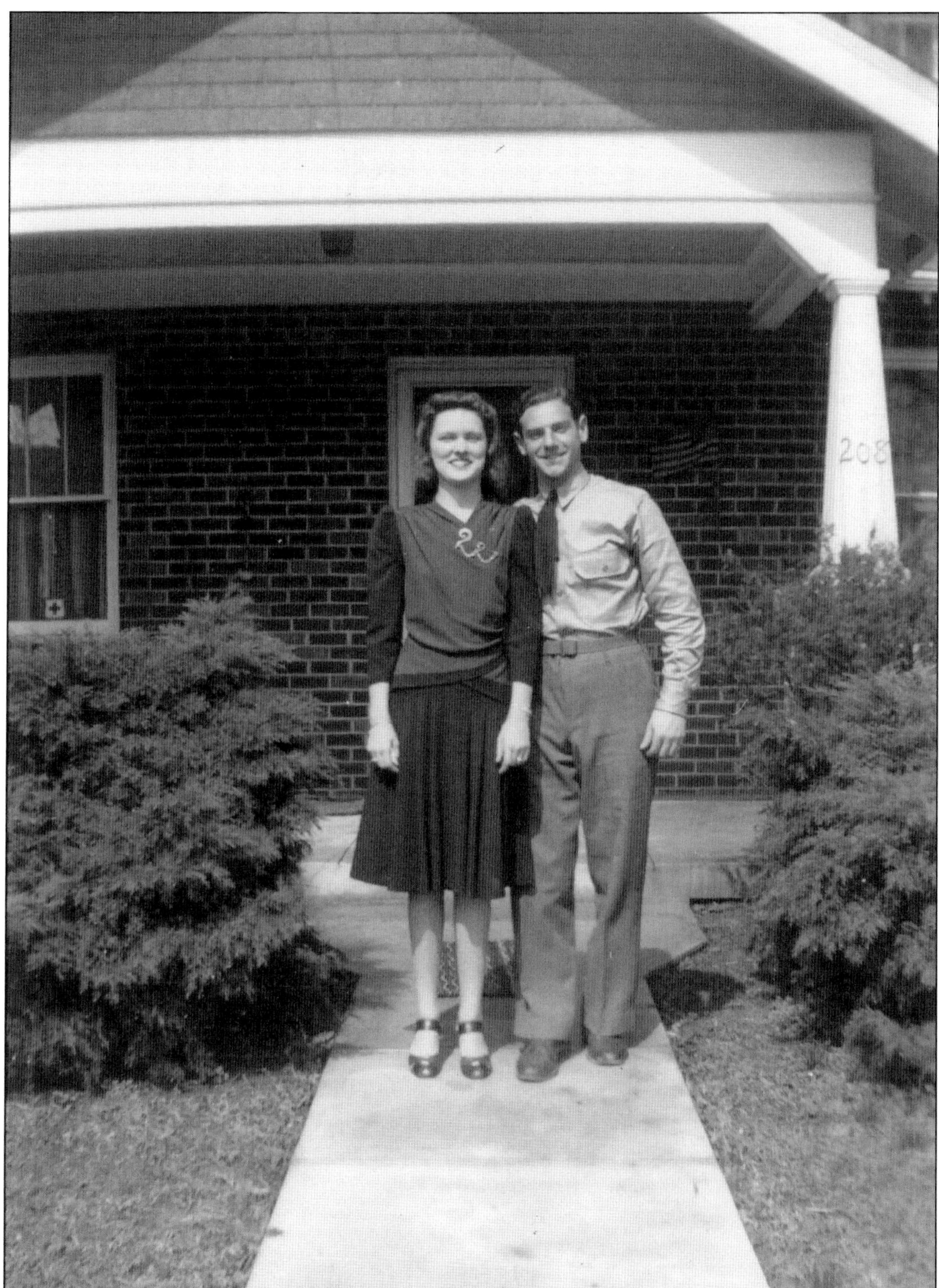

Many houses in the Woodbine community, south of Nashville, were typically modest but well-kept brick or wood bungalows. On a spring day in 1942, Jewell Earline Waggoner and her husband's friend Larry pose in front of her house on McCall Street. Woodbine was merged into Nashville in 1963. (Frank Holt collection.)

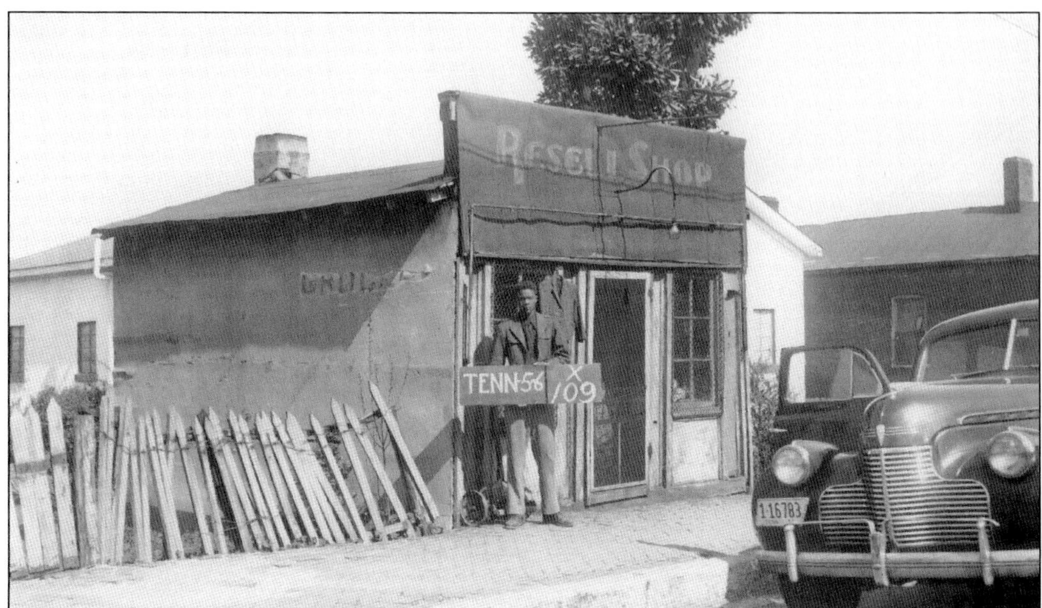

The Federal Housing Act of 1949 gave rise to a major urban renewal program throughout America. During the 1940s and 1950s, many inner-city neighborhoods, including those in South Nashville, were deemed substandard. Many of these structures were without electricity or adequate plumbing. In this 1950 image, an unidentified employee with the Nashville Housing Authority stands in front of a store slated for demolition. (Metro Nashville Archives, MDHA Collection.)

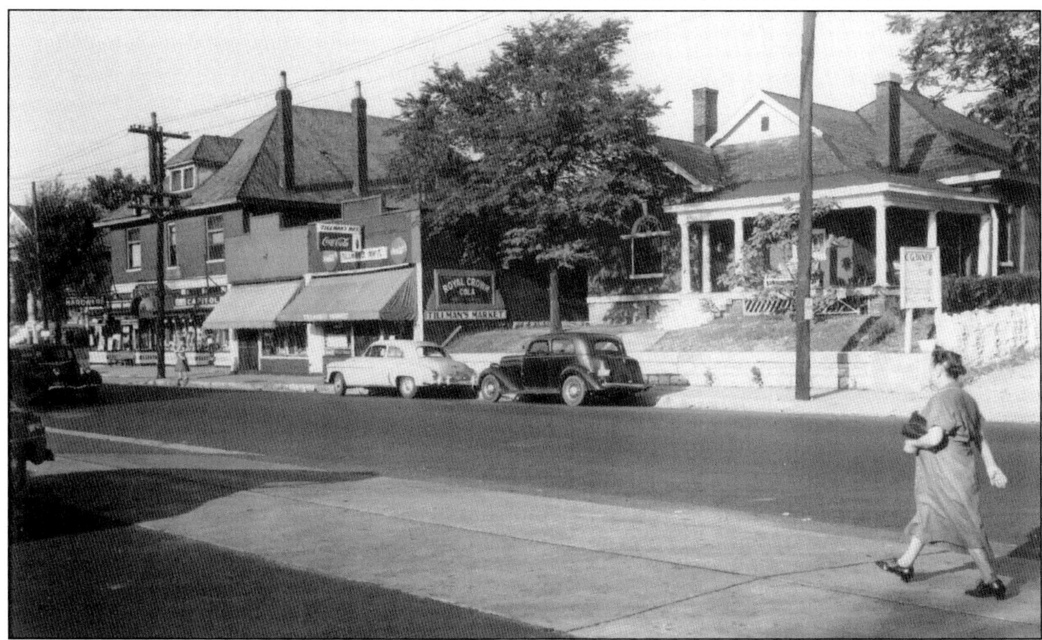

In a time before big chain supermarkets, nearly everyone patronized the local neighborhood store, which in most cases, was just a five-minute walk away. In this photograph, taken during a late afternoon in 1949 at Sixteenth Avenue South near Grand, the Belmont Hardware, Capitol Five & Ten store and Tillman's Market provide an example of street corner convenience. The two houses survive today. (Metro Nashville Archives, MDHA Collection.)

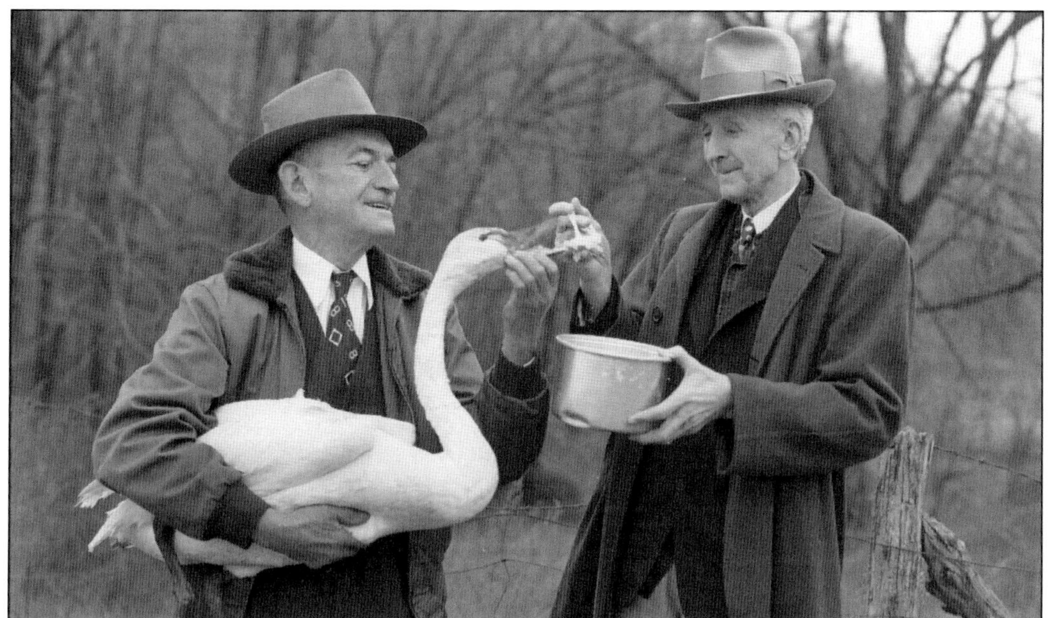

Ornithologists Albert Ganier and Dr. George Mayfield feed a swan, which had been injured, before releasing it on Radnor Lake in December 1951. The lake, south of Nashville, was built by the Louisville & Nashville Railroad in 1917 as a reservoir, supplying water for its locomotives at its nearby rail yard. The lake became a wildlife sanctuary and park in 1973. (Tennessee State Library and Archives.)

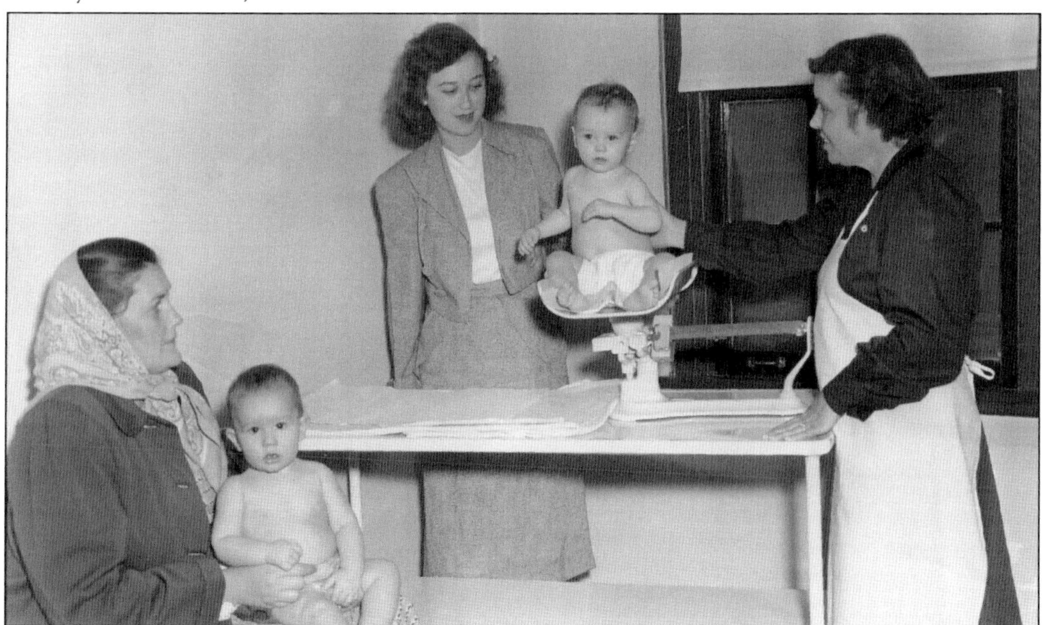

For many years the Davidson County Health Department sponsored public health services for families. The "well baby" clinic provided routine physical checkups, immunization shots, and medical advice for children from infancy to school age. In this 1950s image, a mother watches as her baby is weighed by a health department employee at one of the 14 clinic locations. (Metro Nashville Archives, MDHA Collection.)

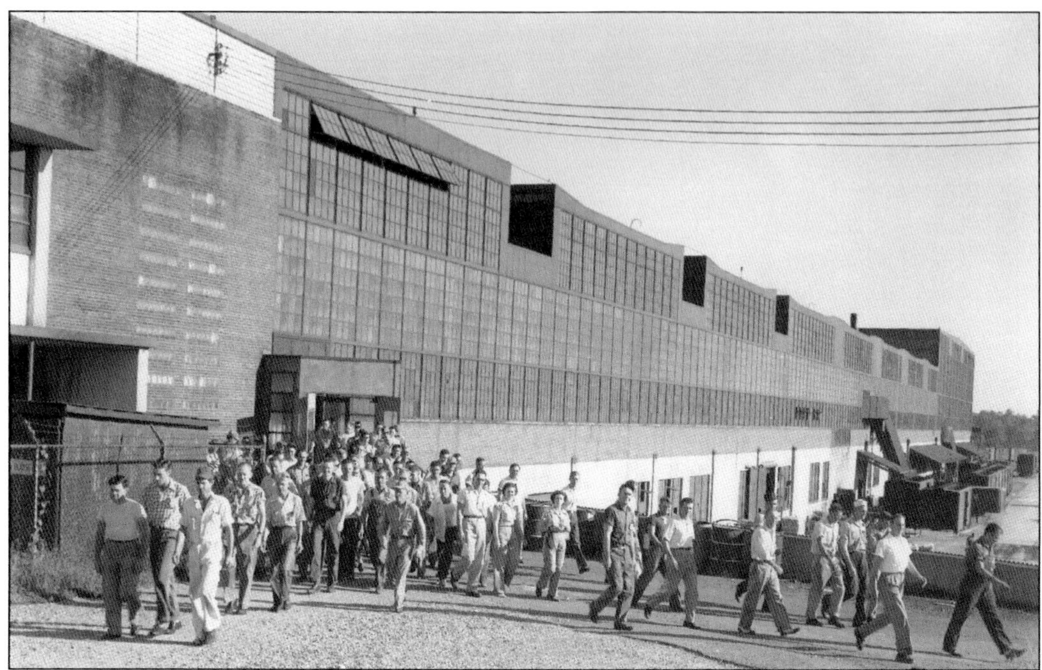

For many years, Avco Manufacturing Corporation was one of Nashville's largest employers. Its history in Nashville can be traced back when it started as Stinson Aircraft Company in 1939. Over the next eight years and a series of mergers, the name was changed to Avco Manufacturing Corporation in 1947. During the next several decades, Avco would manufacture a variety of products that included aircraft wings and parts, farm machinery, and freezers. In the view above, workers file out of the Nashville plant during shift change in 1952. Below, employees work on an assembly line of electric freezers in an image recorded around the same time. (Both, Tennessee State Library and Archives, Department of Conservation Collection.)

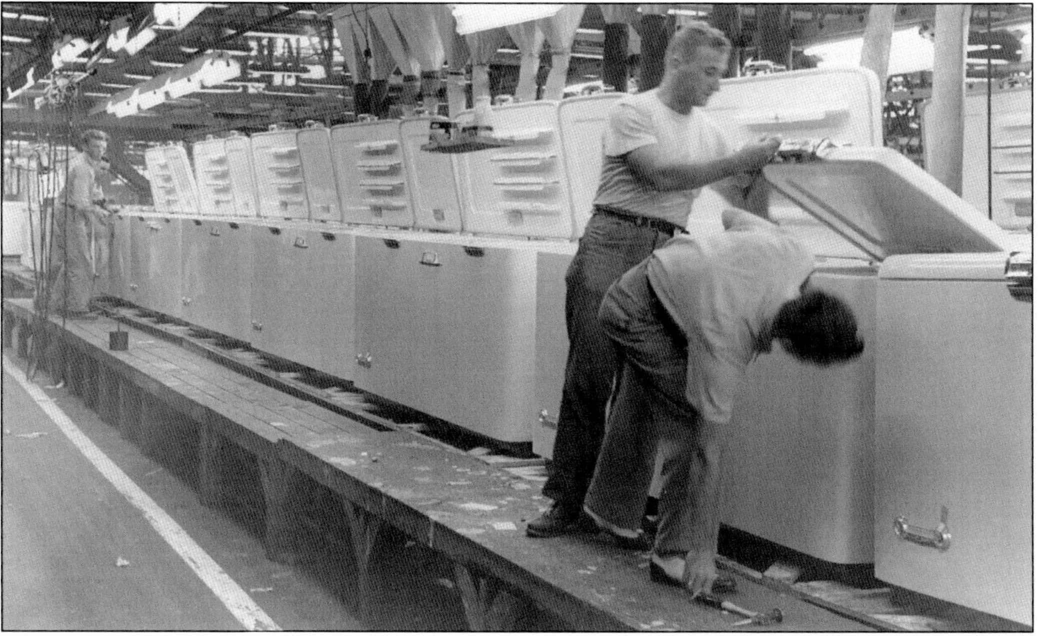

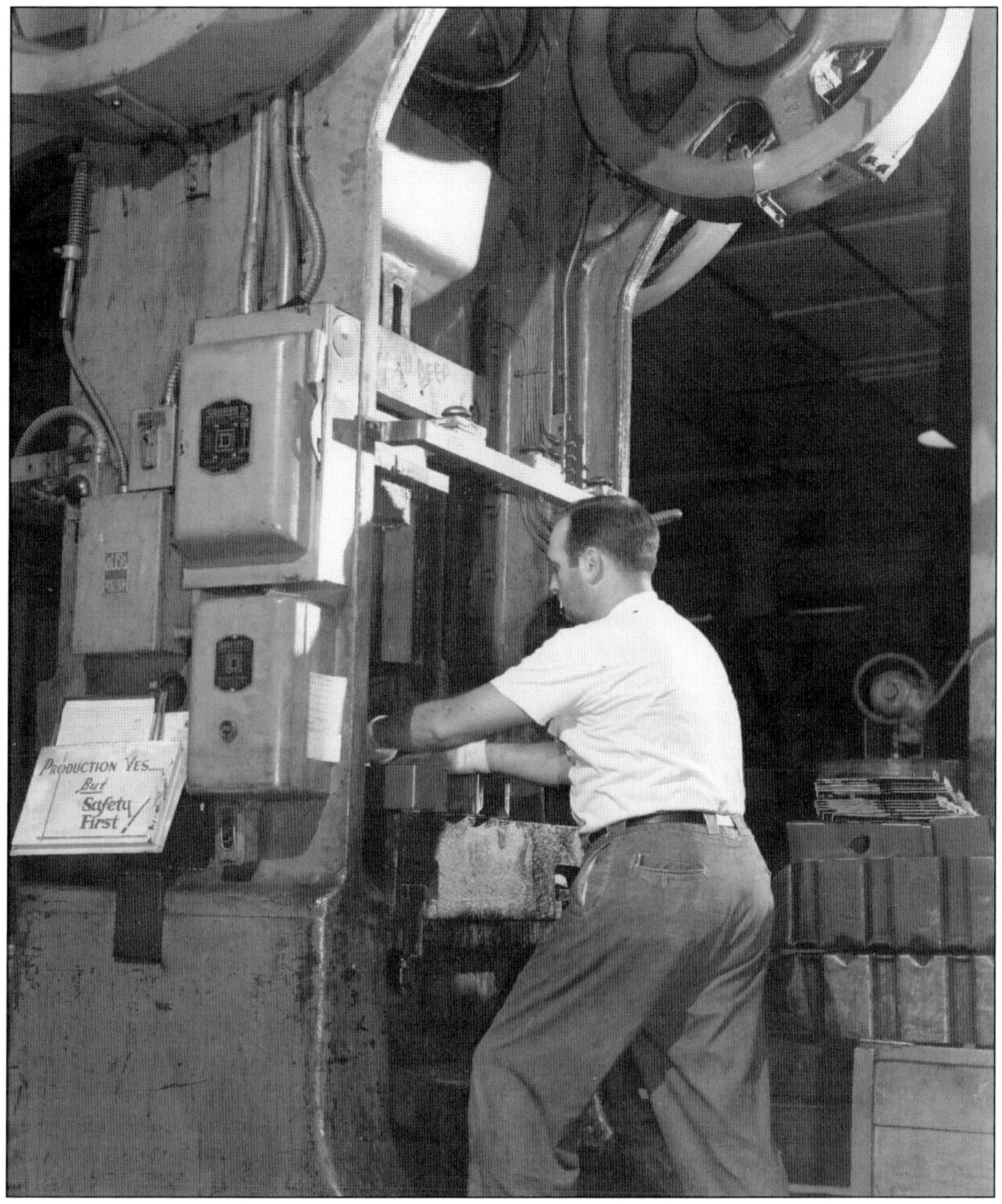

An employee at Avco Manufacturing, also recorded at the Nashville plant in 1952, uses a large hydraulic press to stamp out parts. (Tennessee State Library and Archives, Department of Conservation Collection.)

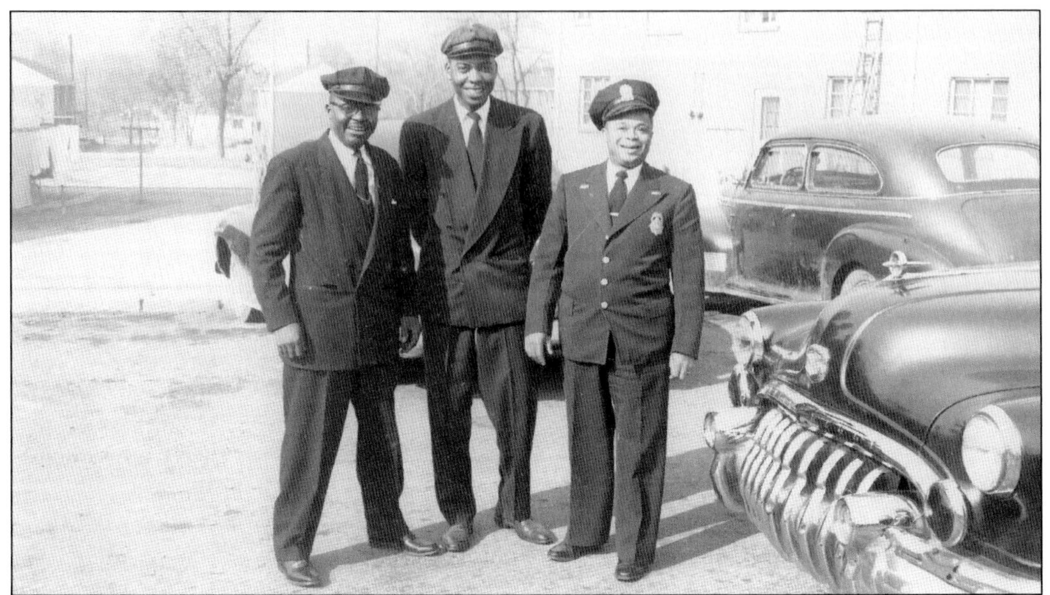

Historically, South Nashville, like other sections of the city, has been made up of many unique and distinctive neighborhoods with strong bonds between friends and family. Two city employees and a Nashville police officer, all unidentified, pose for a city photographer at the J.C. Napier homes during the early 1950s. (Metro Nashville Archives, MDHA Collection.)

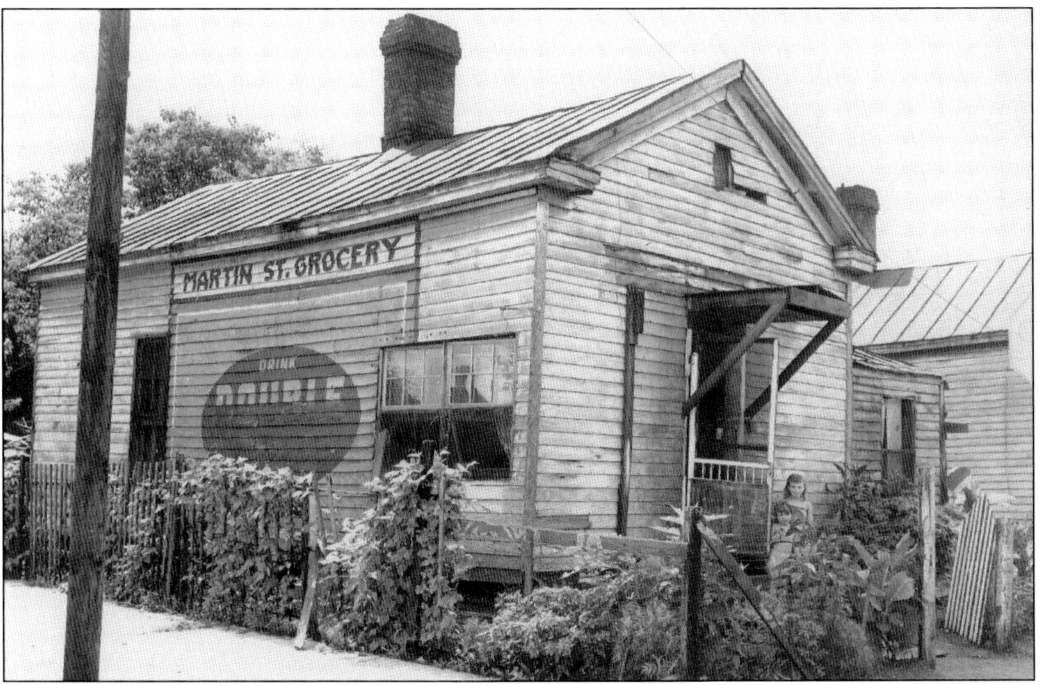

For much of the 20th century, residences throughout Nashville's inner city neighborhoods consisted of simple clapboard shotgun-style houses with tin or tarpaper roofs. Many of these structures were eventually demolished for urban renewal projects. One building, a former market, near Martin and Humphreys Streets, had become a residence by the time this scene was recorded in 1953. Two girls mug for the photographer. (Metro Nashville Archives, MDHA Collection.)

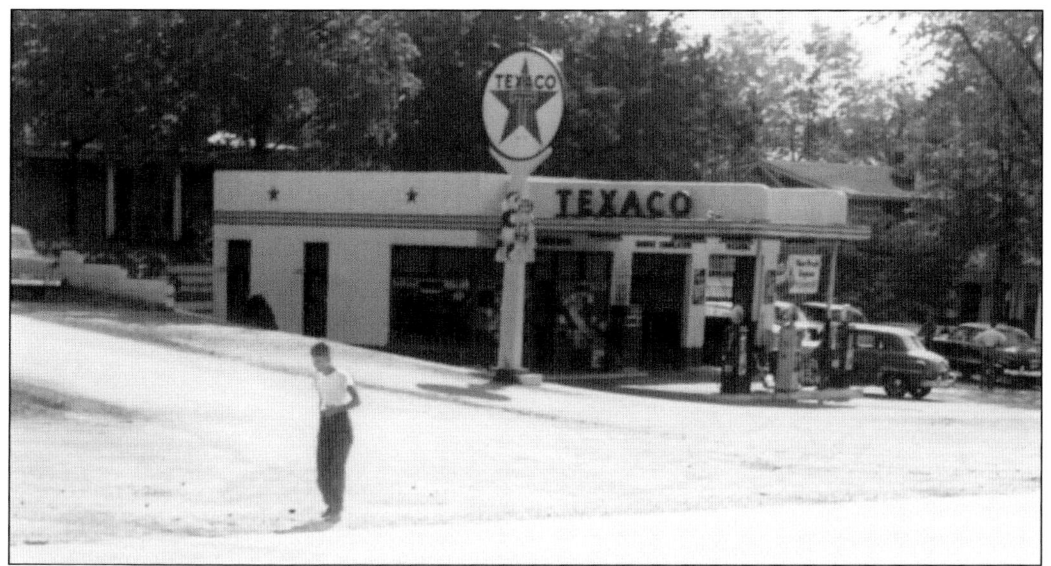

During the 1950s, numerous road-widening projects were underway on South Nashville's arterial streets. This was followed by the construction of interstate highways during the 1960s. It was not until recent years that sidewalks were added to primary streets. During a hot summer day in the early 1950s, a young boy walks down Nolensville Road near Elberta Street in the Woodbine community. (Metro Nashville Archives, MTA Collection.)

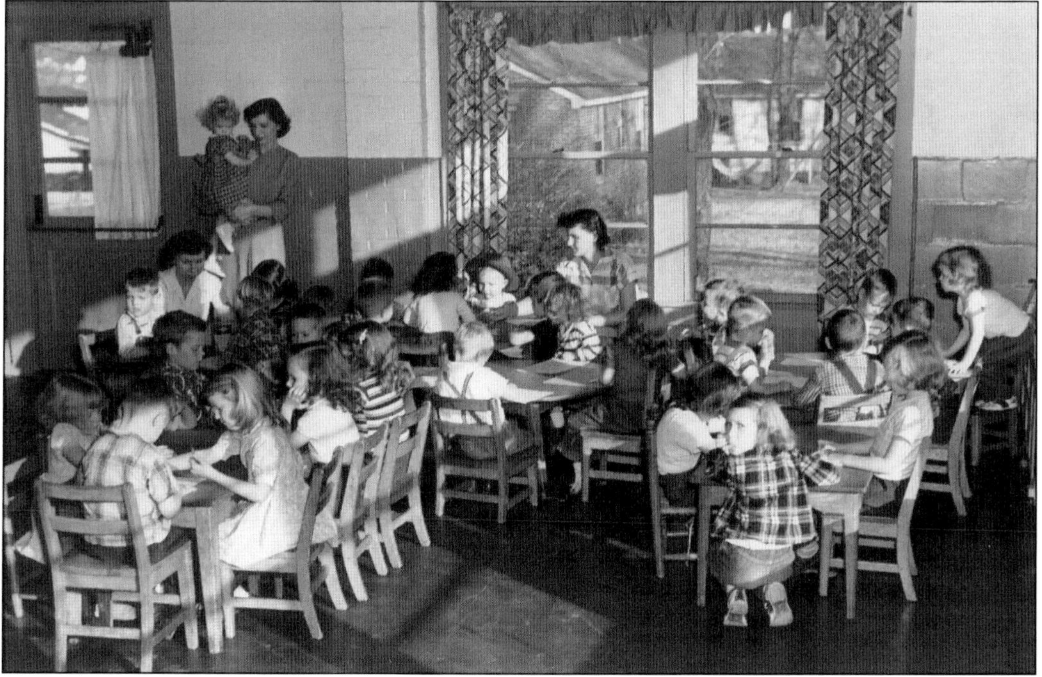

As affordable housing projects were being opened across Nashville during the 1940s and 1950s, it was necessary to have social services such as clinics for infants and children, meal preparation, day care, and other programs for residents needing assistance. This view shows the kindergarten class at the Vine Hill homes in South Nashville during the 1950s. (Metro Nashville Archives, MDHA Collection.)

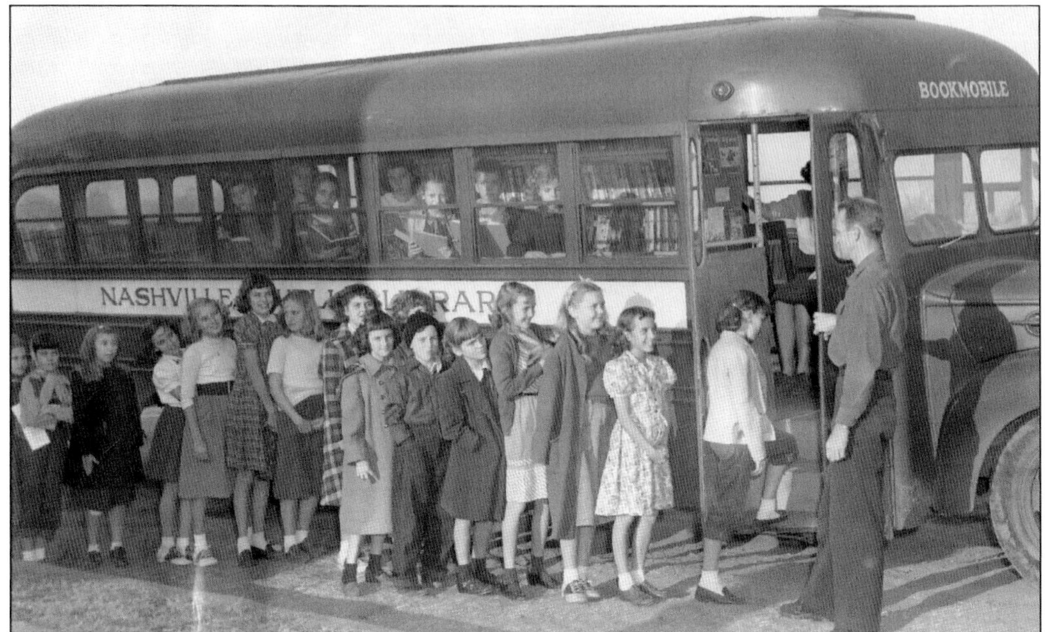

A welcome and familiar sight for Nashville-area school children and all book enthusiasts was the Nashville public library's bookmobile. The bus, a small library on wheels, traveled a regular weekly route stopping at schools, community centers, and even factories. It was a vital service of the library, reaching the outlying sections of the city. (Metro Nashville Archives)

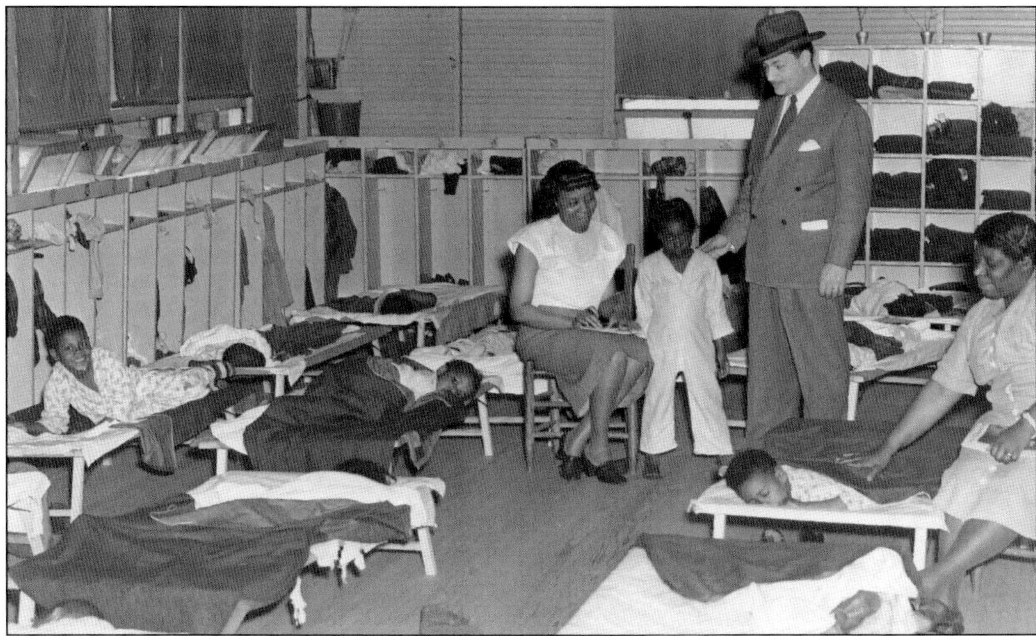

For many years, the South Street Community Center served residents in much of South Nashville. Opened in 1942 in the old Lawrence Elementary School as a day care and nursery school for children of working mothers, the facility later served as an education center for school-aged children and meeting place for adults. During the 1950s, an unidentified official visits the center, chatting with workers. (Metro Nashville Archives, MDHA Collection.)

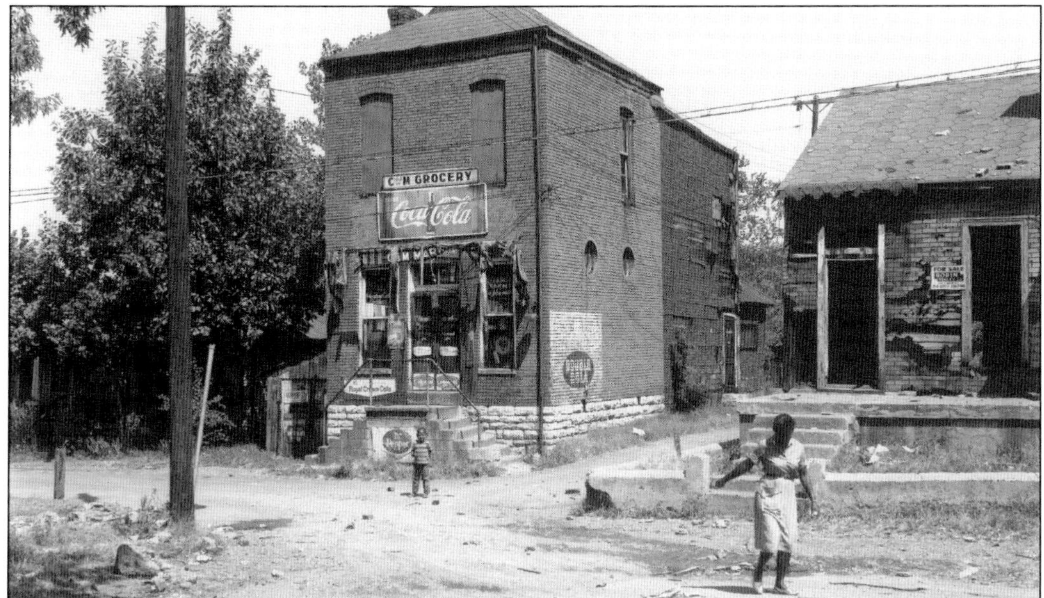

During the 1950s and 1960s, hundreds of commercial and residential buildings south of downtown Nashville were demolished as part of an urban renewal program. The character of neighborhoods was changed forever as newer housing, wider streets and interstate highways replaced older buildings. A mother and her son are seen in front of the C and M Market at Tenth Avenue South and Archer Street around 1965. (Metro Nashville Archives, MDHA Collection.)

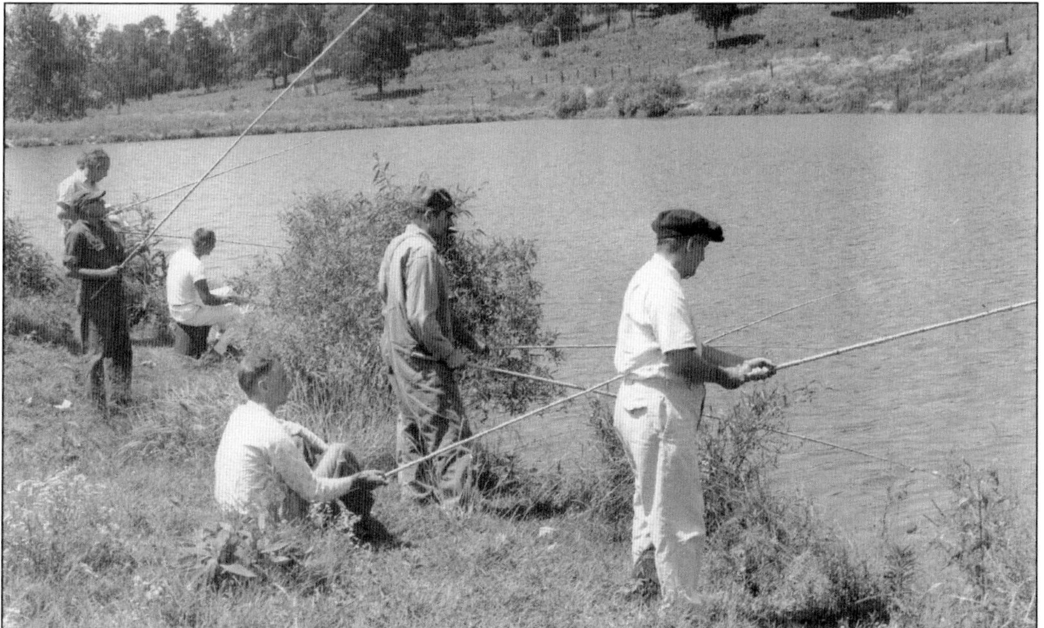

Central State Hospital was middle Tennessee's primary psychiatric facility since the 1840s. The hospital relocated southeast of Nashville to a 1,100-acre site on Murfreesboro Road in 1852, replacing a smaller, antiquated structure inside the city. In this image from 1961, patients enjoy the relaxation of fishing from the hospital-owned pond on the property. (Tennessee State Library and Archives, Department of Conservation Collection.)

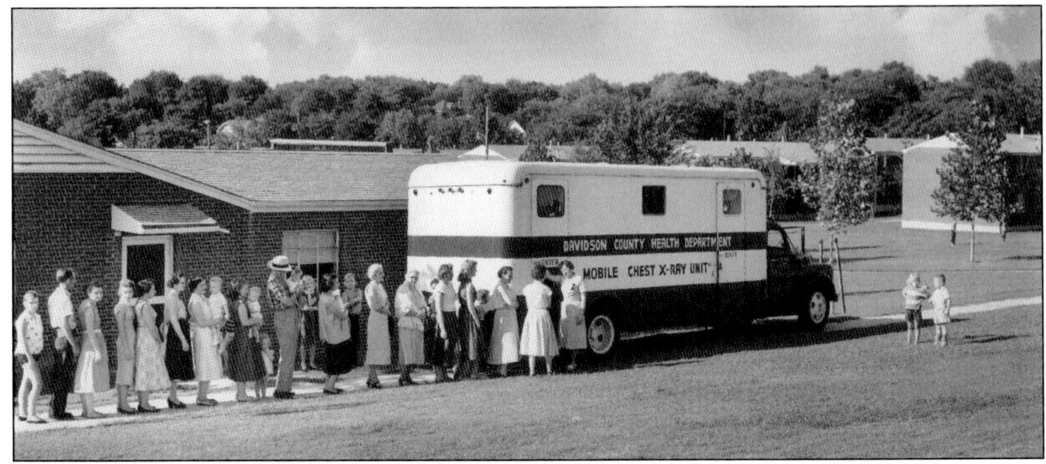

In 1954, the Davidson County Health Department dedicated its new mobile chest x-ray unit to serve the greater Nashville area. The unit was set up at offices, factories, housing developments and other areas with heavily populated areas to stimulate public interest in the drive against tuberculosis. Families wait in line for x-rays at an unknown Nashville housing project during the early 1950s. (Metro Nashville Archives.)

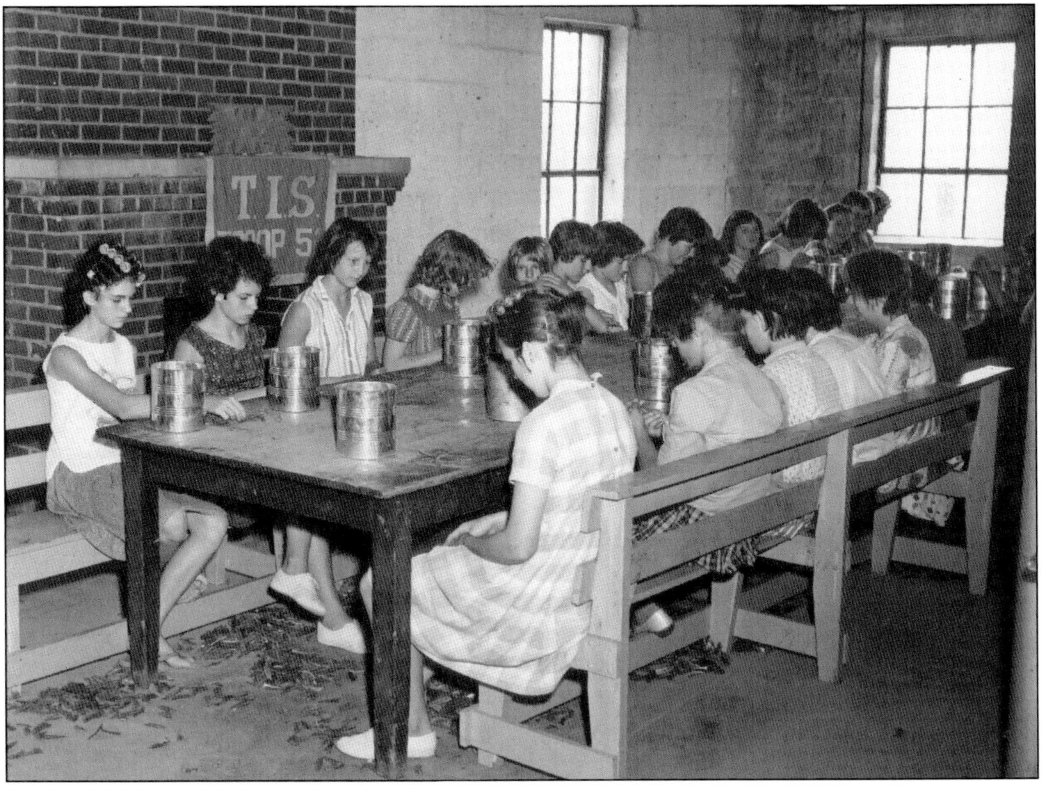

The Tennessee Industrial School (TIS) was begun in 1887 as a state-sponsored school providing care and education for at-risk children from across the state that could not get those necessities from their families. In 1955, TIS changed its name to Tennessee Preparatory School. Teenage students are seen shelling butterbeans for a cannery in this image from 1964. (Tennessee State Library and Archives, Department of Conservation Collection.)

Four

CHURCHES AND SCHOOLS

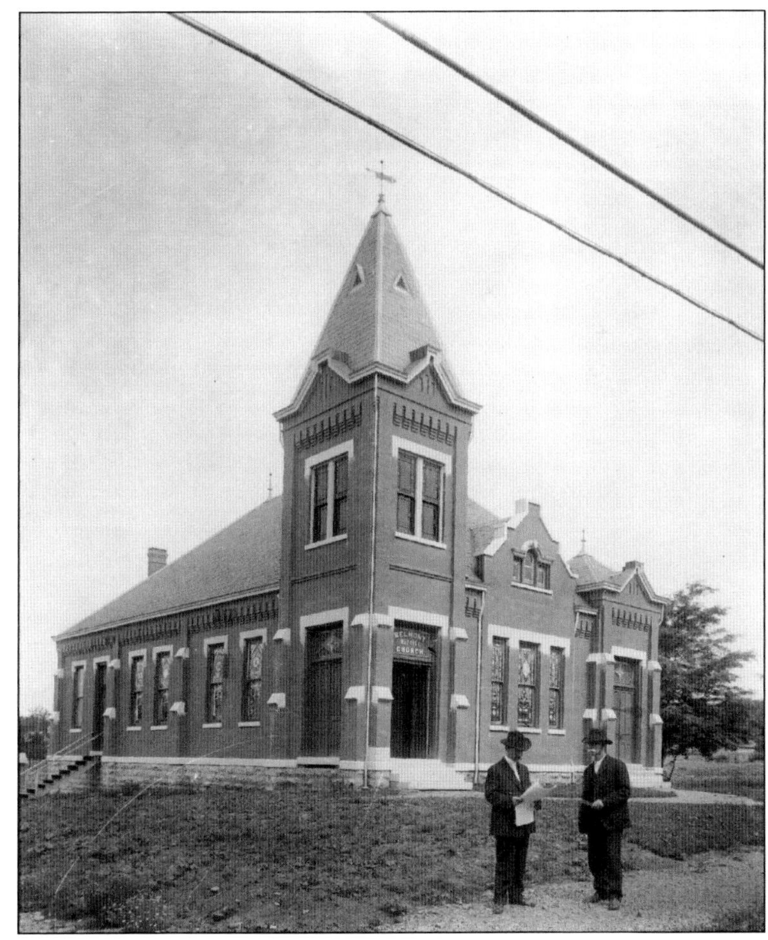

Schools and churches were an important part of life in the early 1900s, as these were places where friends and families could learn and socialize. The 20th-century churches and schools from South Nashville depicted in this chapter offer a variety of architectural styles and history. Belmont Baptist Church, pictured here, opened in 1904 at Twelfth Avenue South and Beechwood Avenue. This building remains in use today. (Tennessee State Library and Archives.)

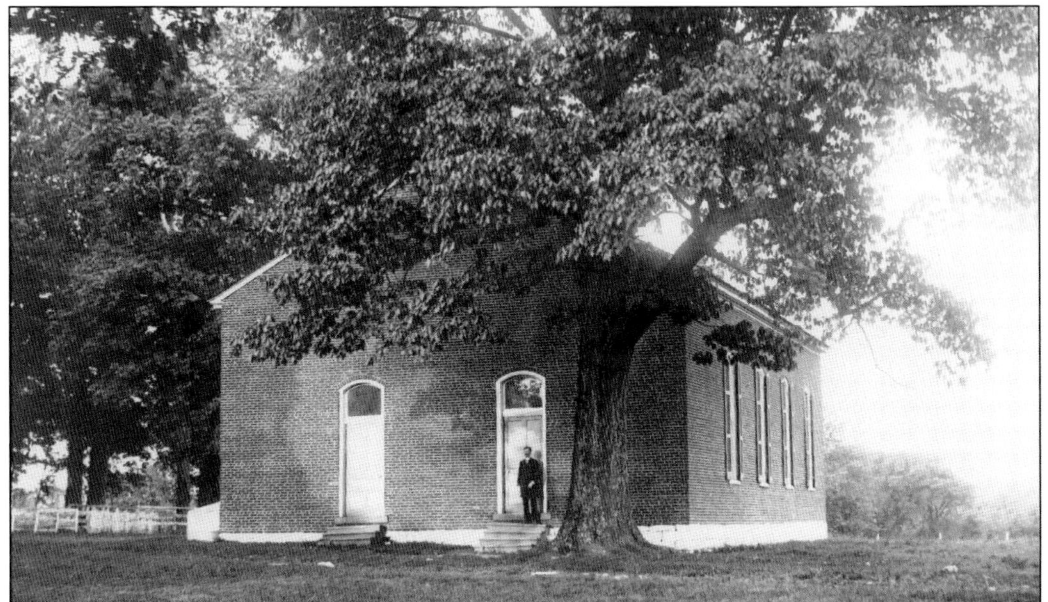

Mill Creek Baptist Church, organized by the Menees and Whitsitt families in 1797, was located on Mill Creek Chapel Road, presently Old Glenrose Avenue, in the Glencliff community. This image was made during the 1890s. The Colonial brick church house was constructed in 1810, replacing the original log building. The church cemetery, situated left, has been partially restored in recent years by historians. (Tennessee State Library and Archives.)

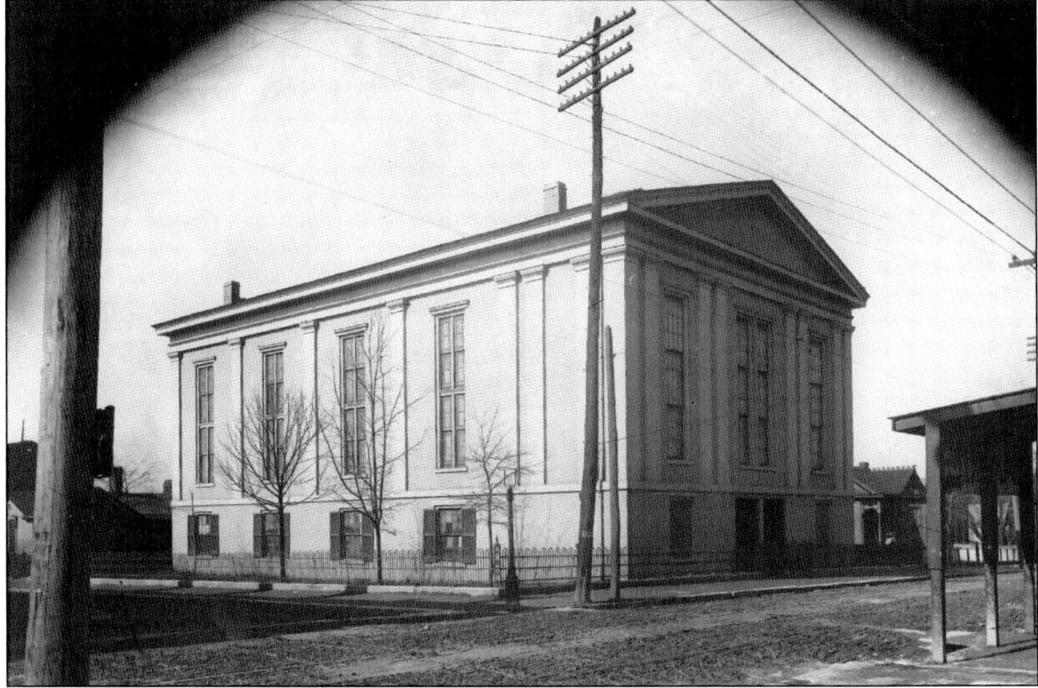

Central Baptist Church, south of downtown Nashville, was once one of the oldest established Baptist churches in the city. The stately building, erected in 1877, was located on Fourth Avenue South at Elm Street. (Tennessee State Library and Archives.)

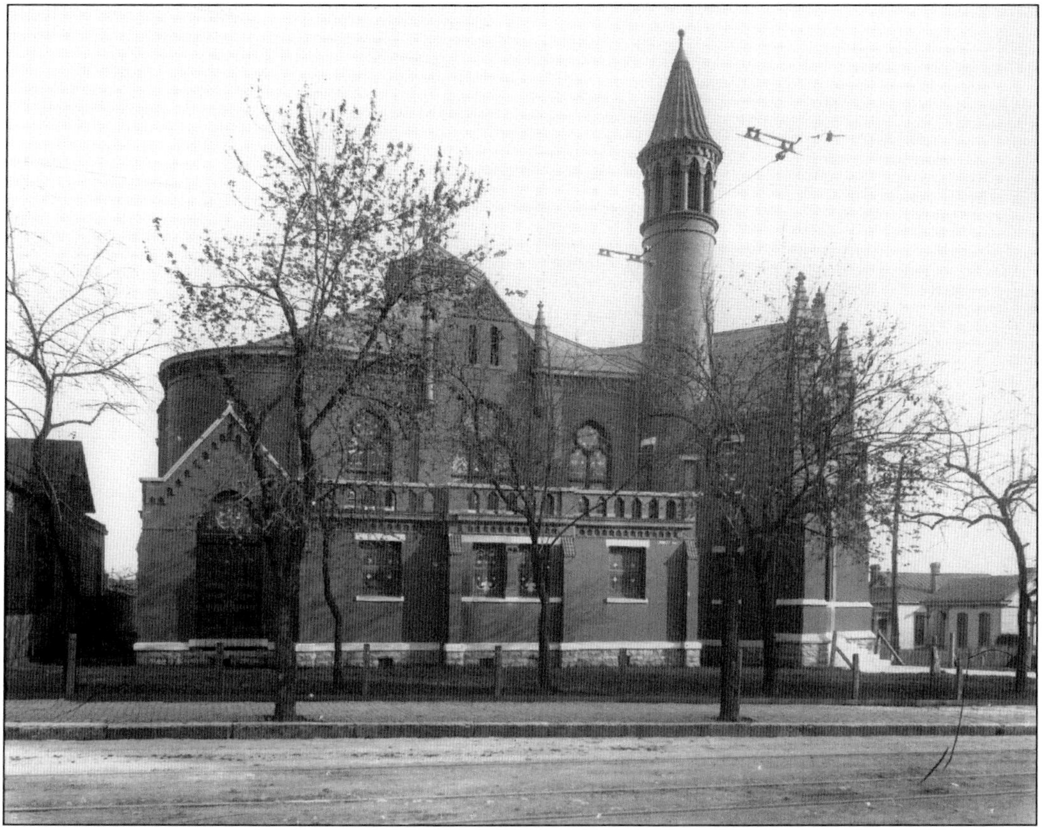

One of the more architecturally striking churches in South Nashville is the Lindsley Avenue Church of Christ, opened in 1895 as the Grace Cumberland Presbyterian Church. The building was sold to the Church of Christ during the 1920s. Located at Fourth Avenue South and Lindsley Street, this two-story Victorian Gothic structure features numerous gables, turrets, pinnacles, and a cupola. (Tennessee State Library and Archives.)

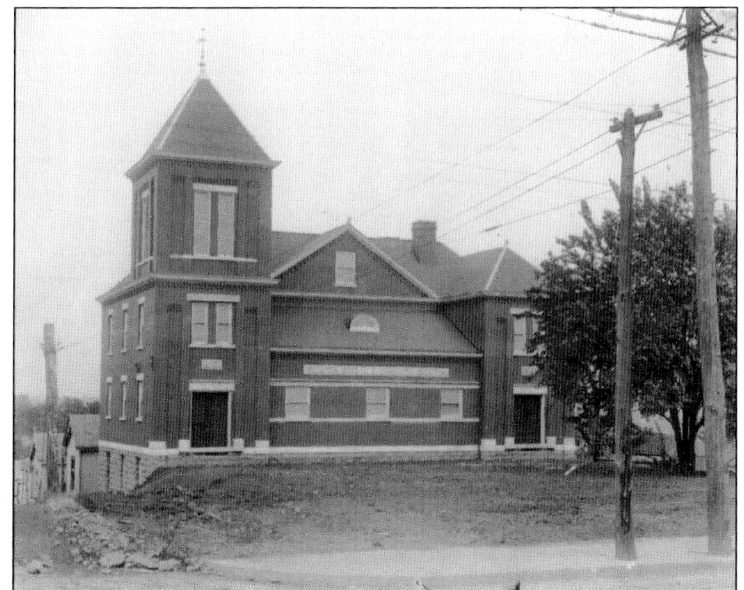

Located at Eighth Avenue South and Hamilton across from the City Reservoir, the South End Methodist Church was an attractive addition to the area when it opened in 1910. South End later merged with another church, relocating across town. The structure survives today but serves as a commercial business. This view was made shortly after construction was nearing completion. (Tennessee State Library and Archives.)

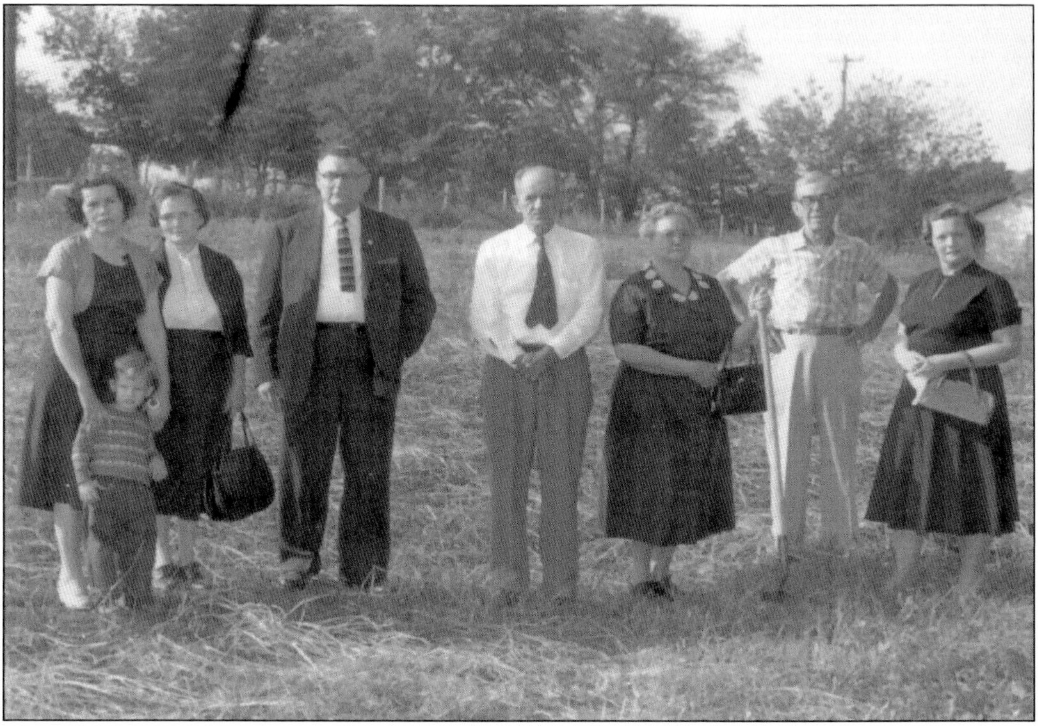

Churches of all denominations could be found across South Nashville, a few, with roots going back to the 19th century. Woodbine Baptist Church, located in the Glencliff community, was founded in 1934. Twenty years later, the congregation had outgrown its building. In 1959, ground was broken for a new church with the surviving charter members present. Shown from left to right are Zora Jackson, nephew Ellis Jackson, Willie Mai Robinson, L.E. Inman, Ed Jackson, Ollie Bell, Jim Bell, and Willie Frakes. Below, the Woodbine congregation poses for a photograph in their new building on Whitsitt Avenue four years later. (Both, Woodbine Baptist Church collection.)

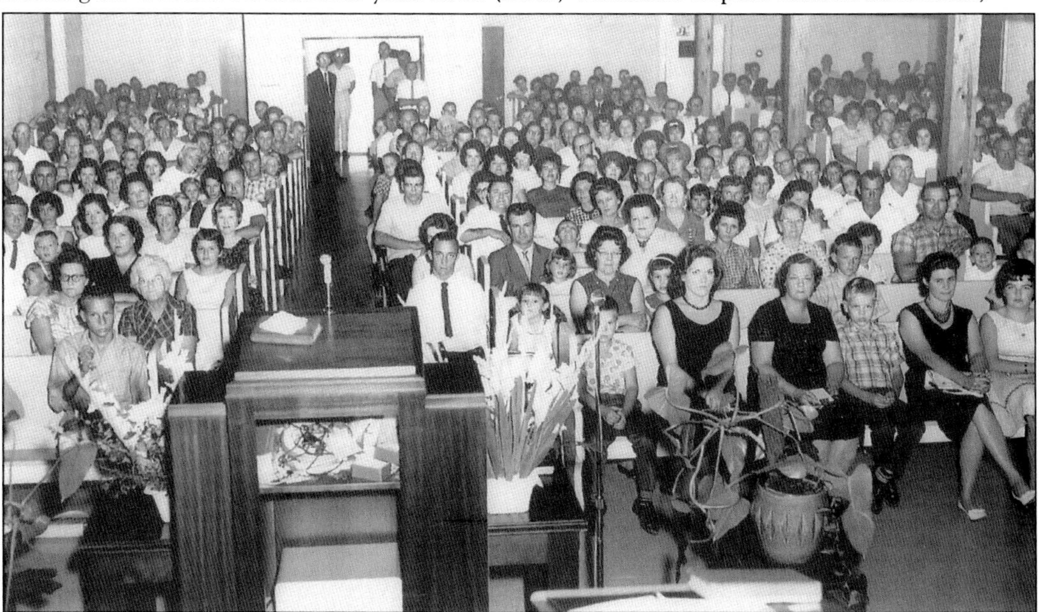

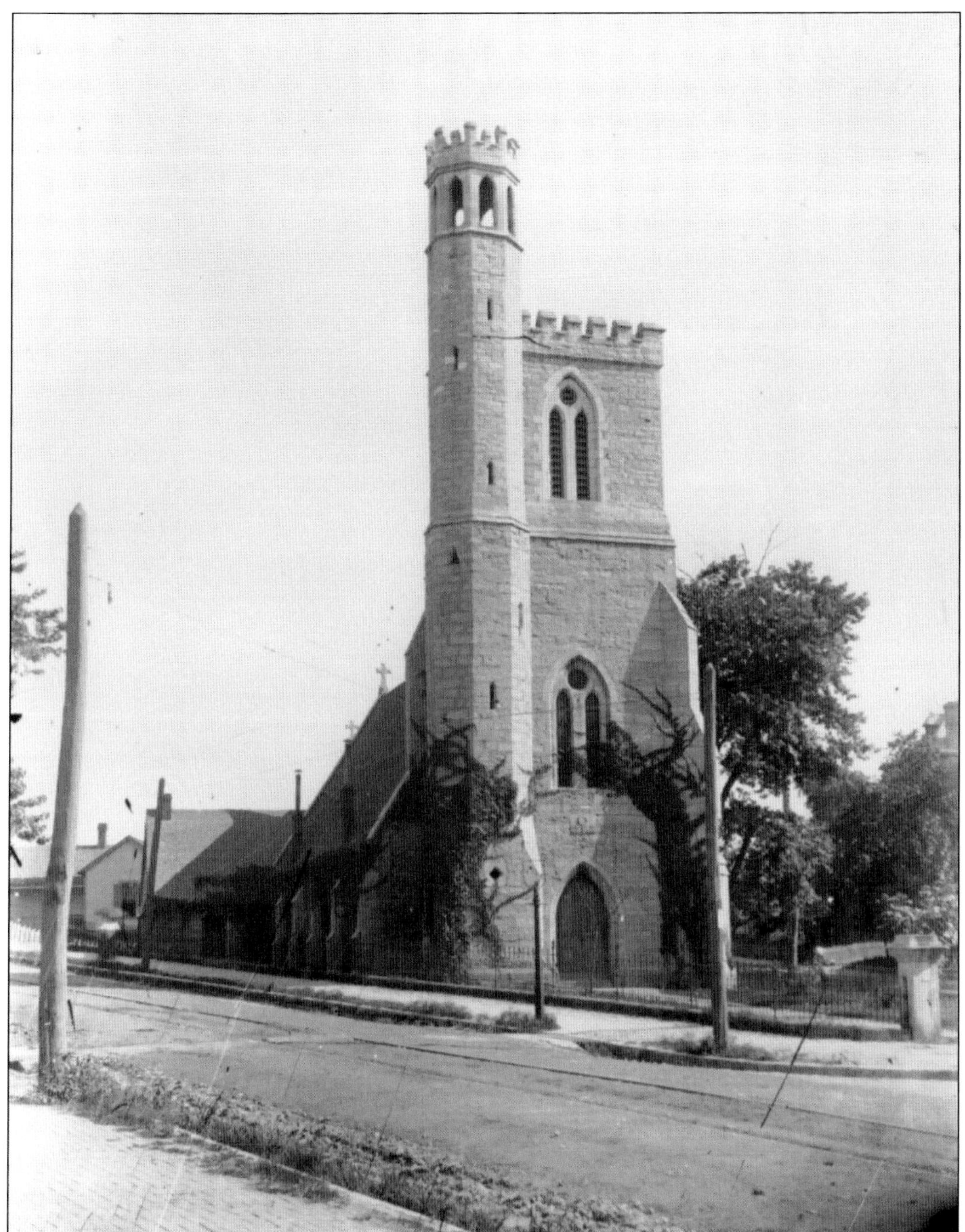

Many of South Nashville's churches experienced changes during the city's history. An example is Holy Trinity Episcopal Church, located at Sixth Avenue at Lafayette Street. Completed in 1852, it was designed in Gothic revival style suggesting an English village church. Holy Trinity has had a predominately black congregation since 1907. During the past 20 years, the neighborhood around the church has undergone extensive redevelopment. This image, recorded around 1920, shows the church with the Sixth Avenue streetcar track in the foreground. (Tennessee State Library and Archives.)

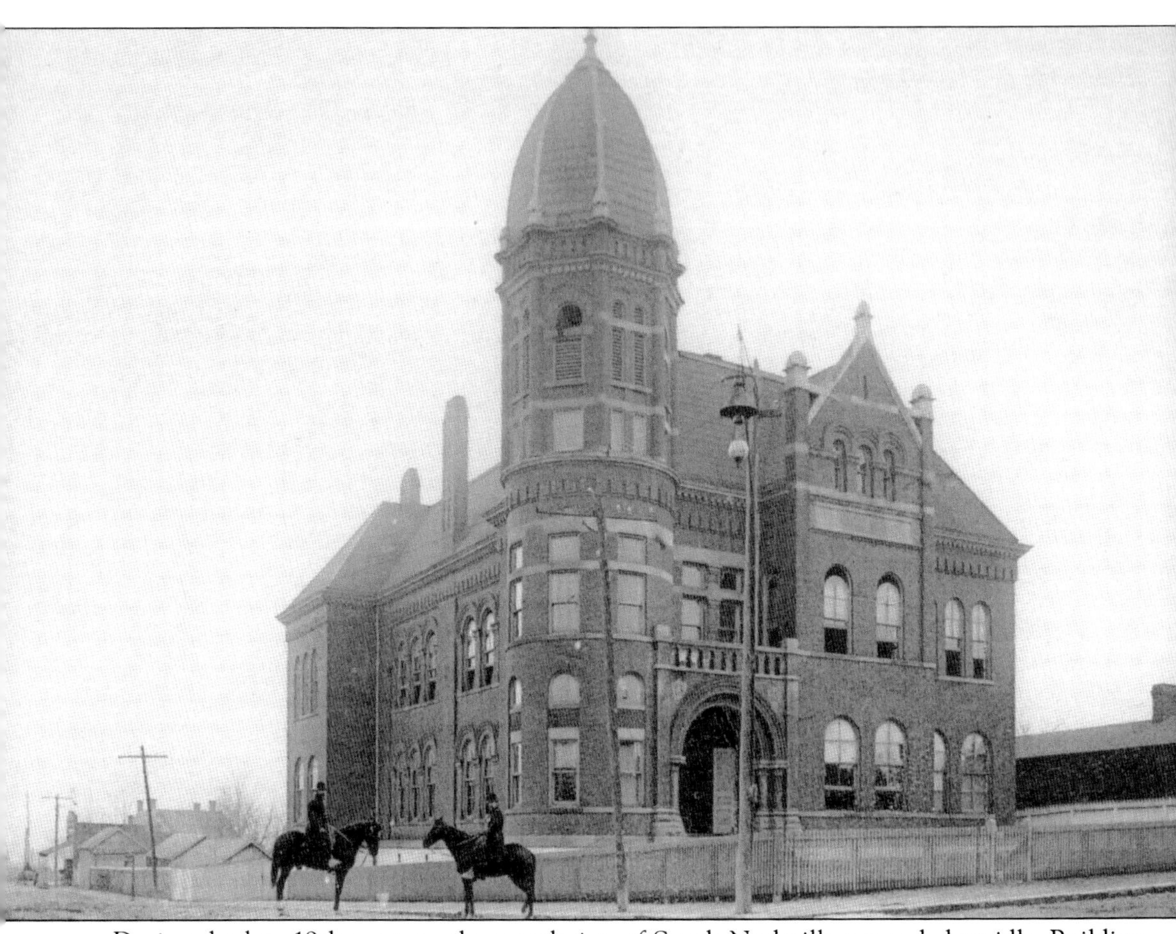

During the late 19th century, the population of South Nashville expanded rapidly. Building enough schools for the additional students was a challenge for the city. Trimble School opened in 1889, replacing a smaller structure on the same site. Located at Market and Chestnut Streets, it was a grand building sporting an ornate tower. Trimble was demolished in 1954 and replaced by Johnson Elementary School the following year. (Metro Nashville Archives.)

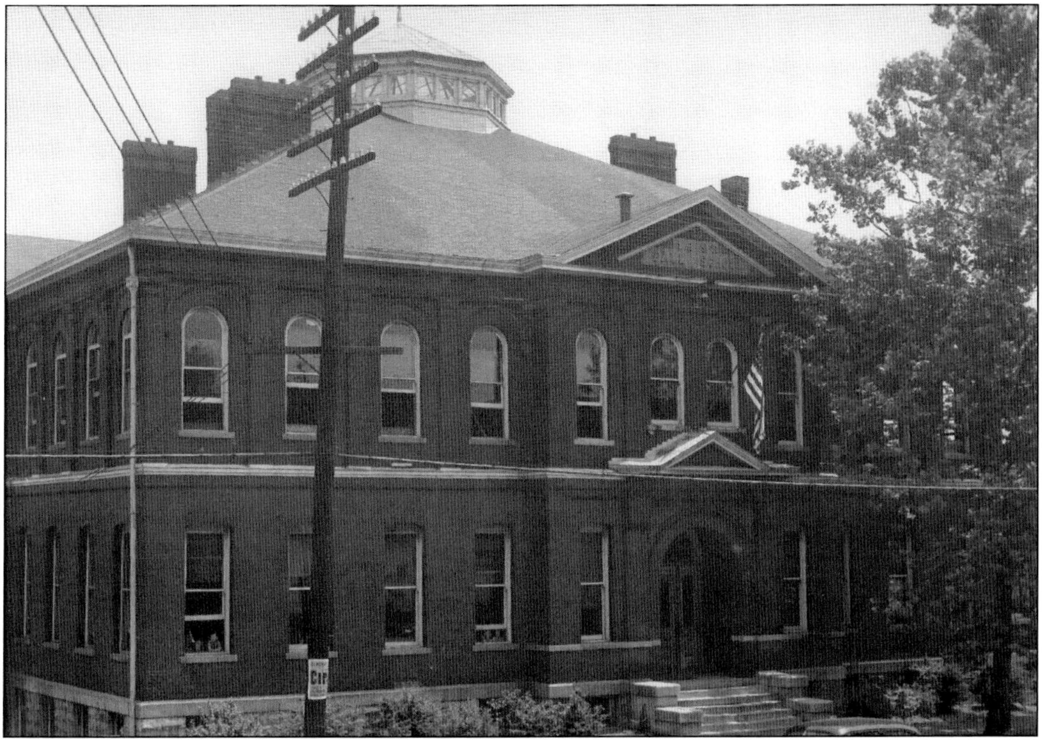

With great fanfare, the Philip S. Fall School was opened in 1898 at a cost of $22,500. Located at the corner of Spruce (later renamed Eighth Avenue South) and Chestnut Streets, this building is 100 feet square, being nearly identical on each side. Below, second graders pose for a class photograph in front of the school in 1914. Fall School was phased out in 1970; after a full restoration, the building was repurposed as a church. (Both, Metro Nashville Archives.)

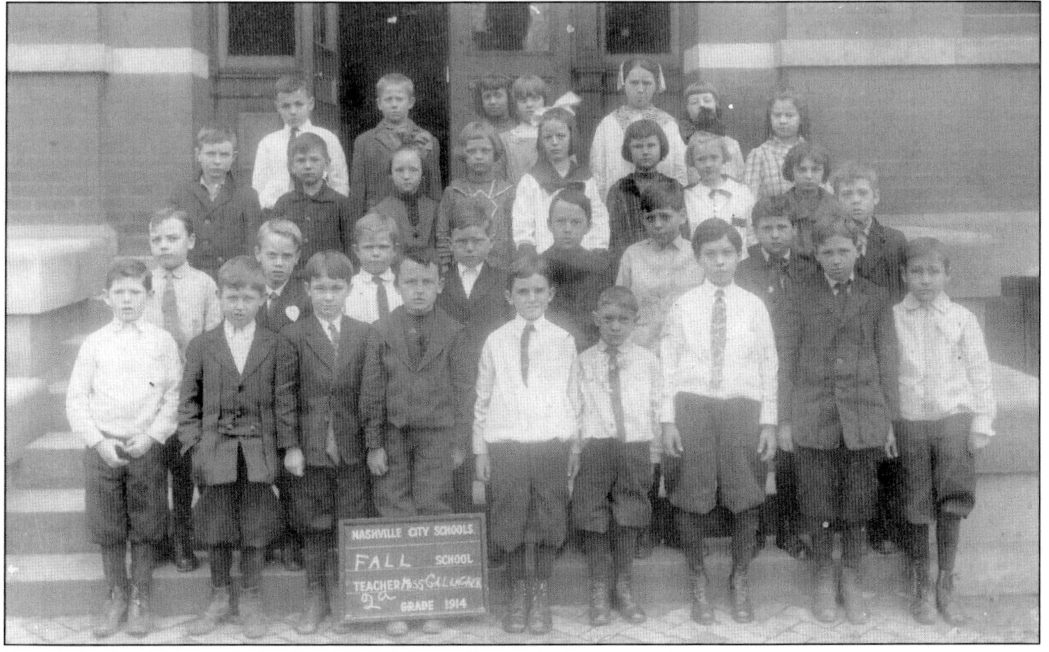

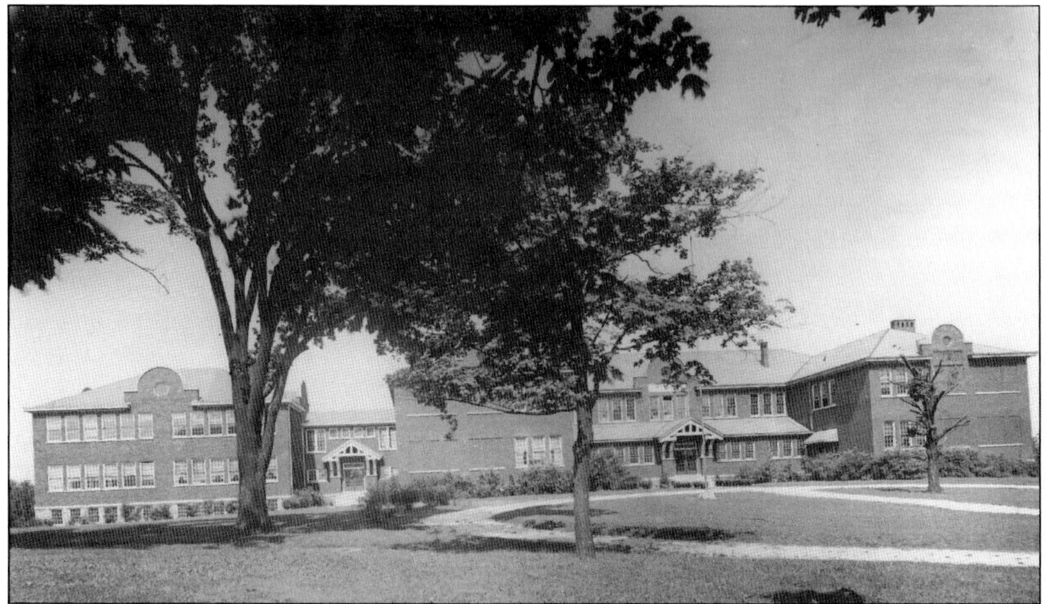

Central High School was located at Rains and Wedgewood Avenues, across the street from the state fairgrounds, and just outside the city limits. It was the first public high school to be located outside the city of Nashville, in what was then rural Davidson County. The school opened in the 1920s and closed in 1971. Below, Central students pose in front of their school. Both images were recorded around 1930. (Both, Tennessee State Library and Archives.)

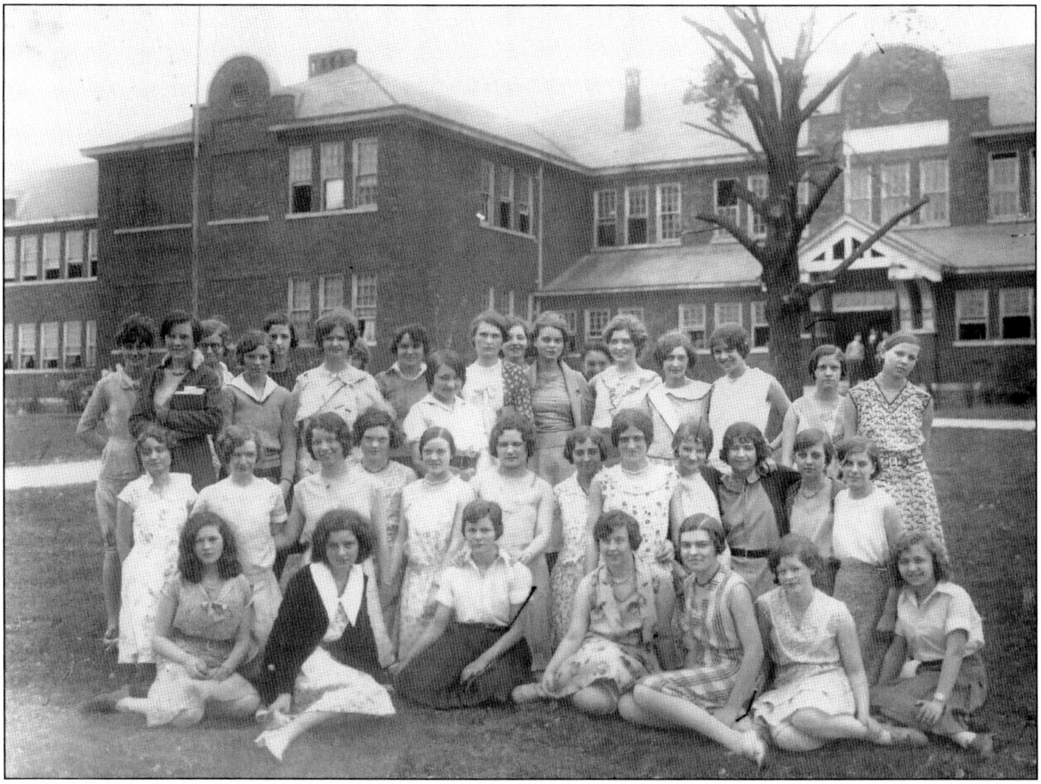

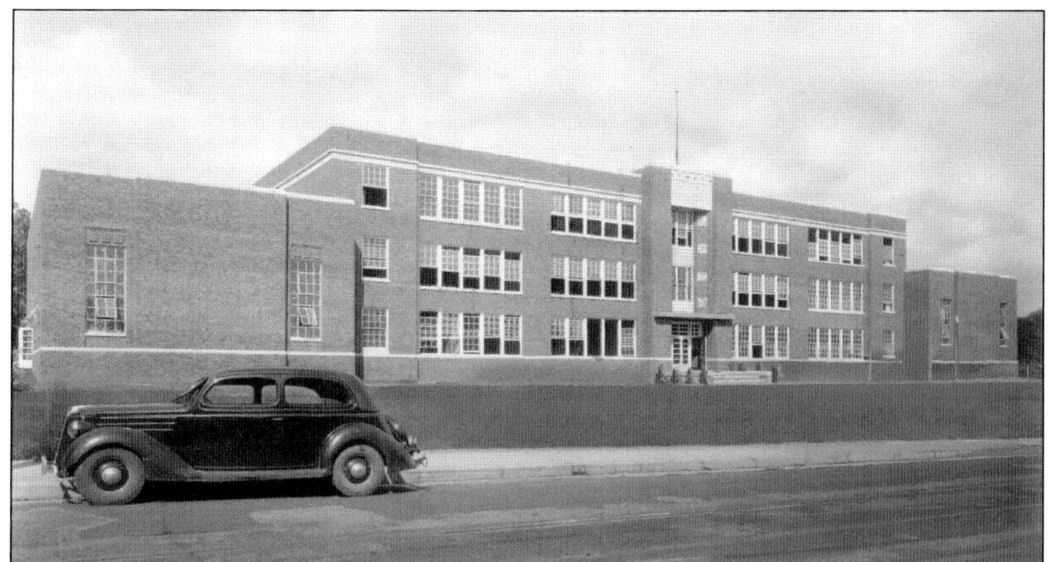

The Waverly-Belmont School, located at Tenth Avenue South and Caruthers Street, was opened in 1937 as a Works Progress Administration project during the Pres. Franklin D. Roosevelt administration. The building was erected to support a burgeoning suburban section in South Nashville, by the same name. After being closed for several years, Waverly-Belmont reopened in 2015 as a technology demonstration school after going through a complete renovation and expansion. (Metro Nashville Archives.)

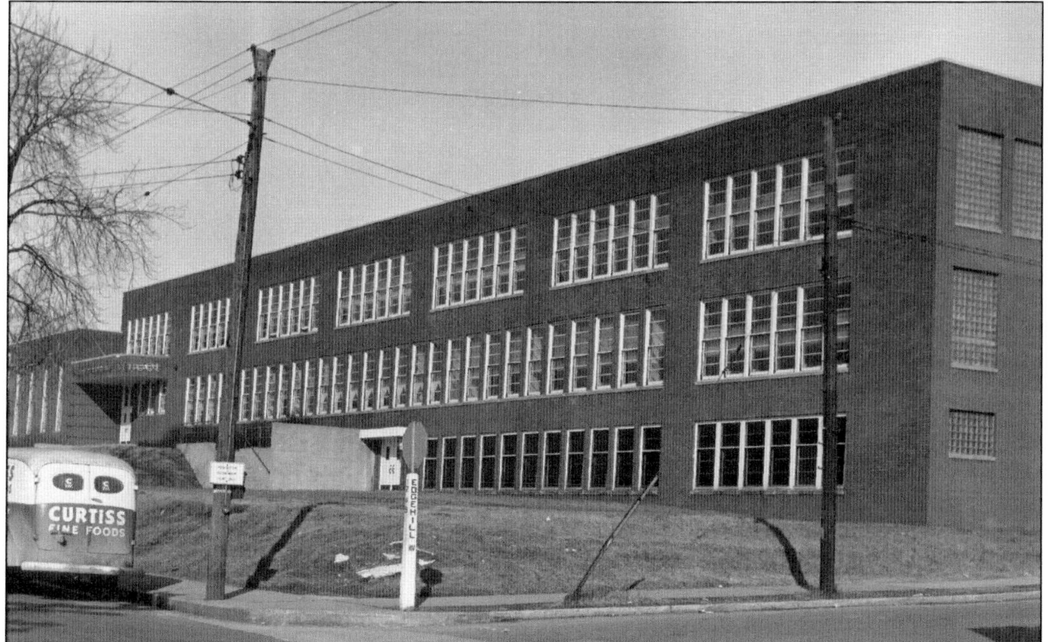

Carter-Lawrence Elementary School is a combination of two previous schools. The building, located at Twelfth Avenue South and Edgehill Avenue, opened in 1940. The design of the school was unique in that it incorporated modern architectural styles, including Art Deco elements and glass-block windows on the south wall. Eight class rooms were added in 1948, followed by a cafeteria in 1959. (Metro Nashville Archives.)

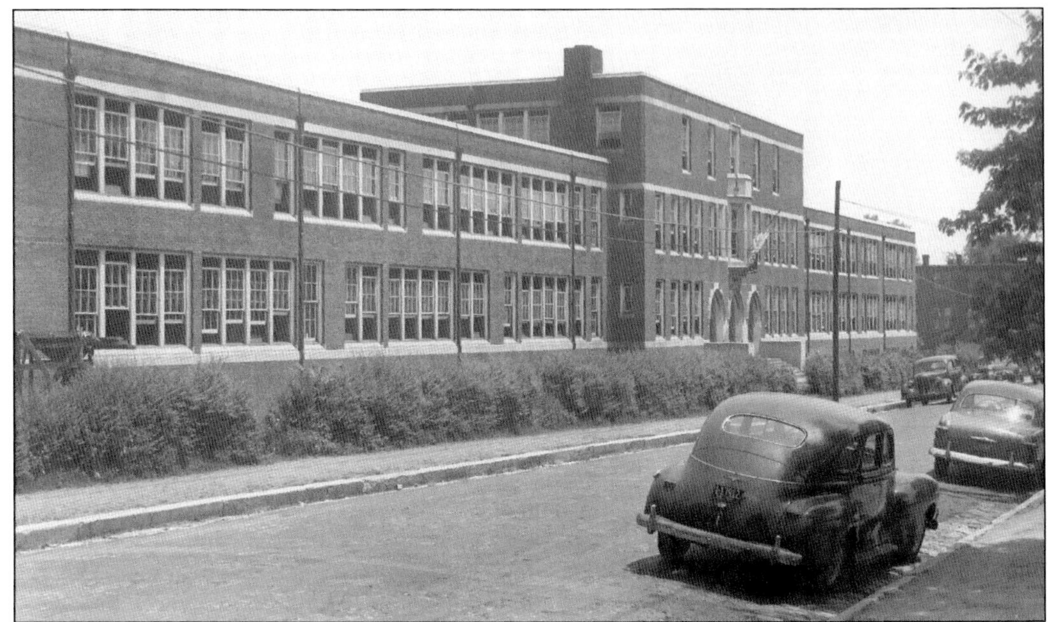

Cameron Junior High School was opened in 1940 to serve African American residents living in South Nashville. The two-story facility was located on First Avenue South and Lafayette Street. The school was expanded in 1954 housing grades 7th through 12th until 1971, when Cameron returned to junior high status. This image shows the school as it appeared in 1949 from the First Avenue side. (Metro Nashville Archives.)

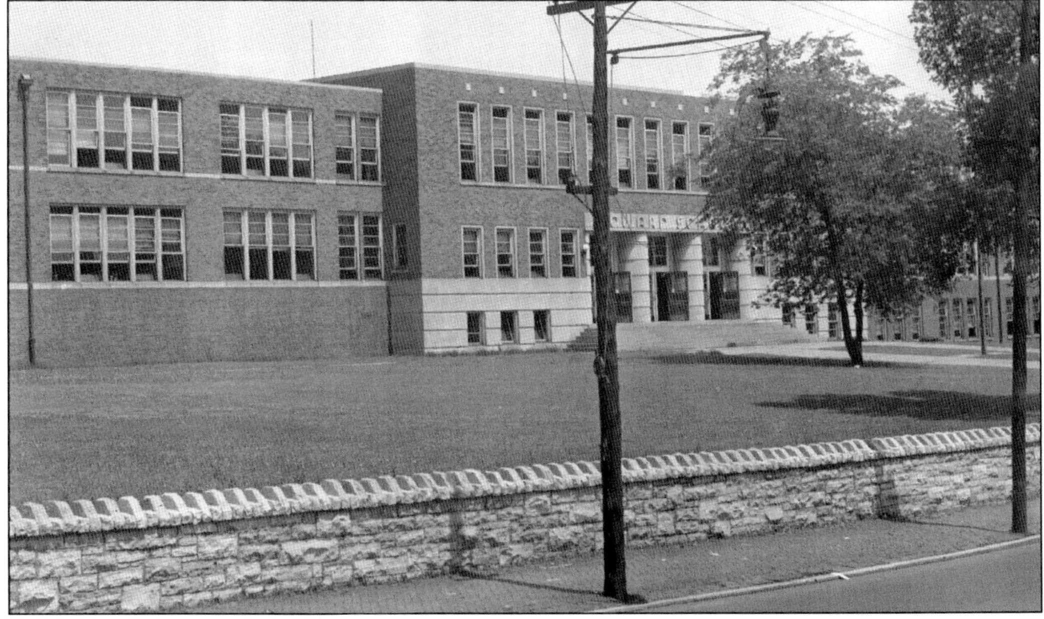

The Howard School Building was built in 1939, replacing an older structure. Located on Second Avenue South, just south of the business district, the facility was designed to serve grades first through twelfth. Howard School was phased out in 1971. The structure survives today as part of the Richard Fulton Campus housing offices of the Metropolitan Government of Nashville and Davidson County. (Metro Nashville Archives.)

Five

Notable Buildings and Landmarks

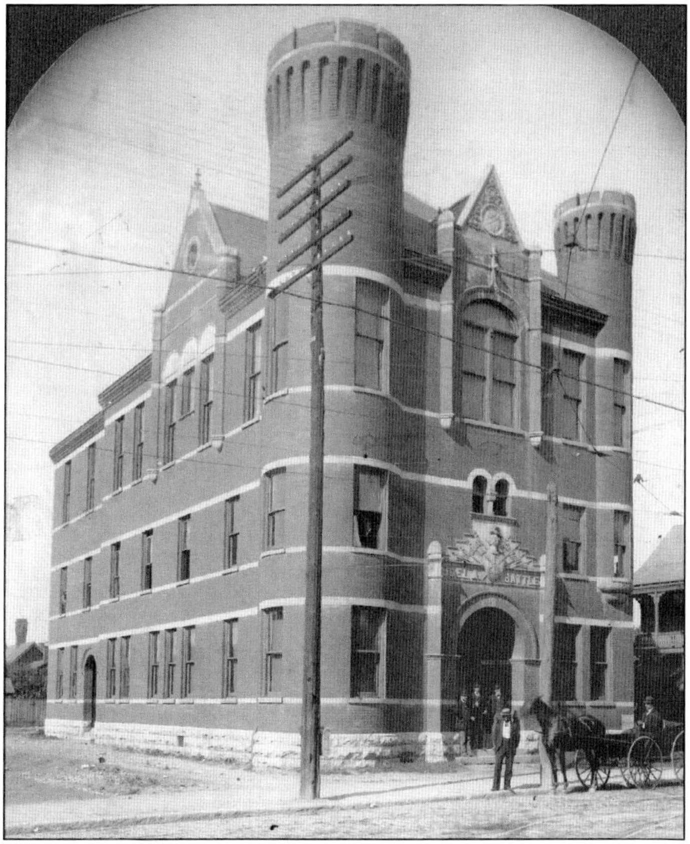

Between 1885 and 1890, the district south of downtown Nashville saw the completion of many distinctive buildings that included the George Reyer Pumping Station, City Reservoir, William Gerst Brewery, and City Hospital. One of the more interesting buildings was the Joel A. Battle Lodge No. 84, Knights of Pythias hall, located at South Market Street and Lindsley Avenue, completed in 1895. (Tennessee State Library and Archives.)

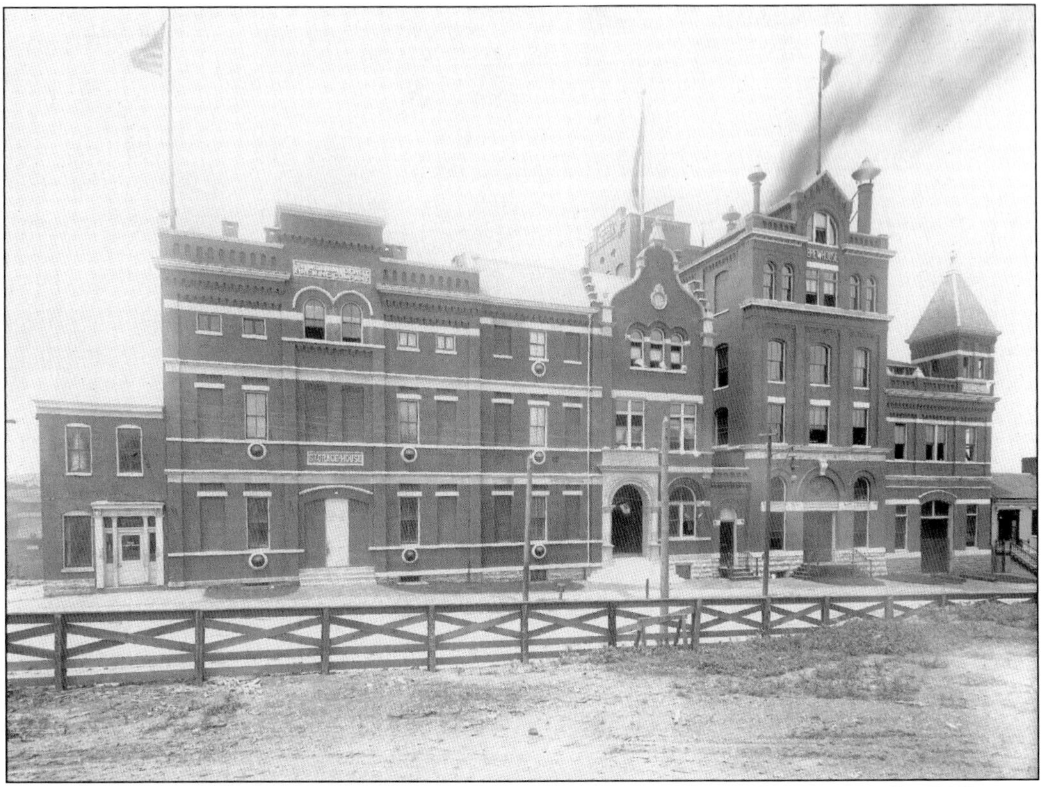

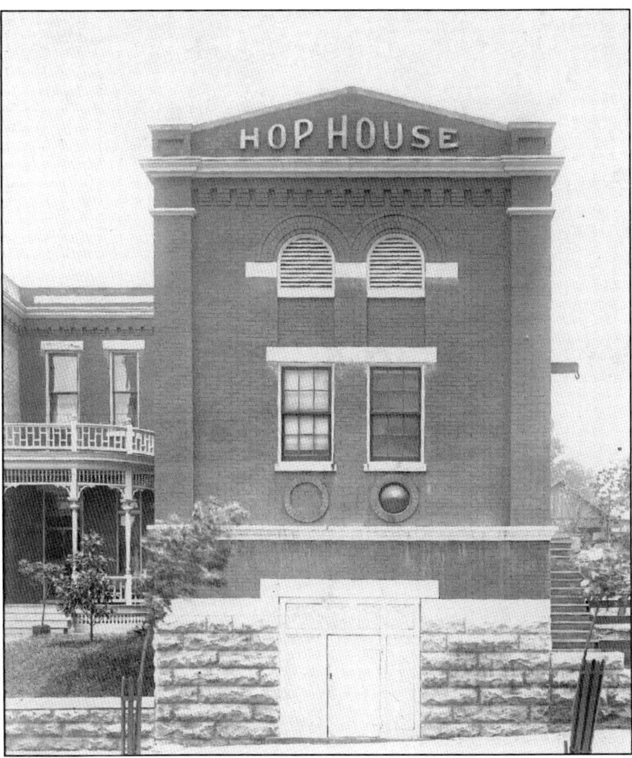

For nearly 64 years, the William Gerst Brewery Company building, located at High and Mulberry Streets, was an impressive South Nashville landmark. The ornate structure, occupying a city block, opened in 1890. The company was the primary brewery in middle Tennessee, before and after the Prohibition era. After struggling for several years due to national competition from larger competing breweries, the Gerst firm shut down in 1954; the attractive building was demolished in 1963. The above image shows the storage house, brew house, and machine house. The sprawling facility also contained fermenting and refrigeration rooms, a boiler house, and offices. In the rear of the brewery were stables for 50 horses. A view of the hop house is shown at left. (Both, Tennessee State Library and Archives.)

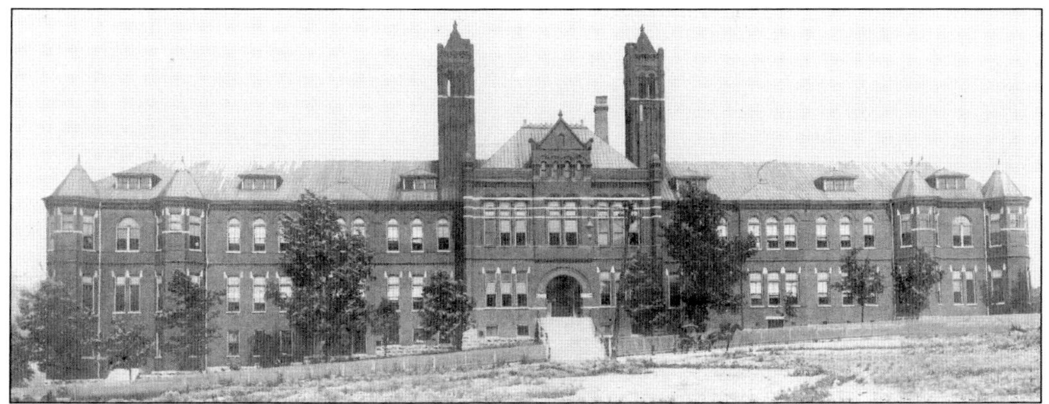

Situated on Rolling Mill Hill on the bluffs over the Cumberland River south of downtown, Nashville's City Hospital was opened in 1890 with one physician, seven nurses, and 60 beds. The view above shows the facility around 1900. In 1932, a four-story addition was opened to relieve the serious overcrowding. In the 1940s scene below, the new brick and concrete addition is visible at left, attached to the front of the original hospital. The other structures at right were added to the compound over the years. The sprawling facility, later renamed Metropolitan Nashville General Hospital, moved from this site to the Meharry Medical College in 1998 after a merger. The former hospital property was later redeveloped into a residential development retaining some of the original hospital buildings. (Both, Metro Nashville Archives.)

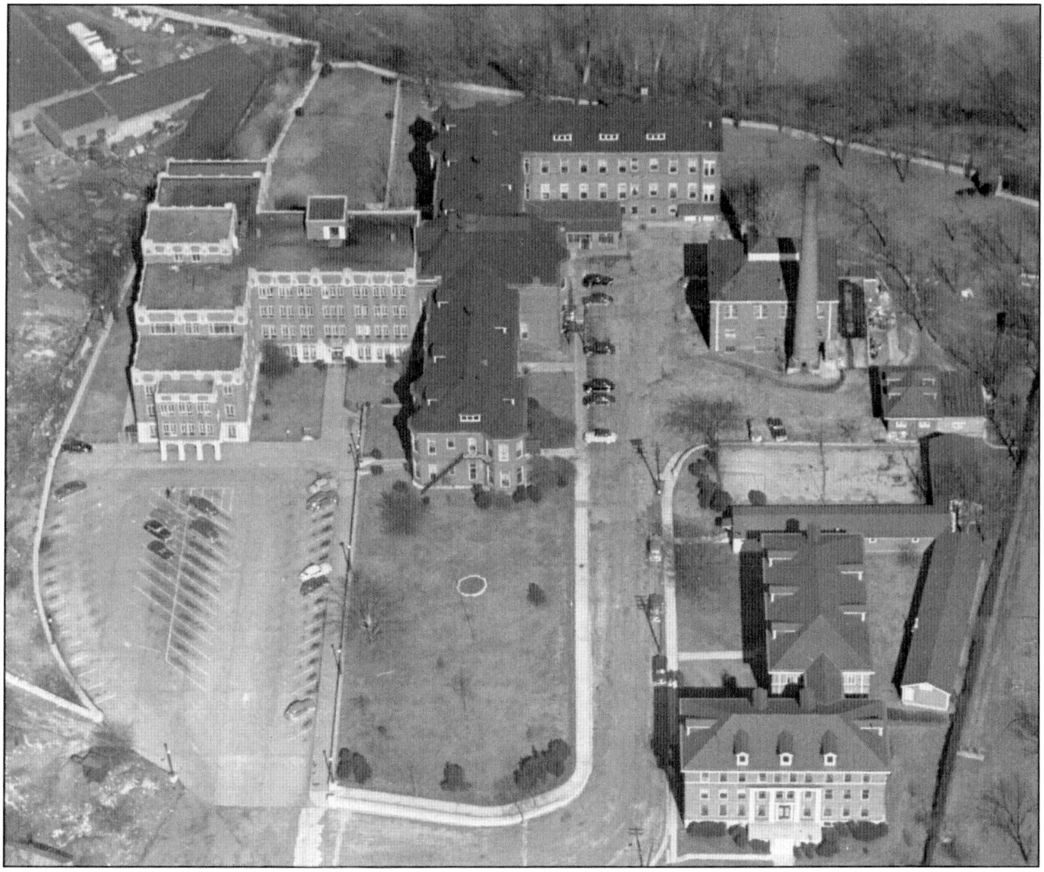

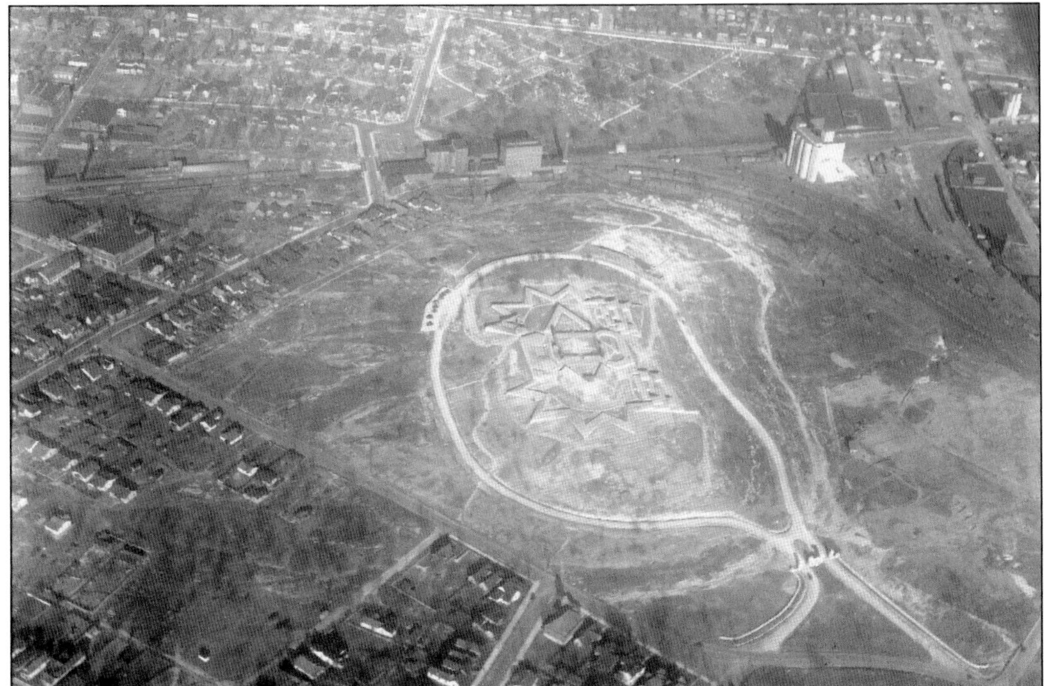

During the Union occupation of Nashville, a large stone fort was built to guard against Confederate attacks. It was located atop St Cloud Hill, and named Fort Negley. Completed in 1862, it was the largest inland fort constructed during the Civil War. After the war, the fort fell into disuse and ruin. During the 1930s the Works Progress Administration reconstructed the abandoned fort, and for a few years it became a public park. However, by the 1940s the park was again abandoned and closed. Decades later the city repaired and stabilized the historic structure, and Fort Negley reopened to the public in 2004. This 1937 aerial view shows the structure as it appeared after the WPA's restoration. Below, another 1937 photograph looks northeast from inside the fort. Factories and other commercial buildings of South Nashville are visible in the distance. (Both, Tennessee State Library and Archives.)

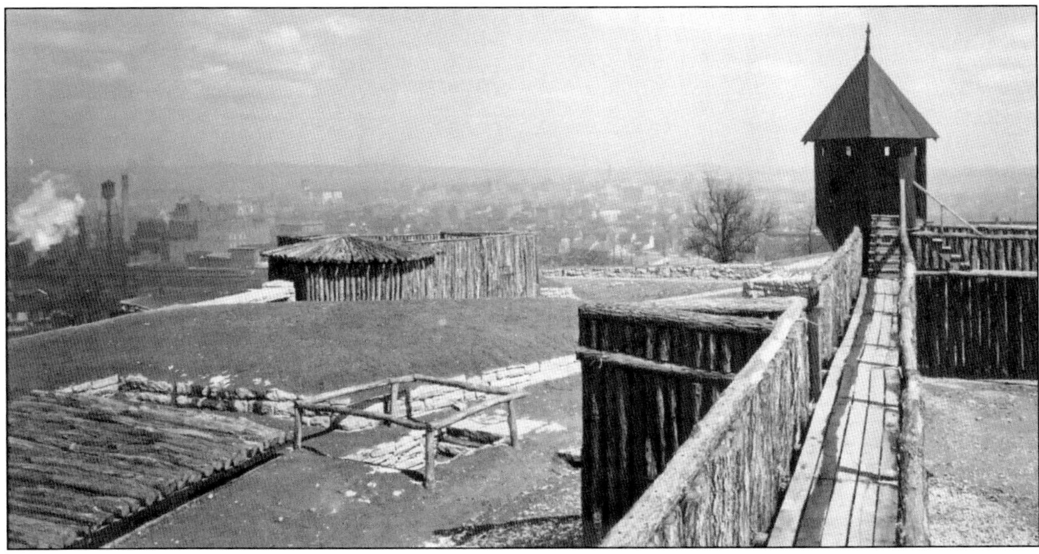

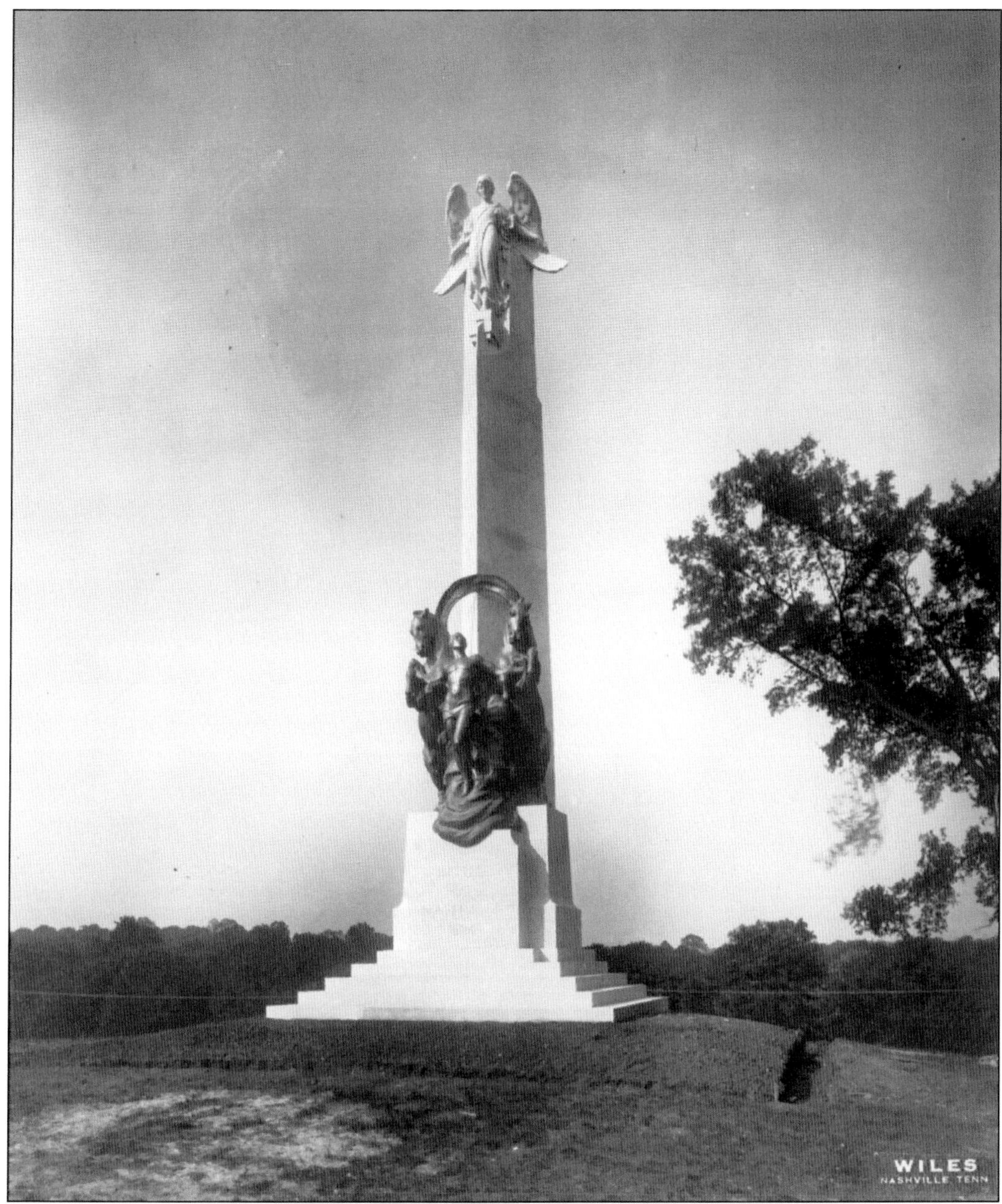

To commemorate the Civil War Battle of Nashville in 1864, the Ladies Battlefield Association commissioned the Battle of Nashville monument by sculptor Giuseppe Moretti. It was dedicated in 1927. Located four miles south of Nashville on Franklin Pike at Thompson Lane, the monument conveys a message of unity, recognizing all Americans who fought in both the Civil War and World War I, featuring a bronze sculpture of a youth and two horses, representing the South and the North, and an angel of peace at the top. The monument sustained substantial damage by a tornado in 1974. After a major highway interchange was built limiting access to the landmark, it was relocated to a park at Granny White Pike and Battlefield Drive and fully restored in 1998. (Tennessee State Library and Archives.)

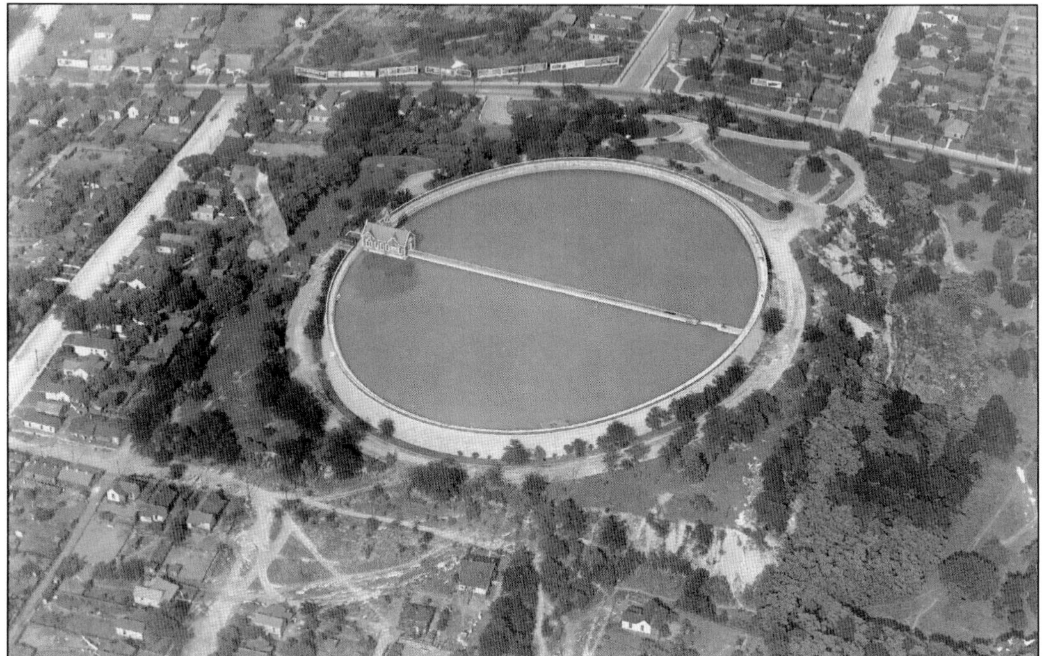

Nashville's City Reservoir remains an impressive sight more than a century after it was opened. Built on top of Kirkpatrick Hill a mile south of downtown, the stone reservoir has been in continuous use since opening in 1889. The structure is divided into two compartments by a partition wall. In this 1930s view facing east, Eighth Avenue is visible at the top. (Metro Nashville Archives.)

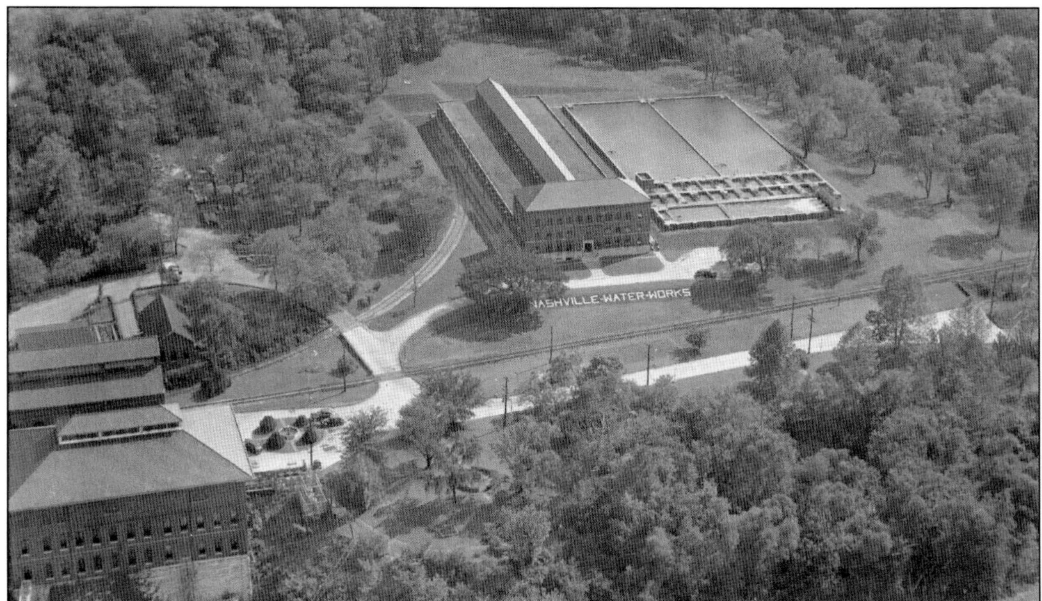

The Omohundro Water Treatment Plant is located east of downtown Nashville along the Cumberland River. The George Reyer Pumping Station, pictured far left, was built in 1889. The water filtration plant (center) was completed in 1929. Today, these buildings remain as an integral part of the city's water system. The Tennessee Central Railway slices between the two structures in this c. 1940 view. (Metro Nashville Archives.)

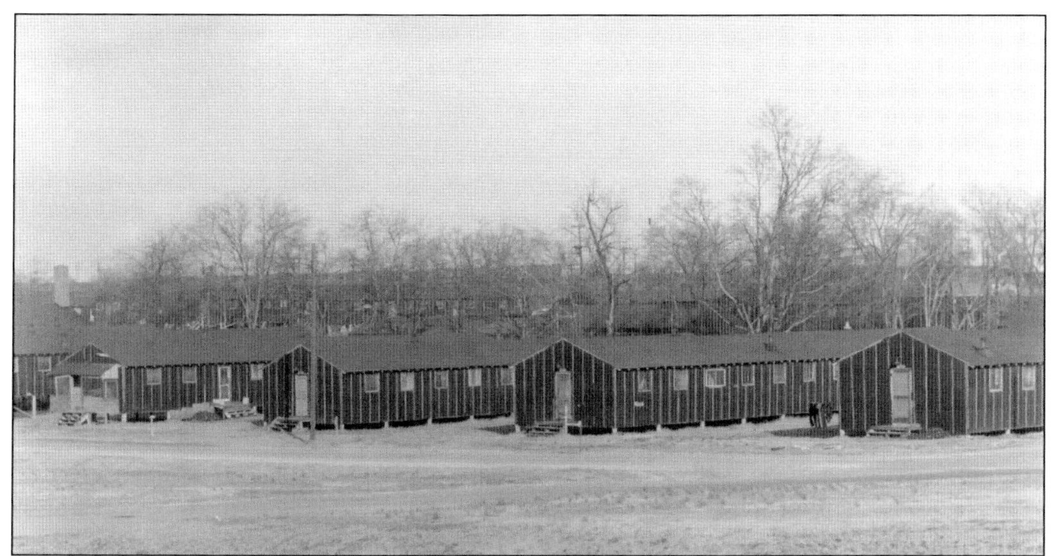

Seven months after the United States entered World War II, the Army Air Forces Classification Center was opened in July 1942. Located on Thompson Lane, the 562-acre center was designed to provide military training to cadets seeking to become pilots, navigators, and bombardiers. In 1945, with the war over and military members returning home, the Navy Separation Center opened in the former Army Air Forces facility for the purpose of processing sailors back to civilian life. The following year, the Navy closed the separation center. In late 1946, the City of Nashville acquired several of the old barracks, converting these into affordable housing units for veterans and their families. These images from the late 1940s show the repurposed buildings after the center had become a housing project. (Both, Metro Nashville Archives.)

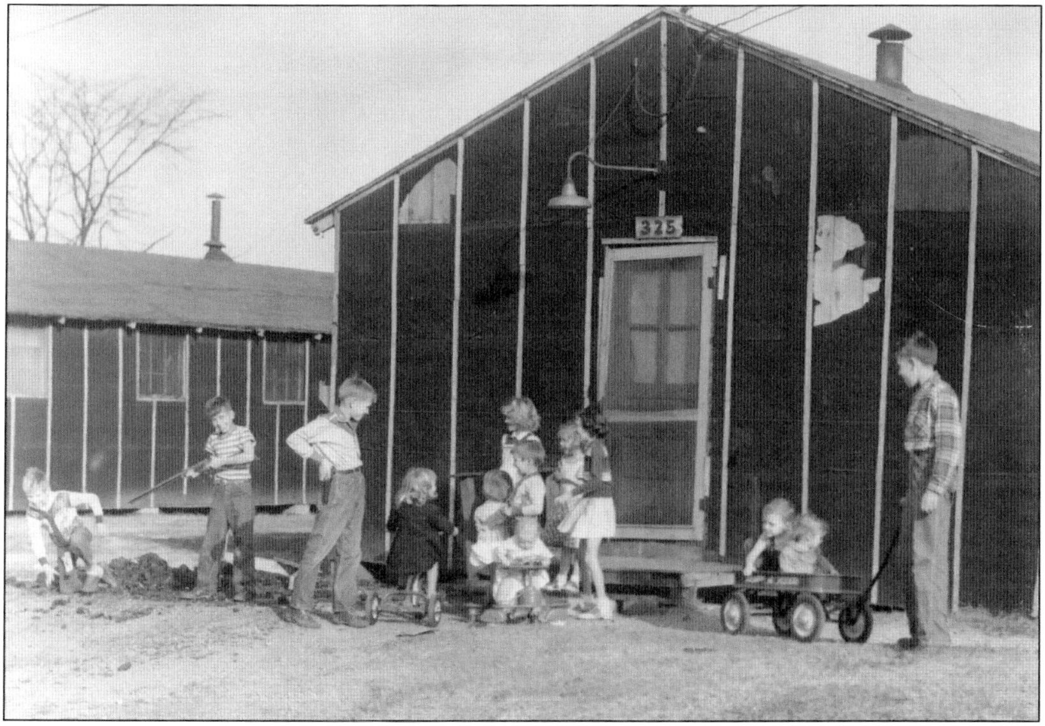

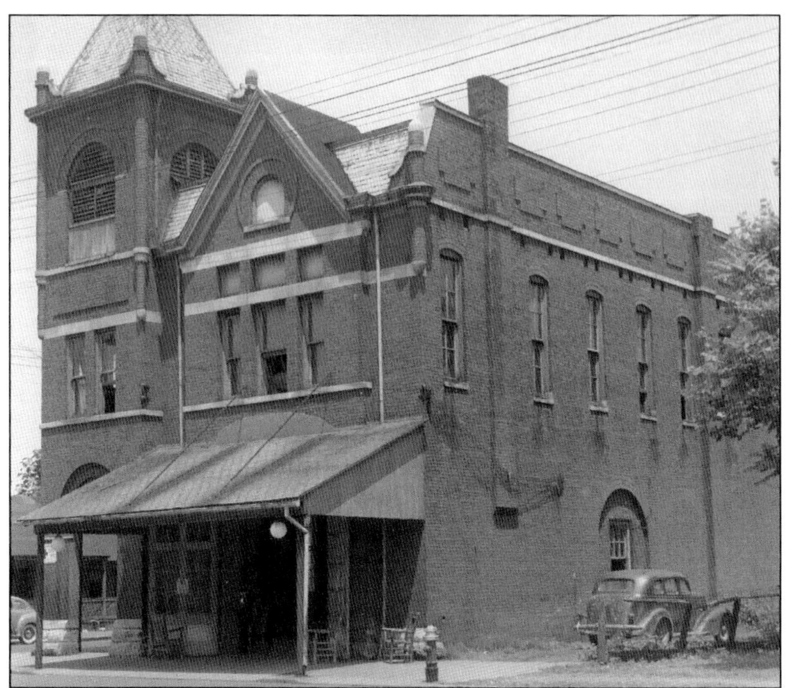

Fire House Engine Company No. 12 was constructed as Hose Company No. 1 in 1892. Located at Wharf Avenue and Fain Street, it is one of the oldest existing fire halls in Nashville. The upstairs housed firefighters while the lower floor stabled the company's two horses. The building served the community for decades before being repurposed as a public library branch in 1993. (Metro Nashville Archives.)

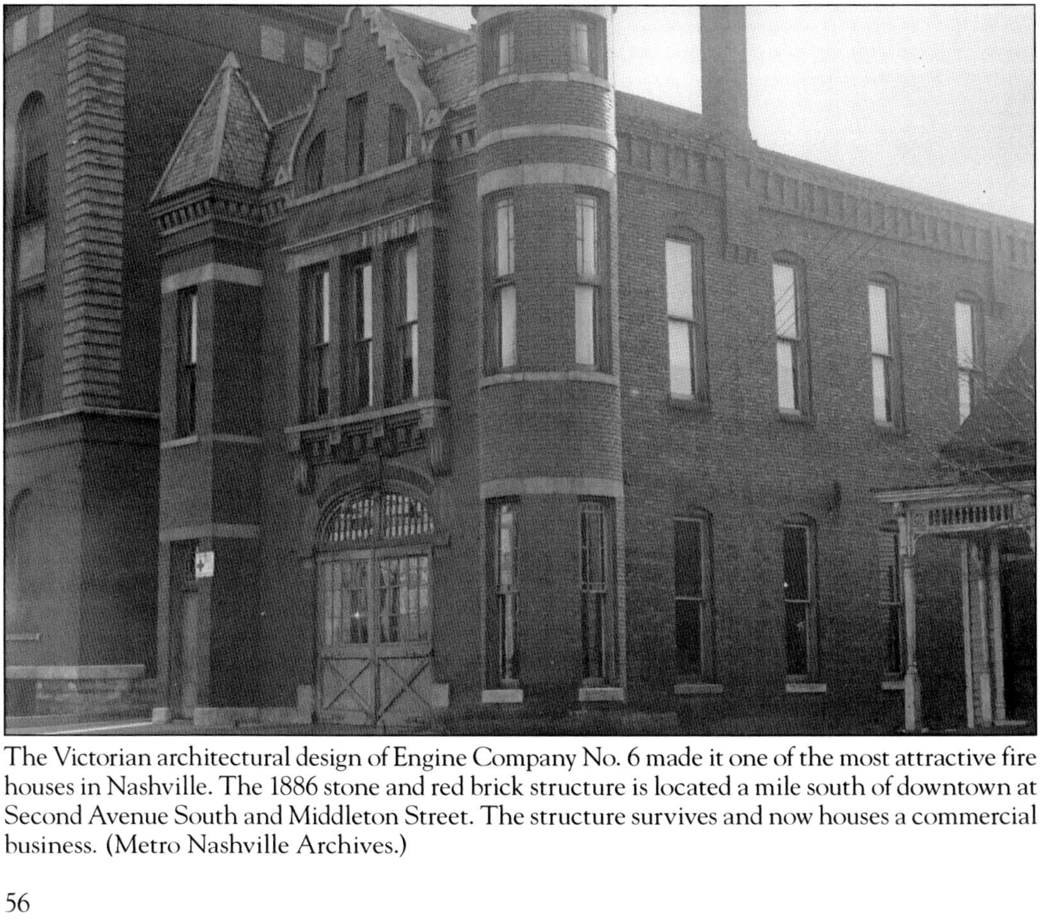

The Victorian architectural design of Engine Company No. 6 made it one of the most attractive fire houses in Nashville. The 1886 stone and red brick structure is located a mile south of downtown at Second Avenue South and Middleton Street. The structure survives and now houses a commercial business. (Metro Nashville Archives.)

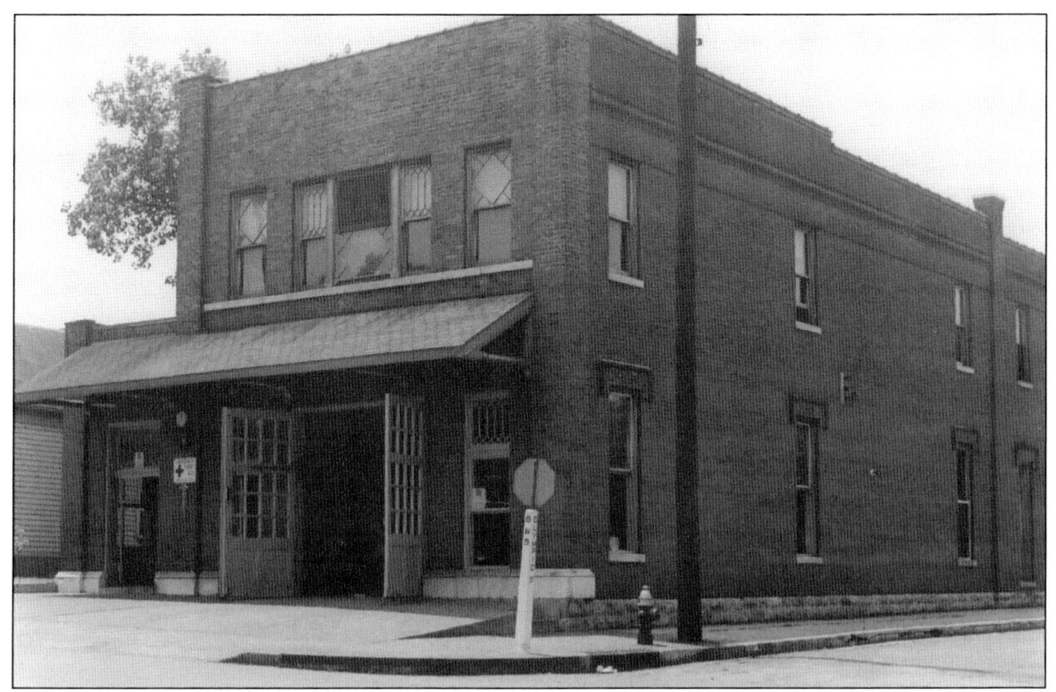

Firehouses have an individual charm and architectural style making each one unique. Engine Company No. 8, located at Eighth Avenue South and Olympic Street, served the Edgehill and Reservoir Park neighborhoods for much of the 20th century. The attractive structure, pictured above in the late 1940s, was ultimately demolished and replaced with a modern facility. Engine Company No. 9, shown below, was located at Fourth Avenue South and McGavock Street, immediately south of downtown Nashville. While not as architecturally stylish as some of the city's other firehouses, it deserves inclusion as a noteworthy structure. The stucco and brick building was replaced by a more substantial structure during the early 1950s. Today, the Schermerhorn Symphony Center occupies this site. (Both, Metro Nashville Archives.)

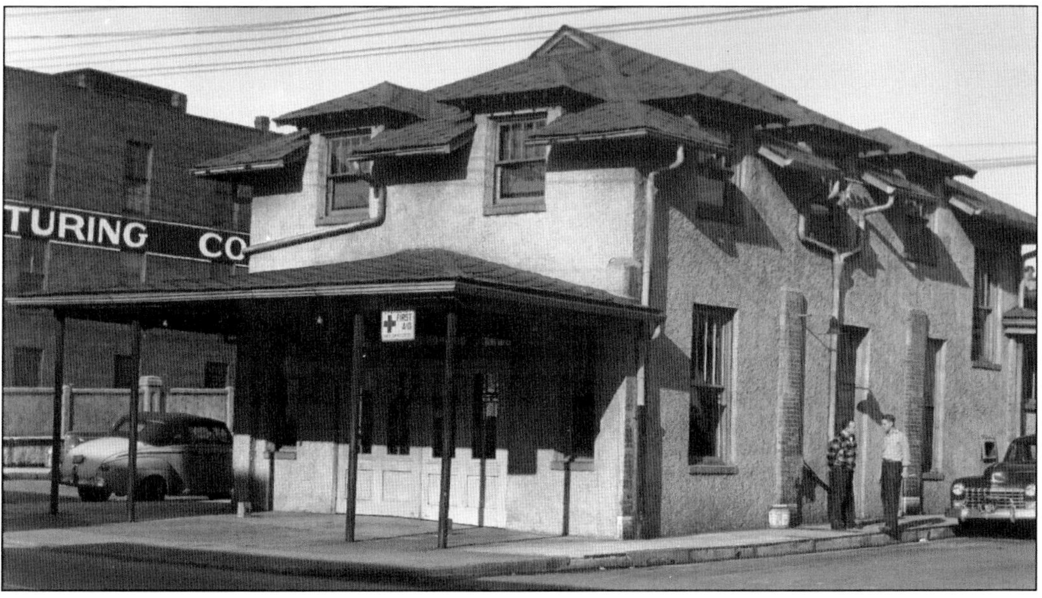

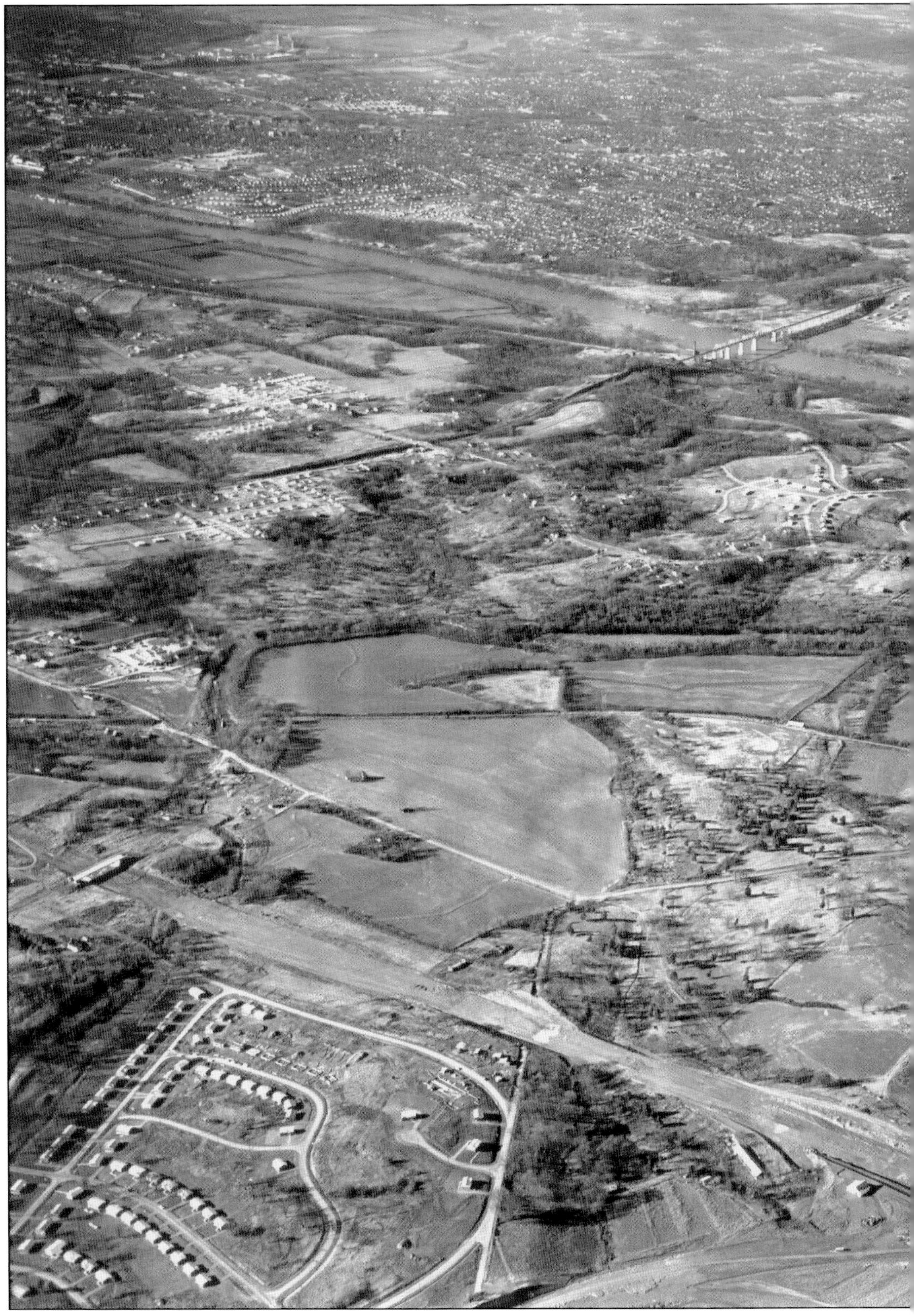

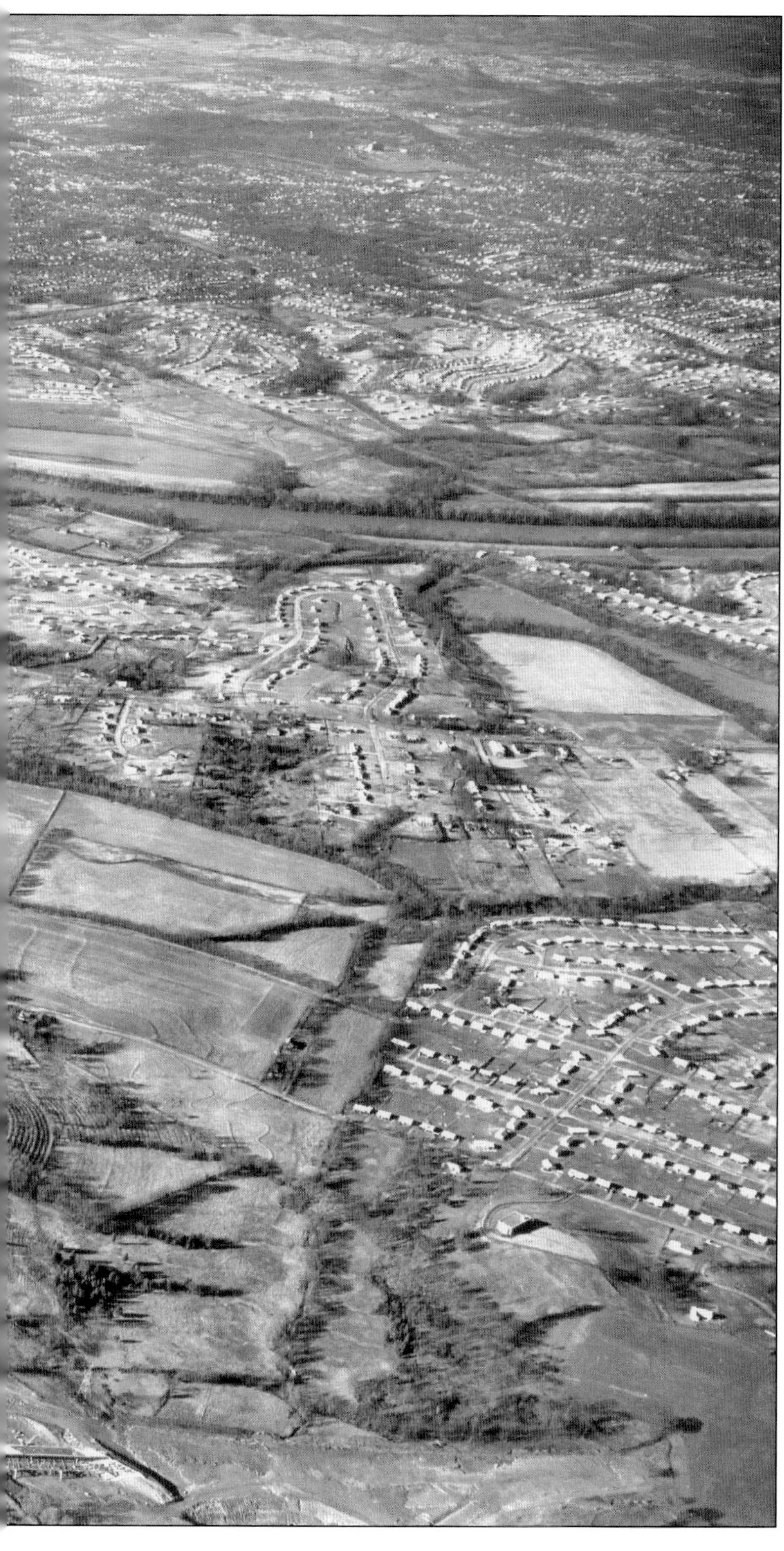

Knapp Farm, or, more correctly, the Knapp School of Country Life, was located to the east of the city. It was a part of George Peabody College for Teachers, which for more than half a century operated it as a demonstration farm. The 300-acre farm contained 25 acres of orchard, a working dairy and a herd of Holstein cattle. By 1965, Peabody's farm had become attractive to developers, who saw it as the largest tract of undeveloped land in Nashville, convenient to the airport and downtown. The cash-strapped college sold it in 1965, and Peabody's bucolic country farm became an urban industrial park. Looking northwest in this 1961 aerial photograph, the Knapp property is bordered on the west and north by Mill Creek, with the Cumberland River visible at the top. Interstate 40, then under construction, can be seen below. (Metro Nashville Archives.)

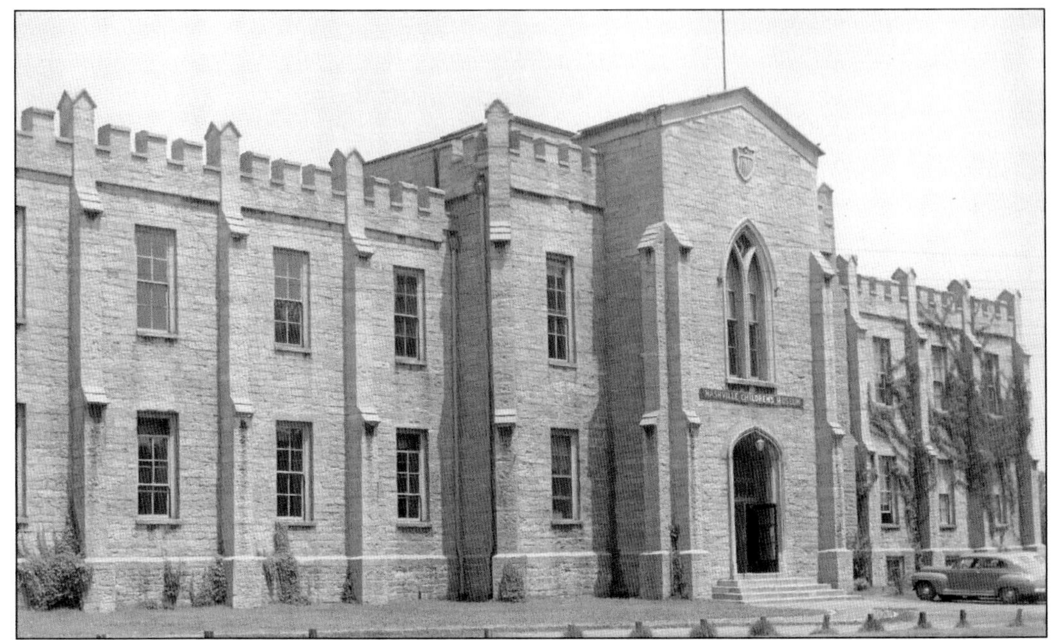

Lindsley Hall is one of the oldest municipally owned buildings in the city. The Gothic Revival–style structure was designed by Nashville architect Adolphus Heiman in 1853 as part of the University of Nashville. Over the years, it has served many functions. Many local residents remember the building when it served as the Nashville Children's Museum from 1944 to 1973. The pre–Civil War era building now houses city offices. (Metro Nashville Archives.)

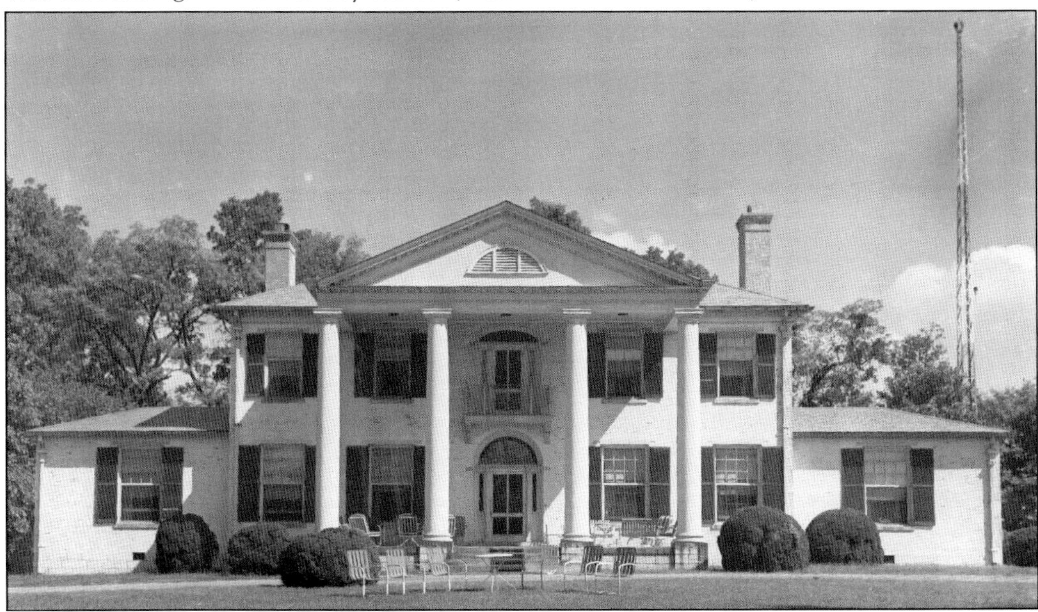

For many years, the Colemere Club was a private club on Murfreesboro Road located in the Colemere mansion. Built in 1931 by the Dempsey Weaver family to replace a home destroyed by fire, the Colonial-style house was the center of many social events. In 1940, the city purchased it for future airport expansion. Later, the mansion was leased to the new Colemere Club, made up of political and civic leaders. Today, a local restaurant leases the mansion. (Metro Nashville Archives.)

Six

The Tennessee State Fair

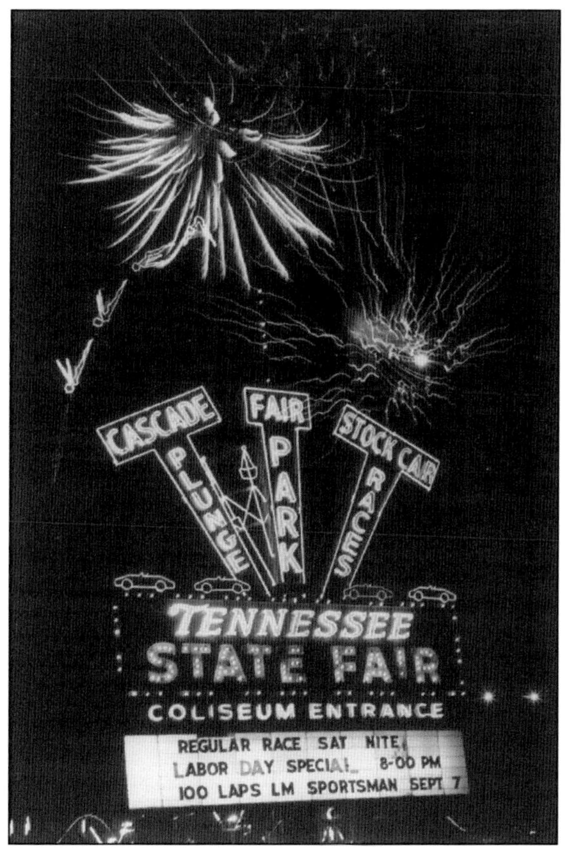

For more than a century, the Tennessee State Fair has been a popular destination each September when thousands of visitors descend on the event from near and far. Located just outside Nashville's pre-1963 city limits, the fairgrounds was not only the site for the annual state fair, but also home to three popular summer attractions. Cascade Plunge was a popular swimming pool and water park for more than half a century. Fair Park, opened in 1952, was Nashville's only amusement park for many years, an attraction that featured rides, concessions and an impressive wood roller coaster. The fairground was also a favorite with racing enthusiasts with its regularly scheduled stock car races and demolition derbies. The animated neon sign at the fairground entrance welcomes visitors in this 1965 scene. (Metro Nashville Archives.)

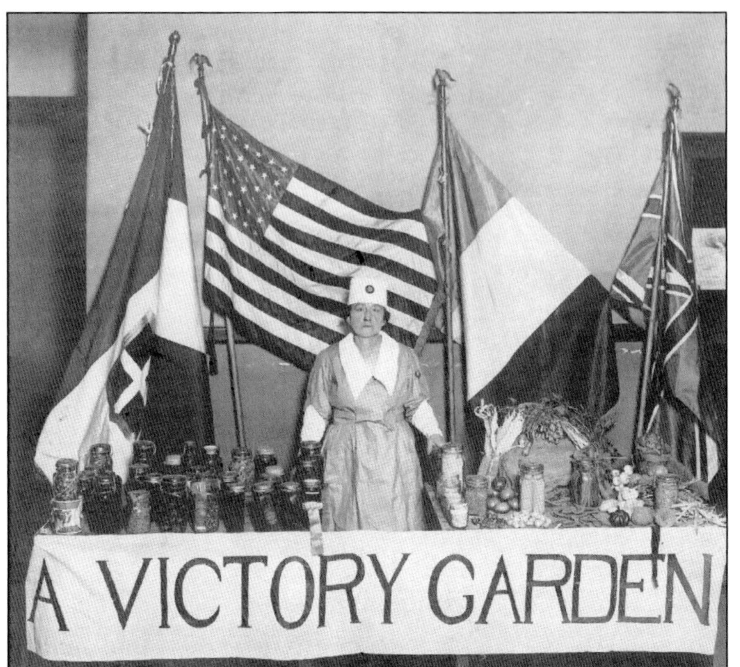

The Tennessee State Fair provided people from across the state an opportunity to display vegetables, livestock and crafts. Mrs. J.H. Matthews was involved in the Victory Garden Association, exhibiting the proper way to successfully set up a garden during World War I. In this c. 1918 scene, Mrs. Matthews shows off samples of her produce and canned goods after winning 14 ribbons for her endeavors. (Nashville Public Library, Special Collections.)

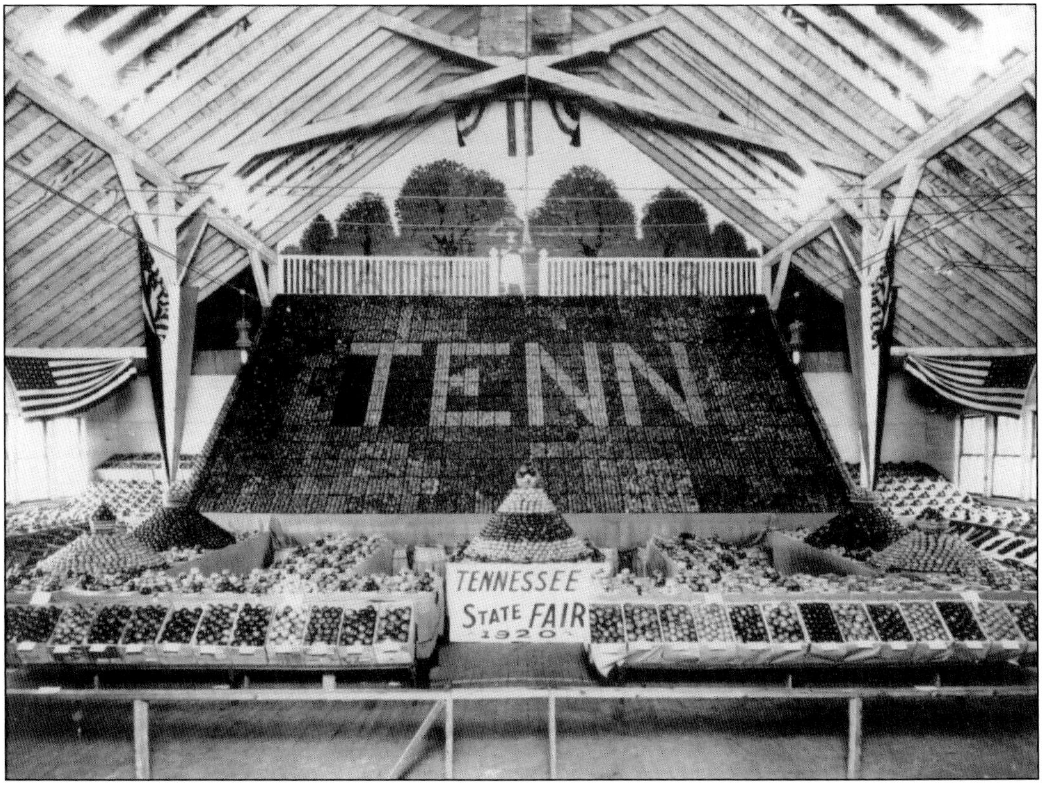

The state fair was an opportunity for Tennessee to show off its products—whether it be livestock, jellies, vegetables or fruit. This 1920 photograph shows an impressive exhibit showcasing the state's apple harvest. (Metro Nashville Archives.)

In 1903, the Tennessee State Fair relocated to South Nashville adjacent to the Cumberland Park horse race track on Nolensville Pike. The event lasted six days, attracting people from across the state as well as other states. This full-page advertisement dates from 1908, the third year for the fair after its move. (Ralcon Wagner collection.)

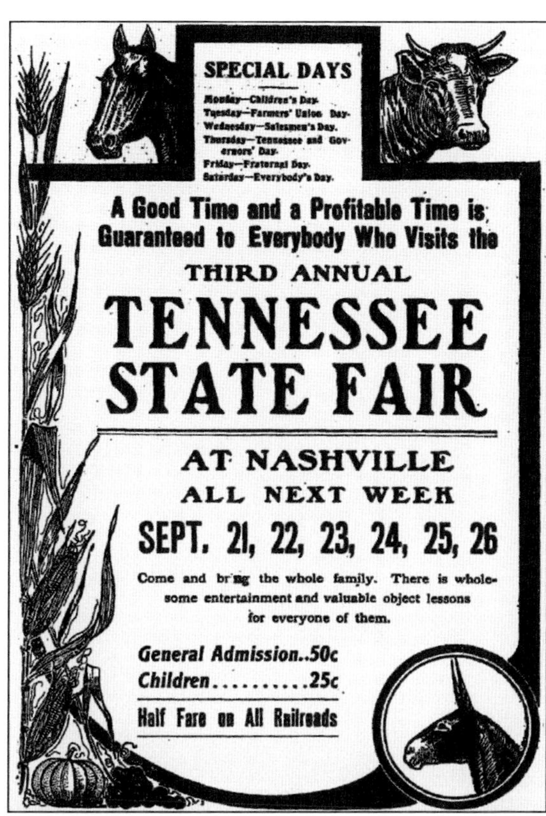

Much of the state fair activities were focused on agriculture. Judging livestock was always a popular attraction. Here, spectators observe a hog-judging competition during the 1930s. (Nashville Public Library, Special Collections.)

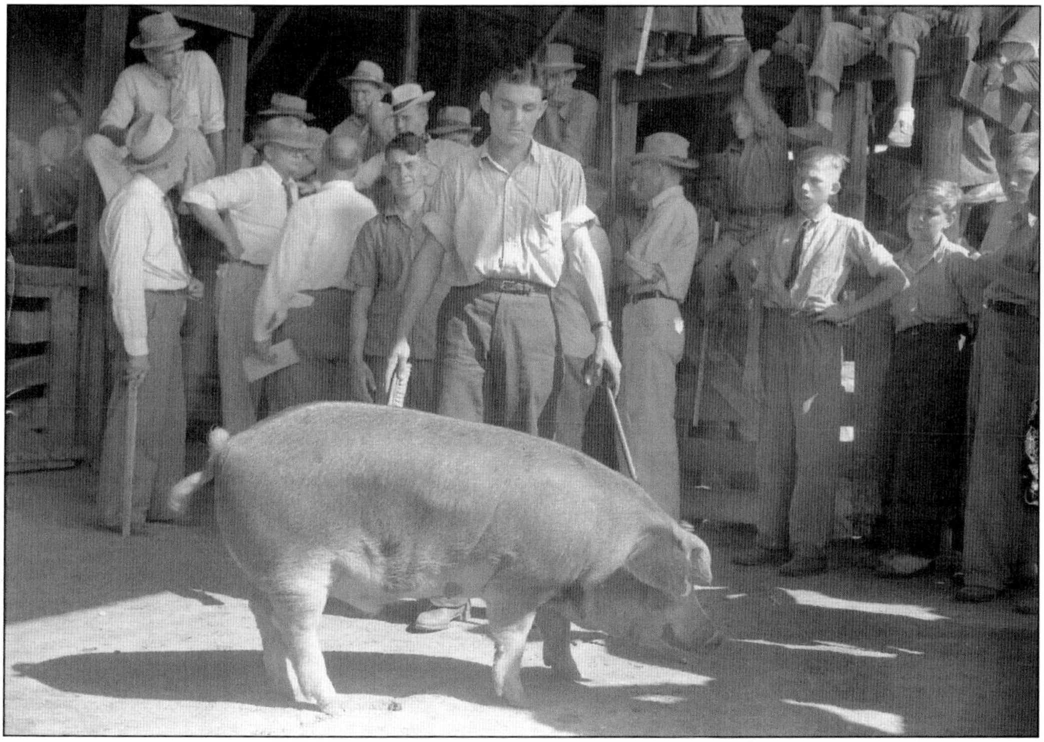

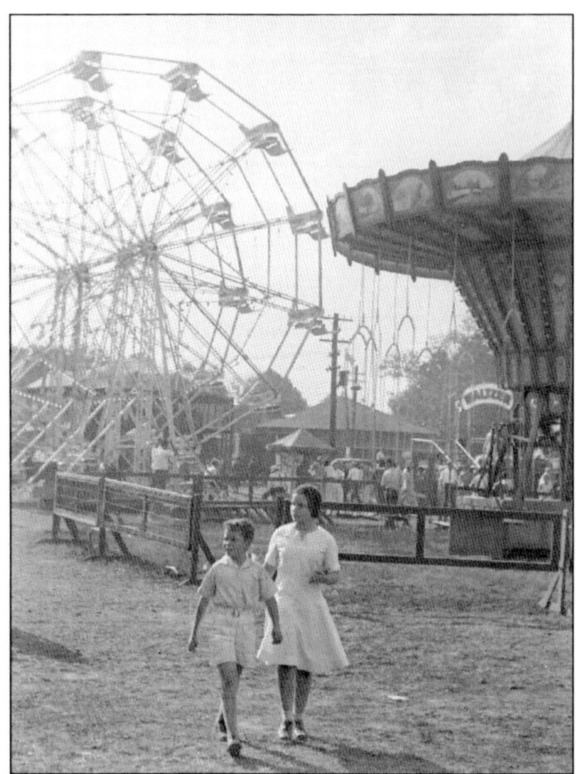

The Midway was always a popular attraction for children of all ages. A couple of youngsters spend time exploring the sights and sounds of the rides. (Metro Nashville Archives.)

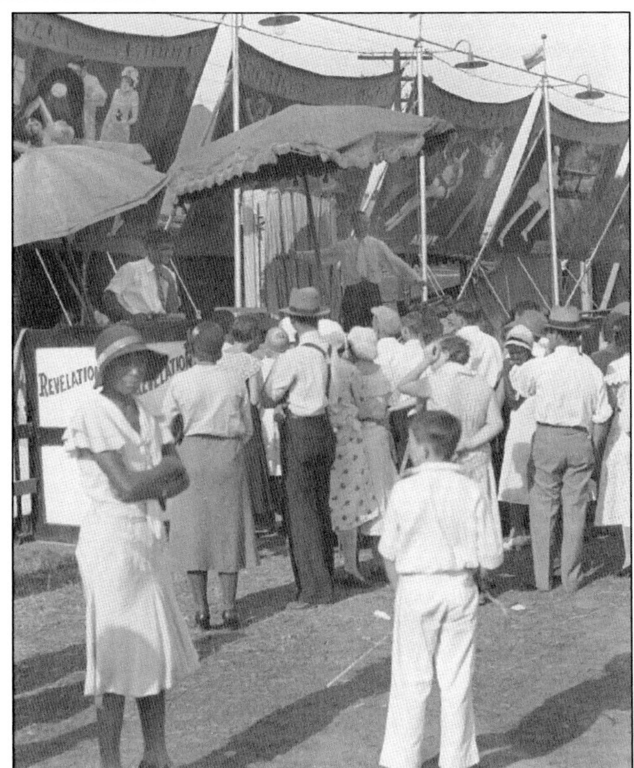

An evangelist and carnival barker compete for the attention as a crowd gathers on the Midway. Such sights were typical at the state fair. (Nashville Public Library, Special Collections.)

During a windy afternoon, three women take in the carnival-like atmosphere of the Midway at the 1931 fair; it had been a strong attraction for visitors who traveled hundreds of miles to attend the venue. (Metro Nashville Archives.)

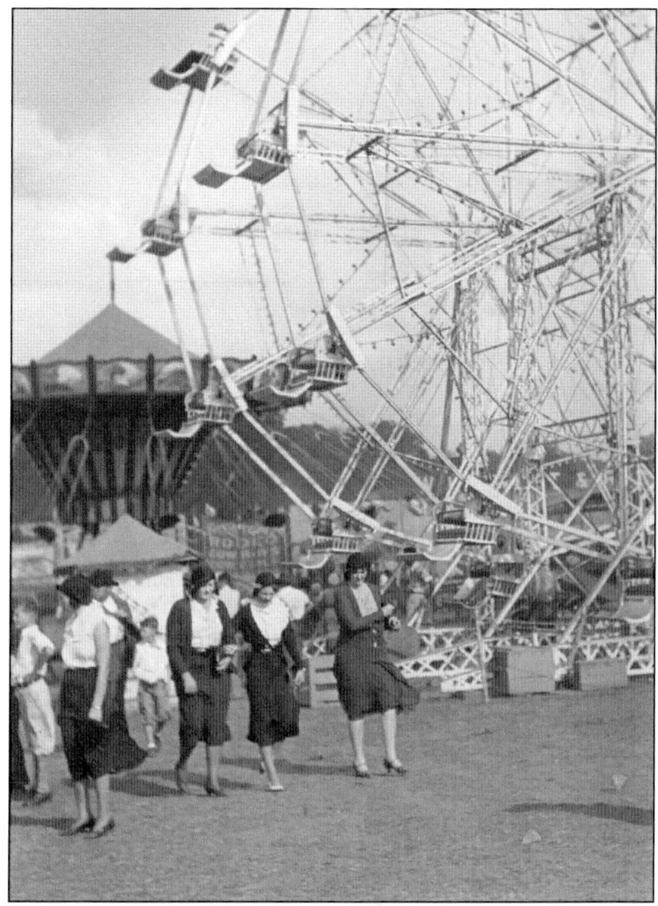

The fair provided youngsters a chance to work with livestock and compete for prizes. A boy struggles to bring his cow back to the stall during the 1937 fair. (Nashville Public Library, Special Collections.)

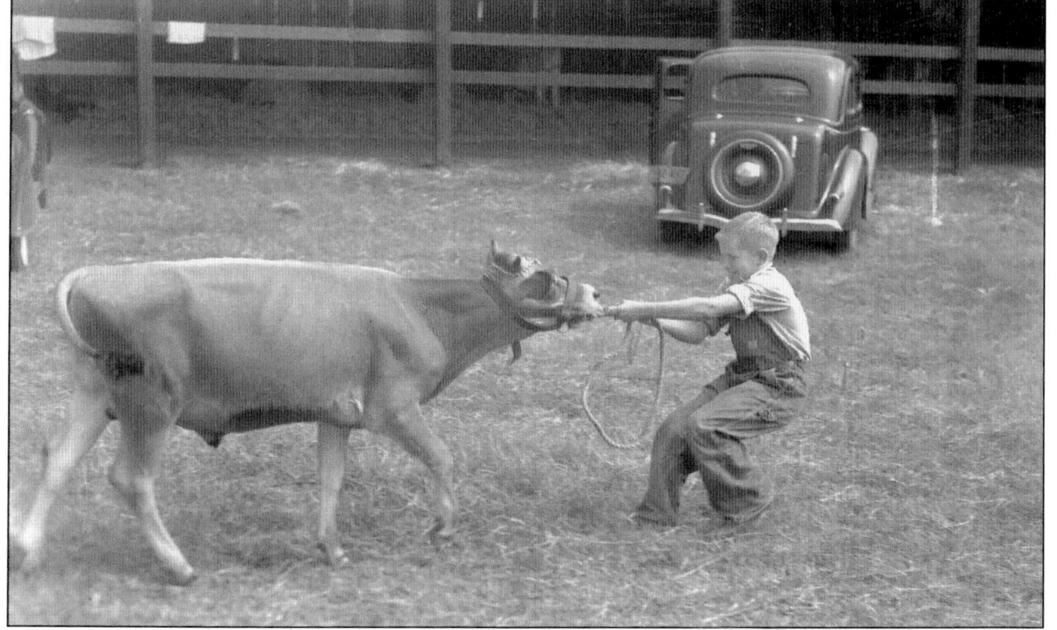

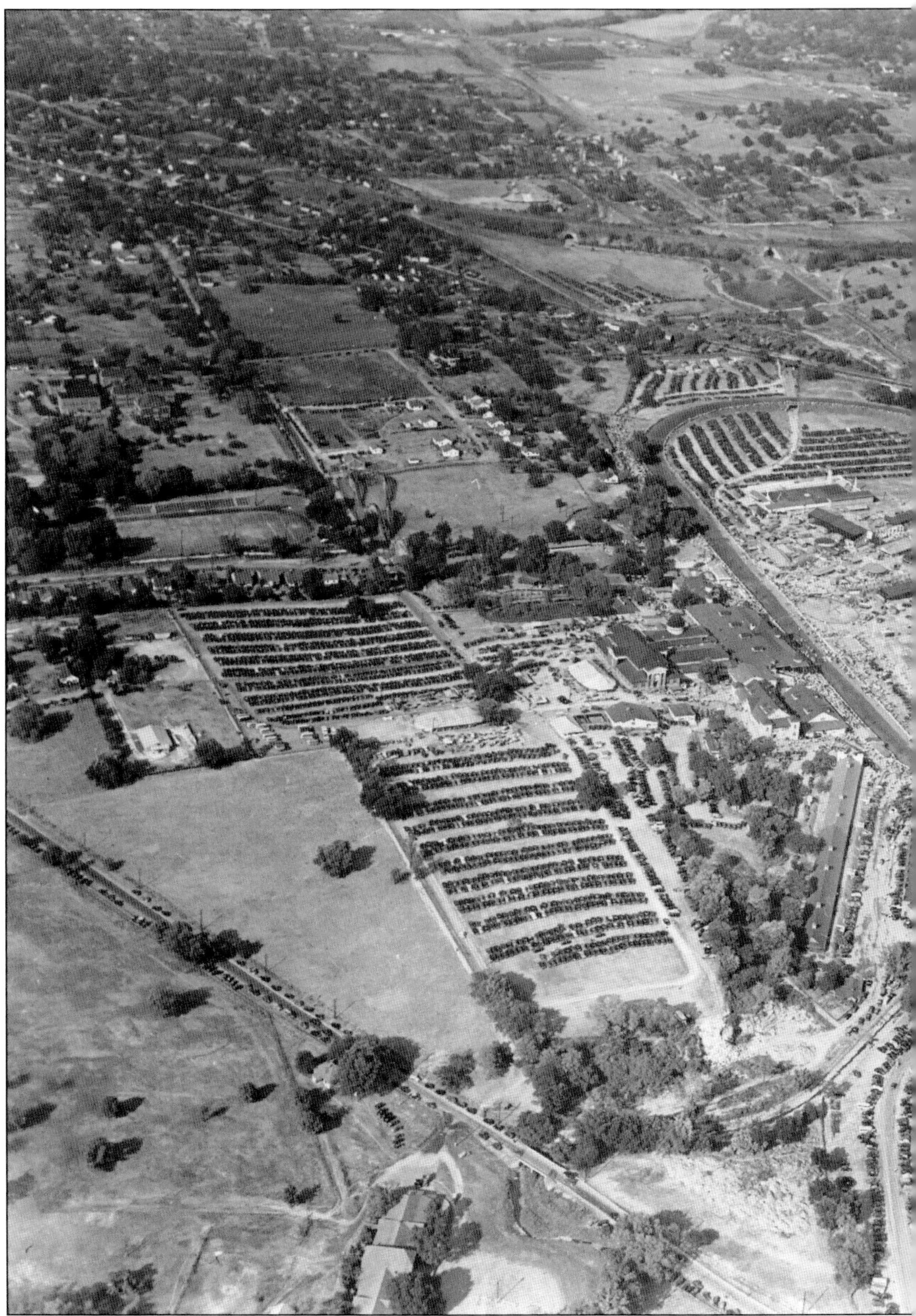

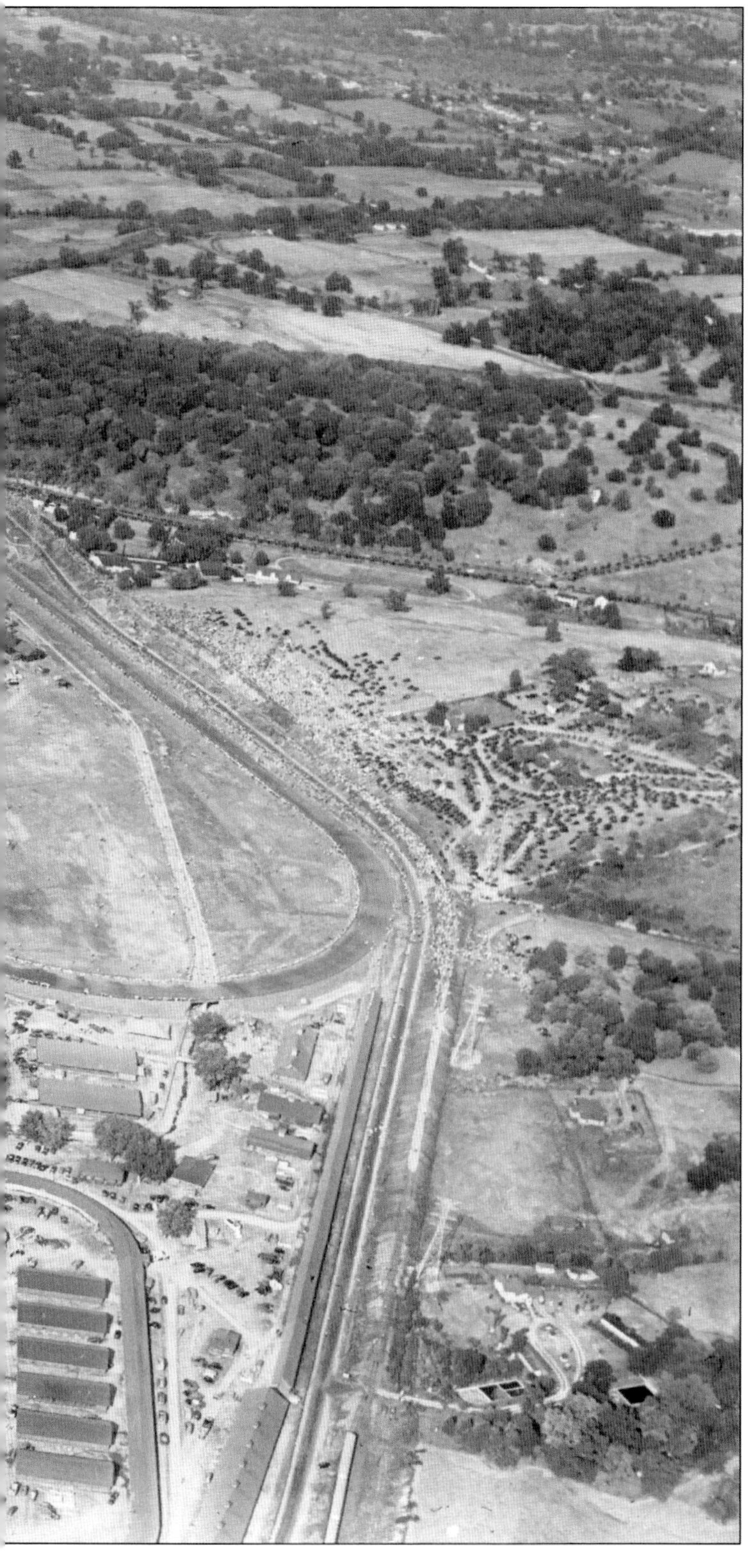

This aerial view from 1940, facing northeast, shows the Tennessee State Fair when it was at the height of its popularity. The spacious Cumberland Park track was large enough to accommodate the Midway with its rides and various concessions. The presence of the thousands of cars around the grounds is indicative of how many people were in attendance this day. Nashville's Central High School and its football field are visible at upper left. Nolensville Pike is at the top of this scene. (Tennessee State Library and Archives.)

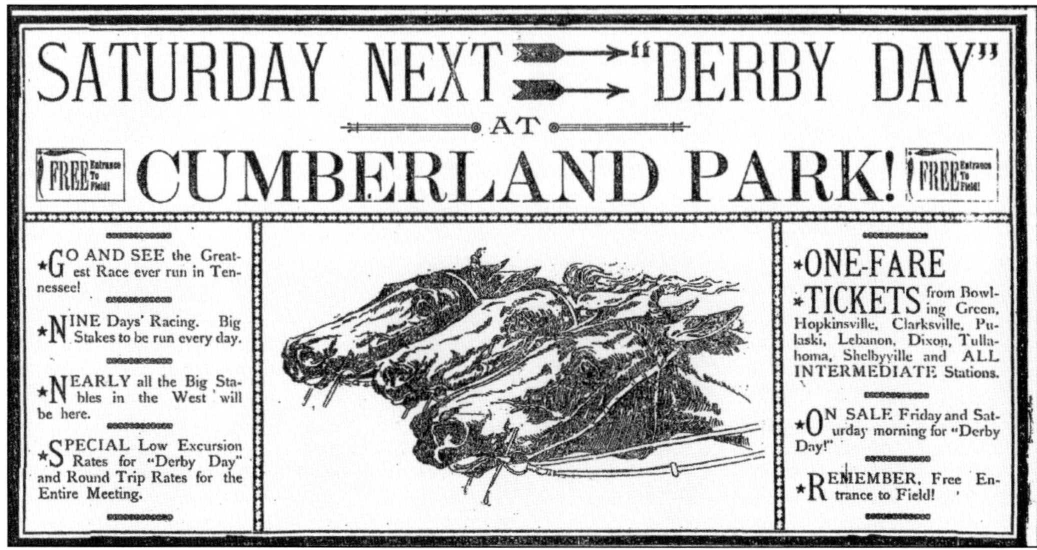

The Cumberland Park racetrack was one of the most impressive courses in the region when it opened 1891, attracting visitors from around the country. While the South Nashville track was historically associated with harness racing, varieties of events, which included thoroughbred and even bicycle races, were held at the site. In 1906, the Tennessee State Fair relocated to the park. A few years later, car races were also added. The one-mile oval track continued in popularity for more than 60 years. In 1956, city leaders felt the land would be better suited for auto races. The dirt track was replaced by a modern half-mile asphalt version and renamed Fairground Speedways. Both stock-car and NASCAR races became an entertainment staple, drawing large audiences. (Above, Ralcon Wagner collection; below, Nashville Public Library, Special Collections.)

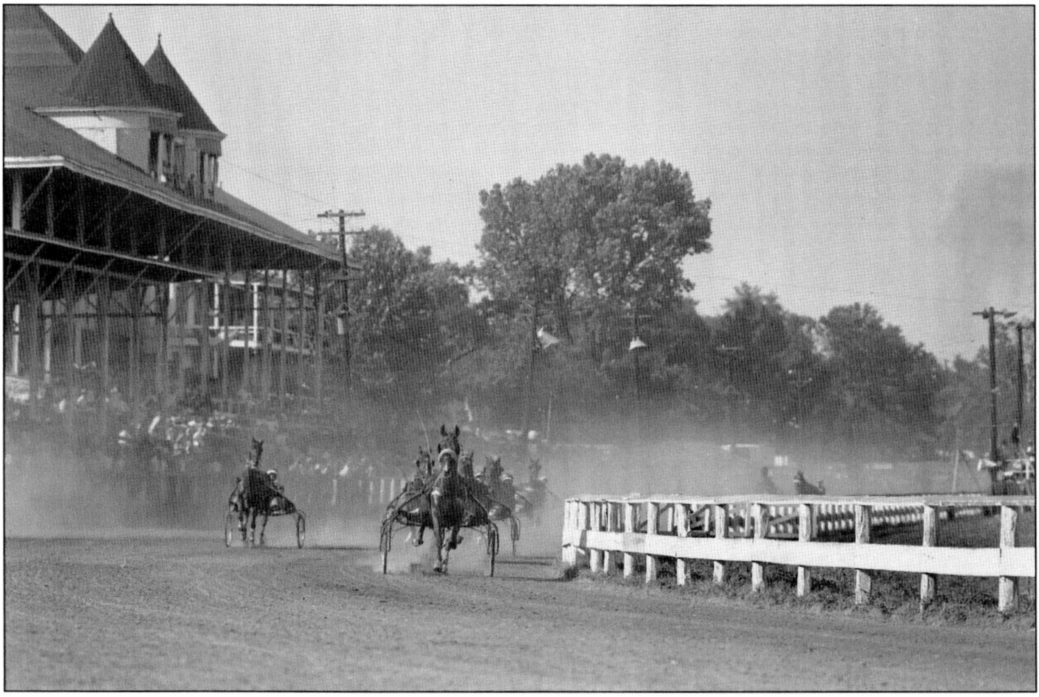

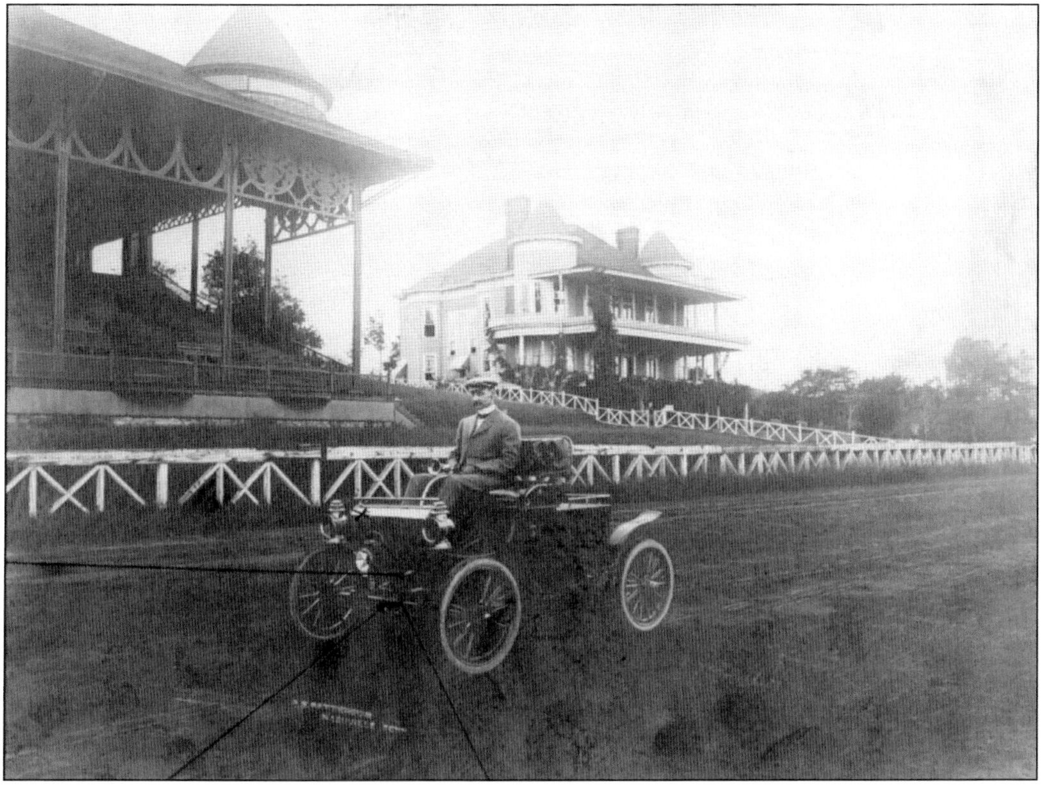

From its earliest days as a horse track, Cumberland Park also hosted car races over its dirt course; the image above, recorded in 1907, is an early example. By the late 1950s, Fairground Speedways was reduced in size, as grandstand capacity was increased to accommodate the added legions of auto racing fans. (Above, Tennessee State Library and Archives; below, Nashville Public Library, Special Collections.)

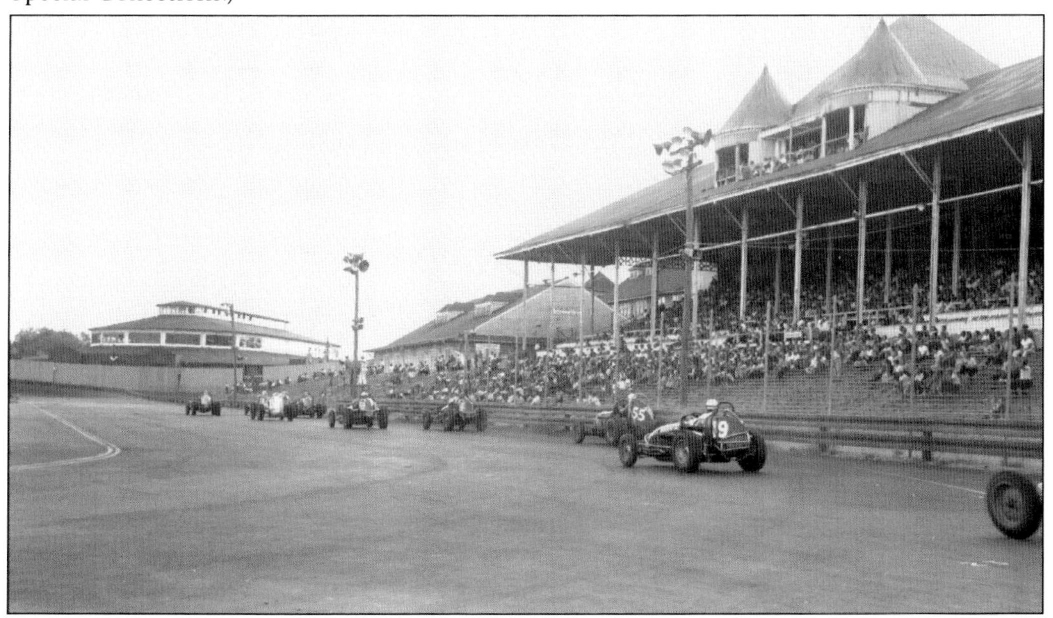

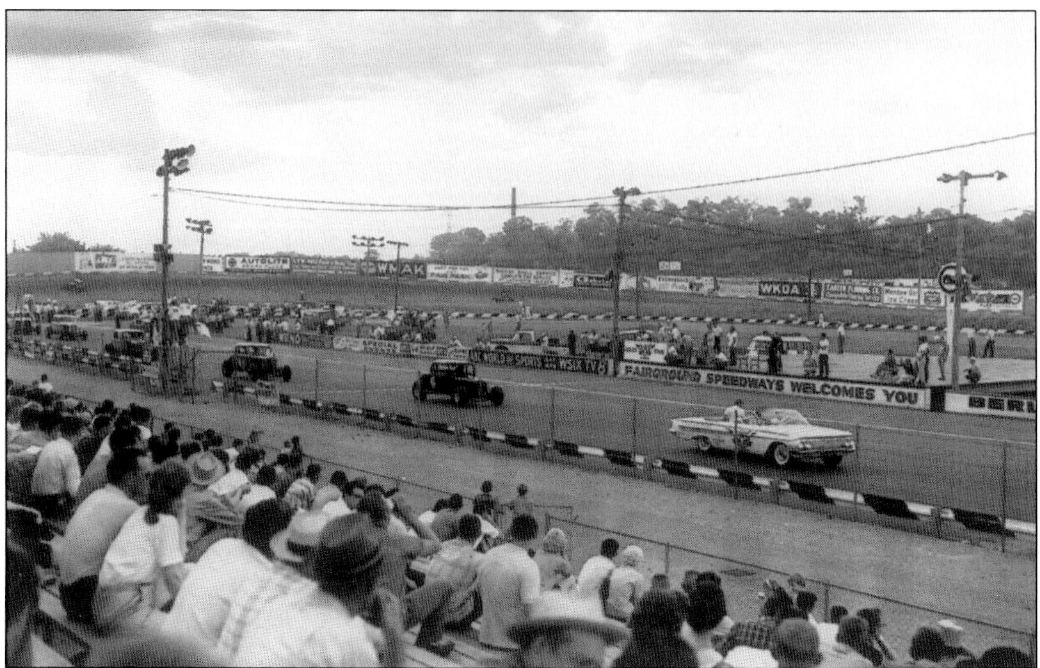

For many years, Fairground Speedway has been a favorite summer destination for racing enthusiasts to take in the sights and sounds of Saturday night stock-car races. On a warm September 1961 evening, the stands are full of racing enthusiast as a stock car race gets underway. (Above, Metro Nashville Archives; below, Nashville Public Library, Special Collections.)

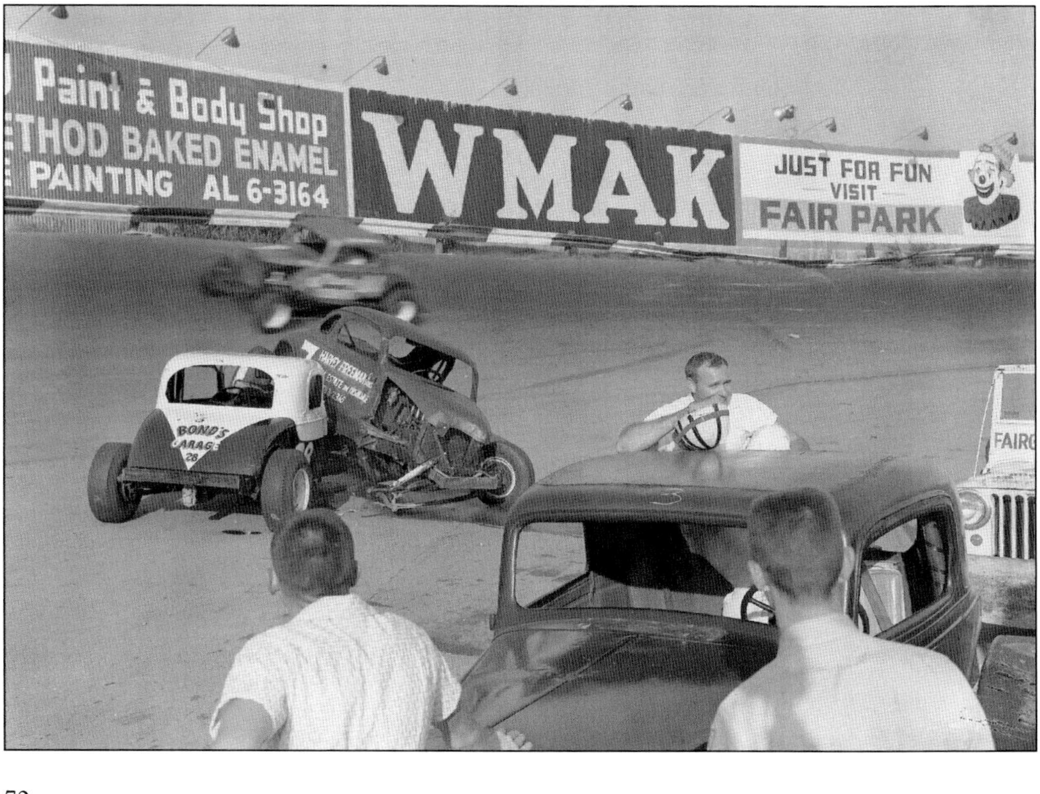

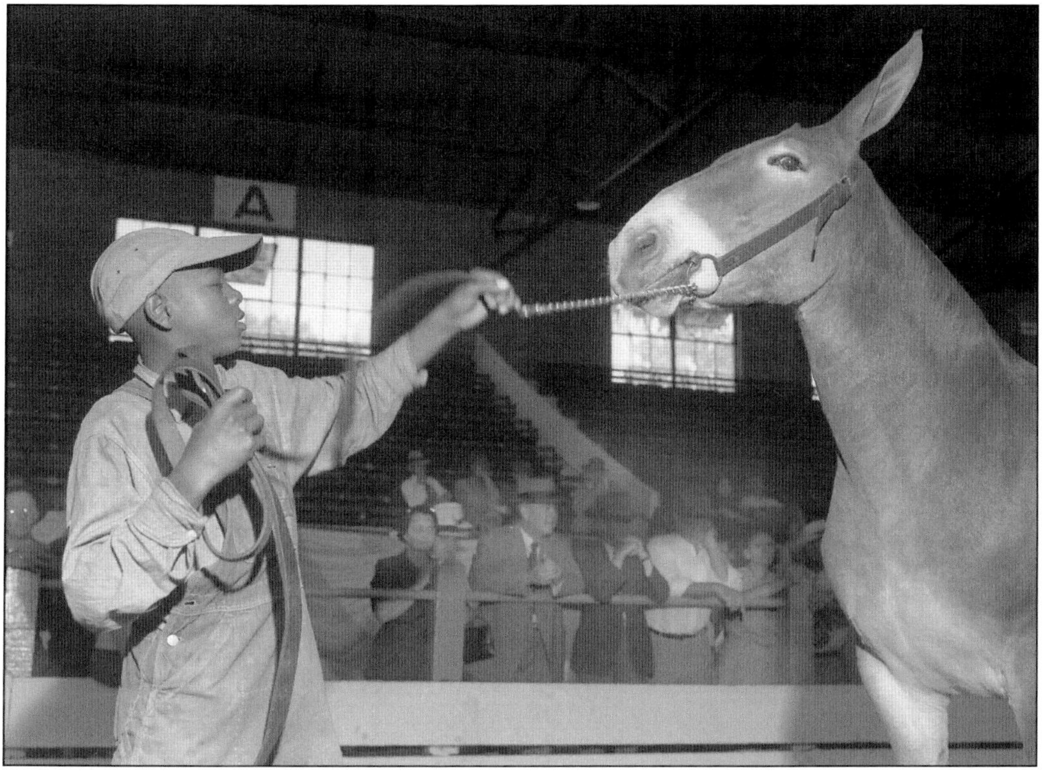

An important part of the fair always involved contestants showing off prized livestock competing for that first- or second-place ribbon, such as these scenes from the 1950s. (Both, Nashville Public Library, Special Collections.)

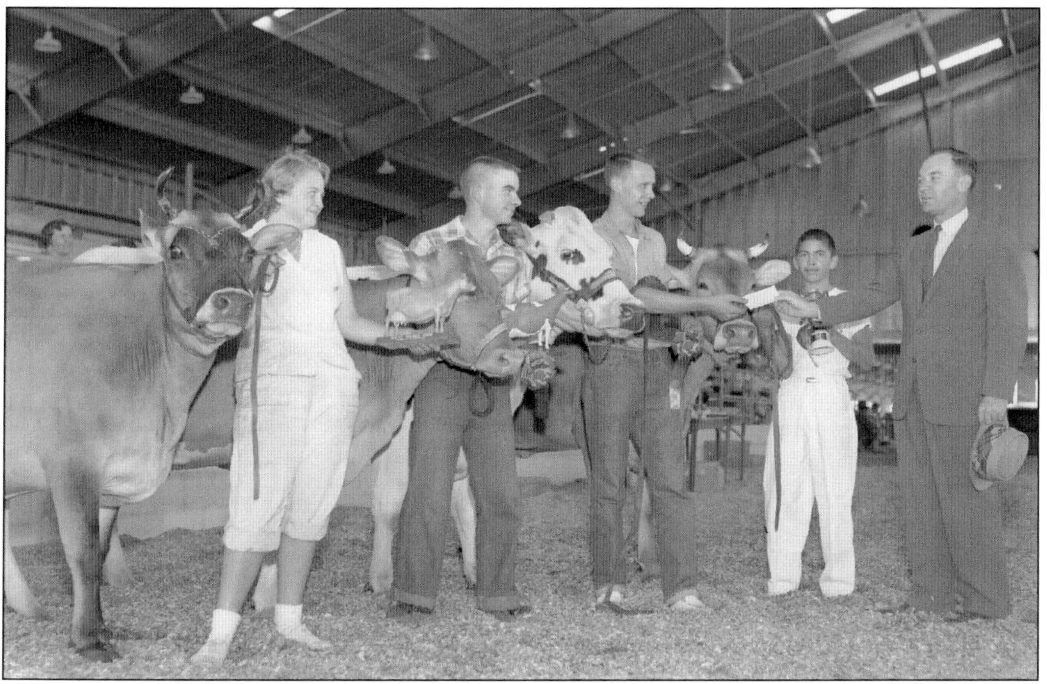

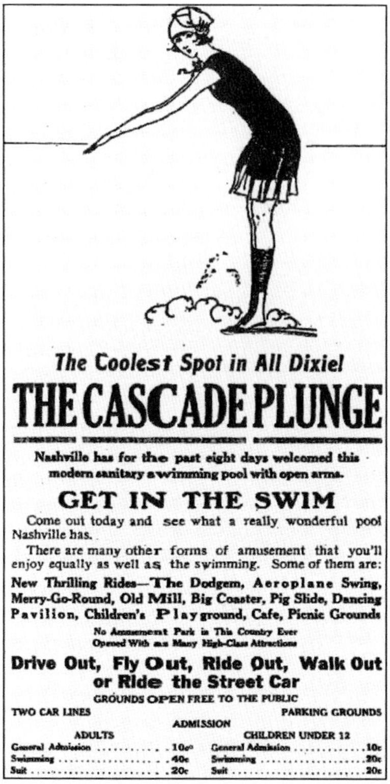

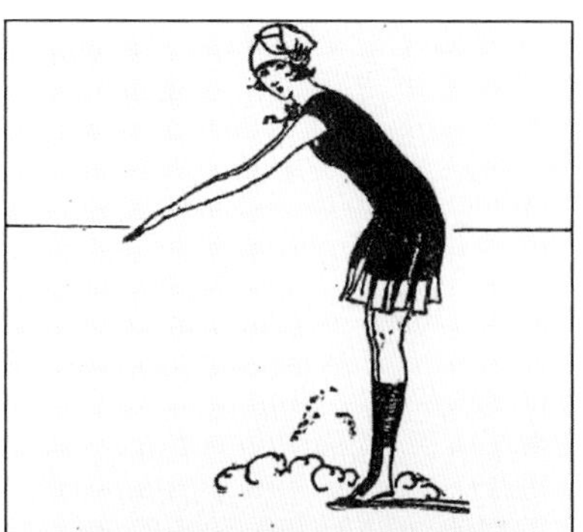

For more than half a century, Cascade Plunge at the Tennessee State Fairgrounds was a favorite place to cool off for people of all ages in an era before air conditioners. In a scene recorded shortly after the facility's opening in 1922, five unidentified Nashville schoolteachers enjoy the water. (Both, Tennessee State Library and Archives.)

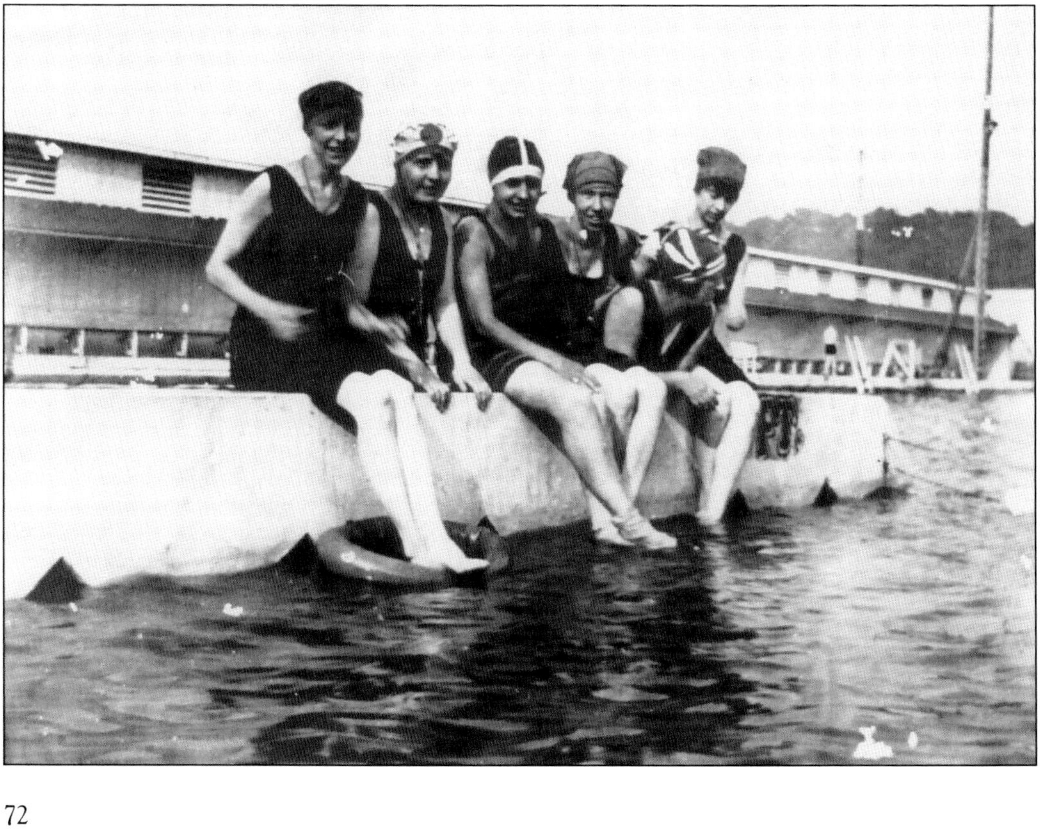

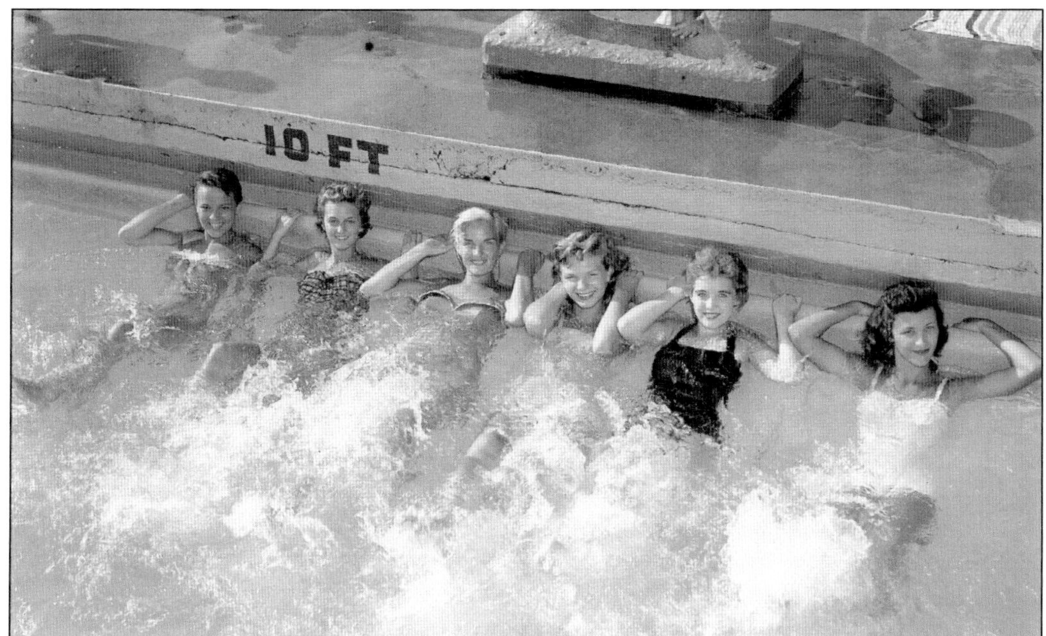

Cascade Plunge along with the adjacent Fair Park evokes great memories for baby boomers who remember spending enjoyable times with friends during hot summer days. The large pool offered something for every age group, including a diving board and slides. After more than 50 years of operation, the popular attraction closed in 1975. (Both, Nashville Public Library, Special Collections.)

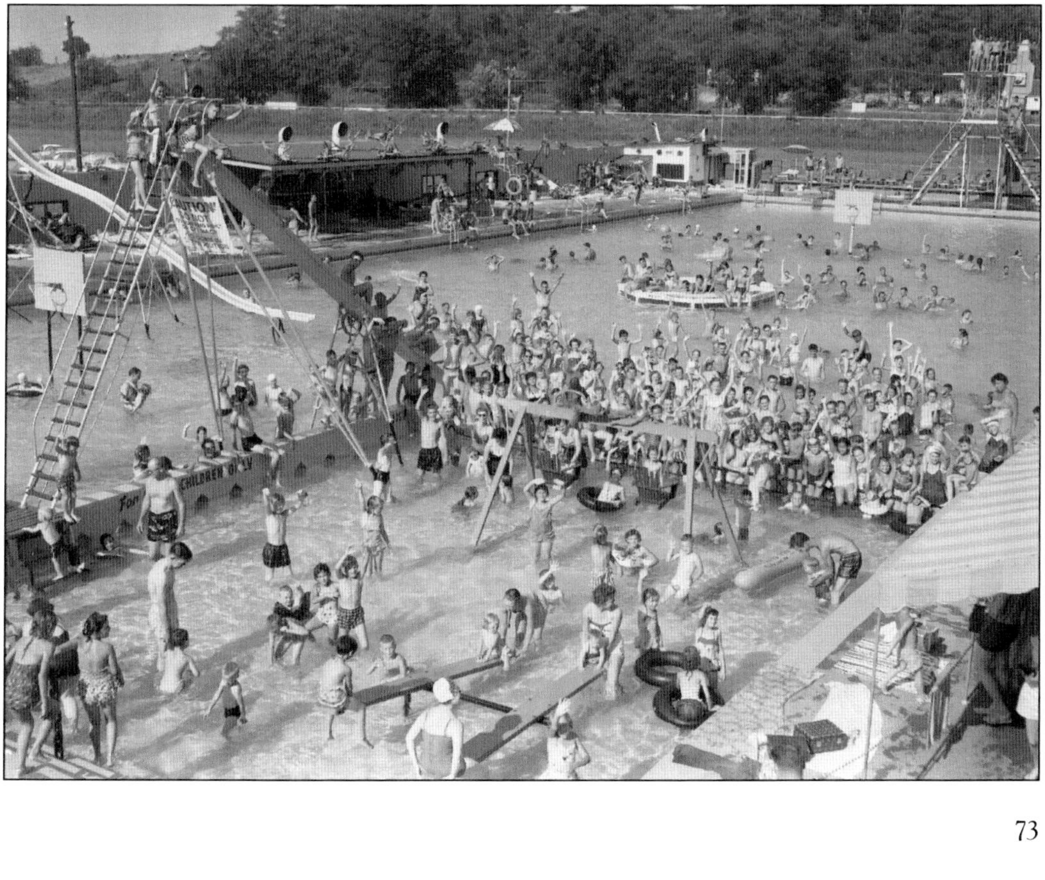

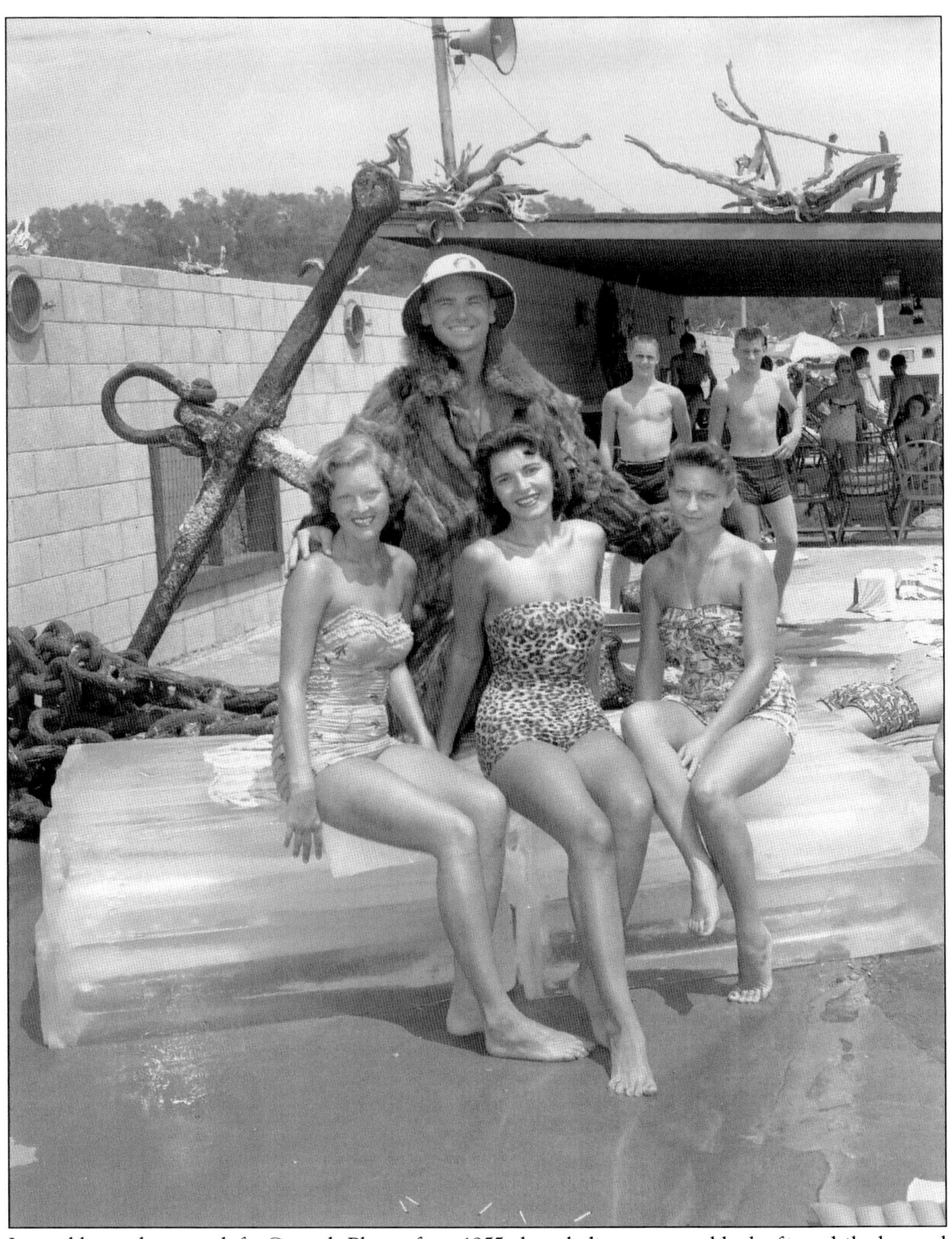

In a publicity photograph for Cascade Plunge from 1955, three ladies pose on a block of ice while the pool lifeguard, wearing a fur coat, joins them. The anchor and pieces of driftwood seen in the background were typical of décor around the water park. (Nashville Public Library, Special Collections.)

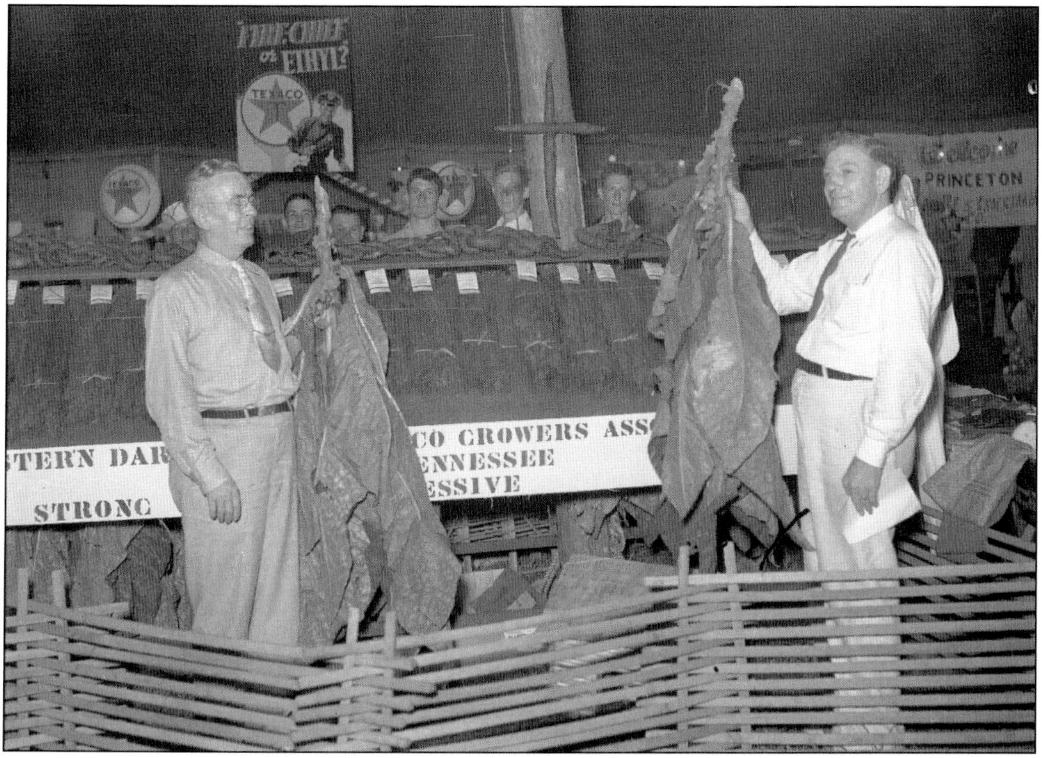

Two judges from the Eastern Dark-Fired Tobacco Growers Association examine tobacco leaves at one of the many agricultural events at the 1937 state fair that attracted fair attendees. (Nashville Public Library, Special Collections.)

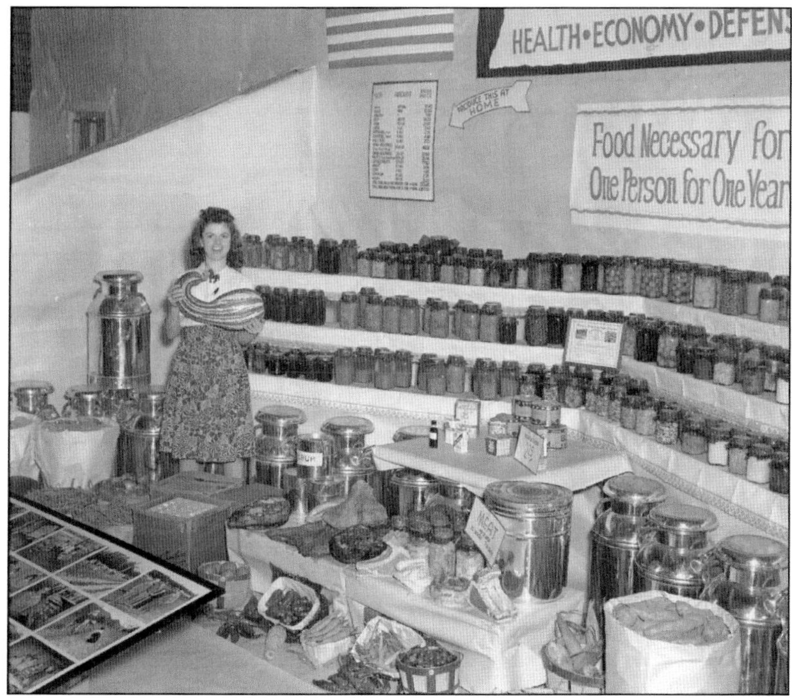

An unidentified young lady from Woodrow, Tennessee, is seen at the Home Food Supply Exhibit during the early 1940s. Conservation of food and other resources played an important role during the war years. The display stressed the importance of producing food by citizens in their own gardens. (Tennessee State Library and Archives.)

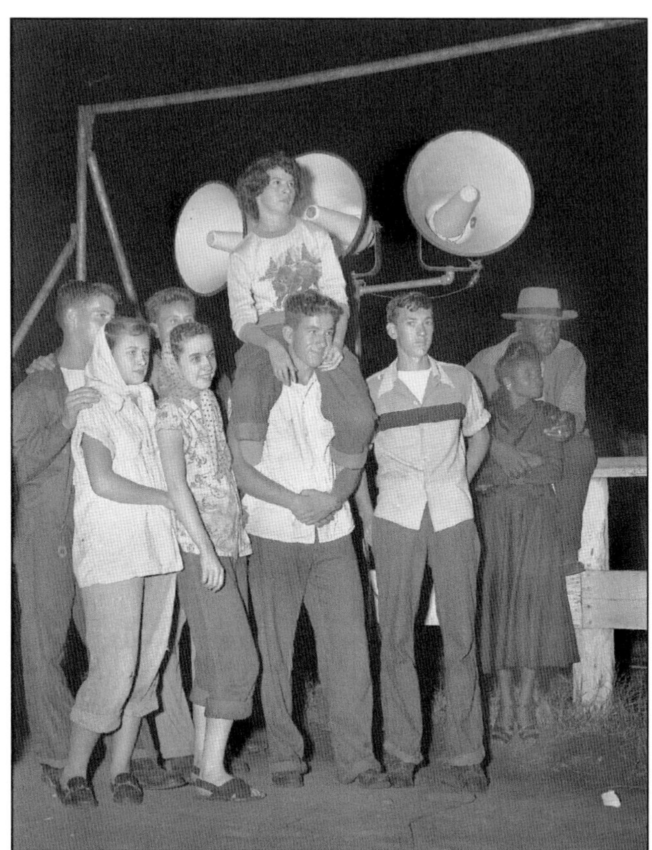

A group of teenagers take in the sights and sounds of the Midway at the 1950 state fair. For decades, fairs and carnivals were a place where men took their dates and youths socialized. (Nashville Public Library, Special Collections.)

In another scene from the 1950 Tennessee State Fair, a young girl on a pony is interviewed by a local radio station. During the years before television, live radio broadcasts from the state fair were common. (Nashville Public Library, Special Collections.)

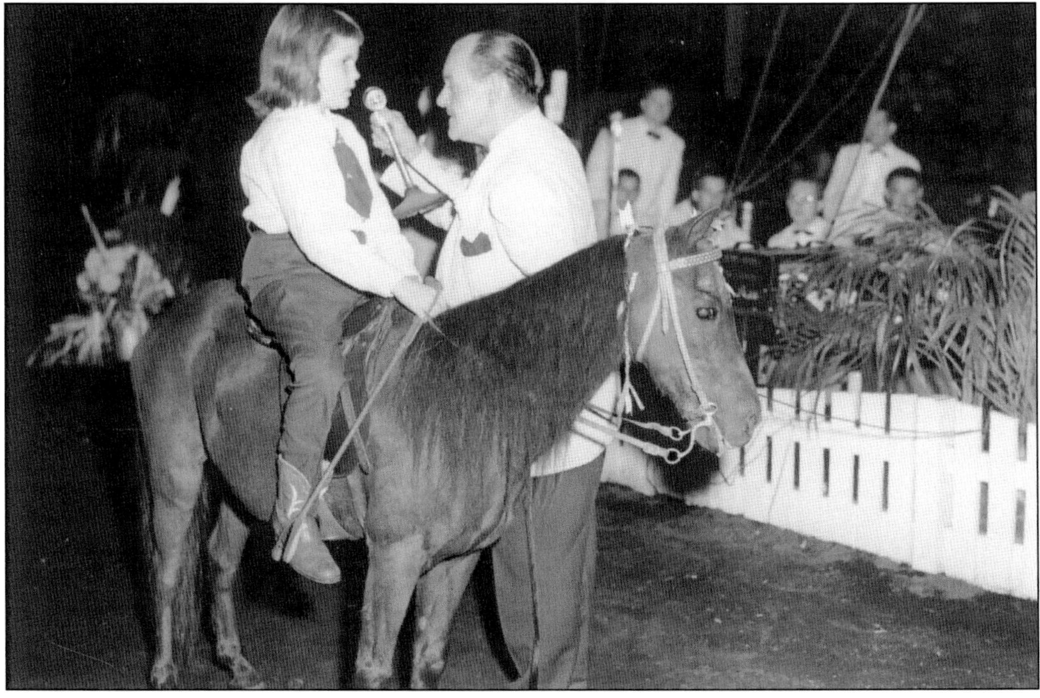

The lights and movement of the carnival rides of the state fair Midway provide children with special memories. A young girl enjoys her cotton candy while watching the surroundings. (Metro Nashville Archives.)

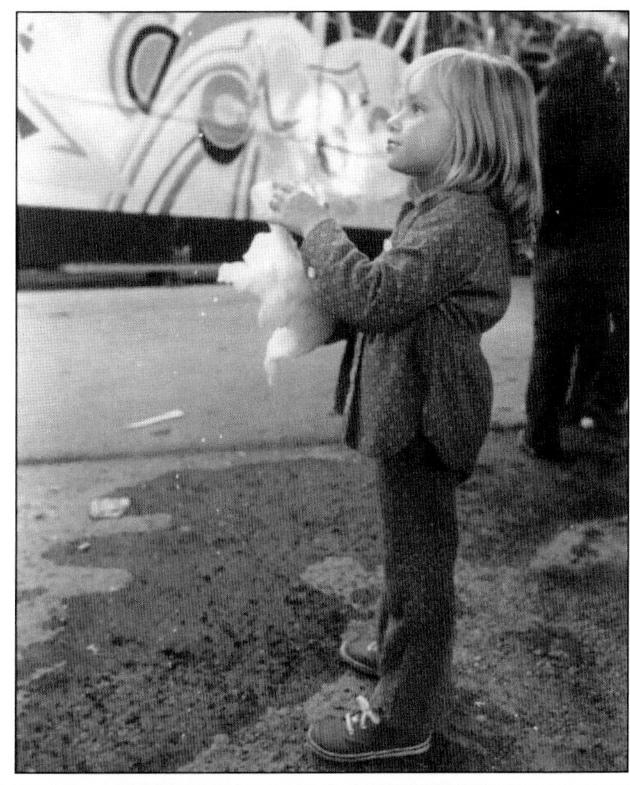

A youth from the Bedford County 4-H Club catches some rest on a bed of quilts and hay bales in a stall with his heifers before his next competition. It was common for contestants to stay close to their animals during competitions. (Nashville Public Library, Special Collections.)

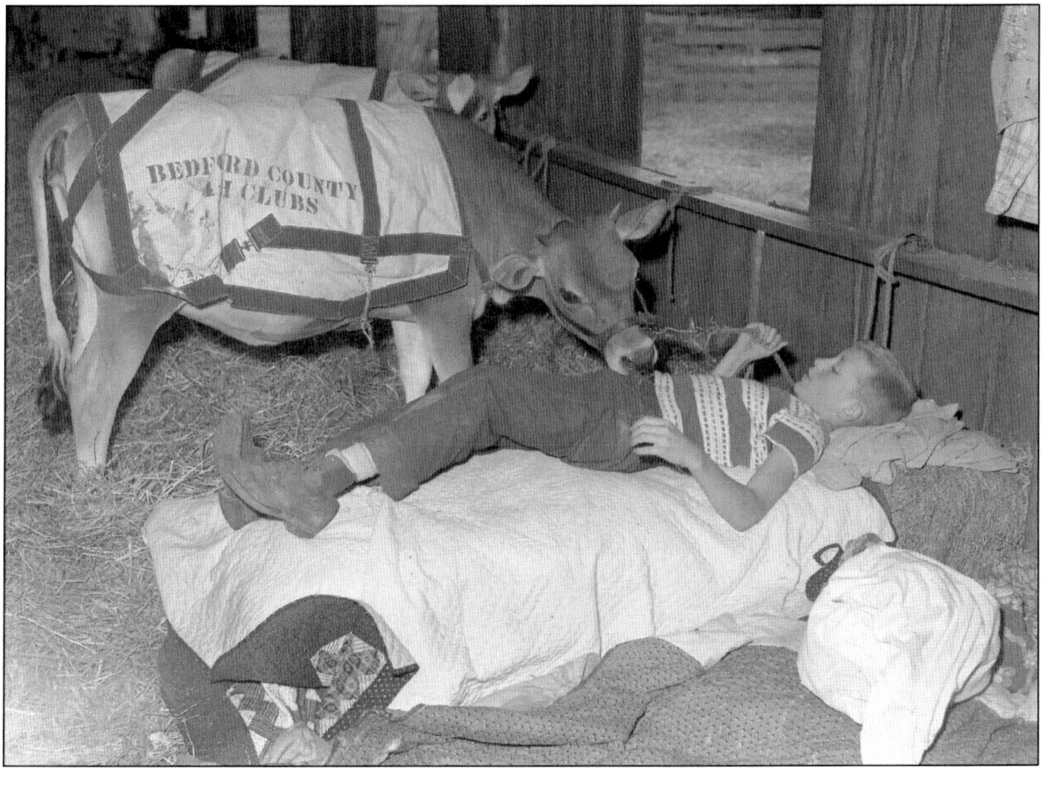

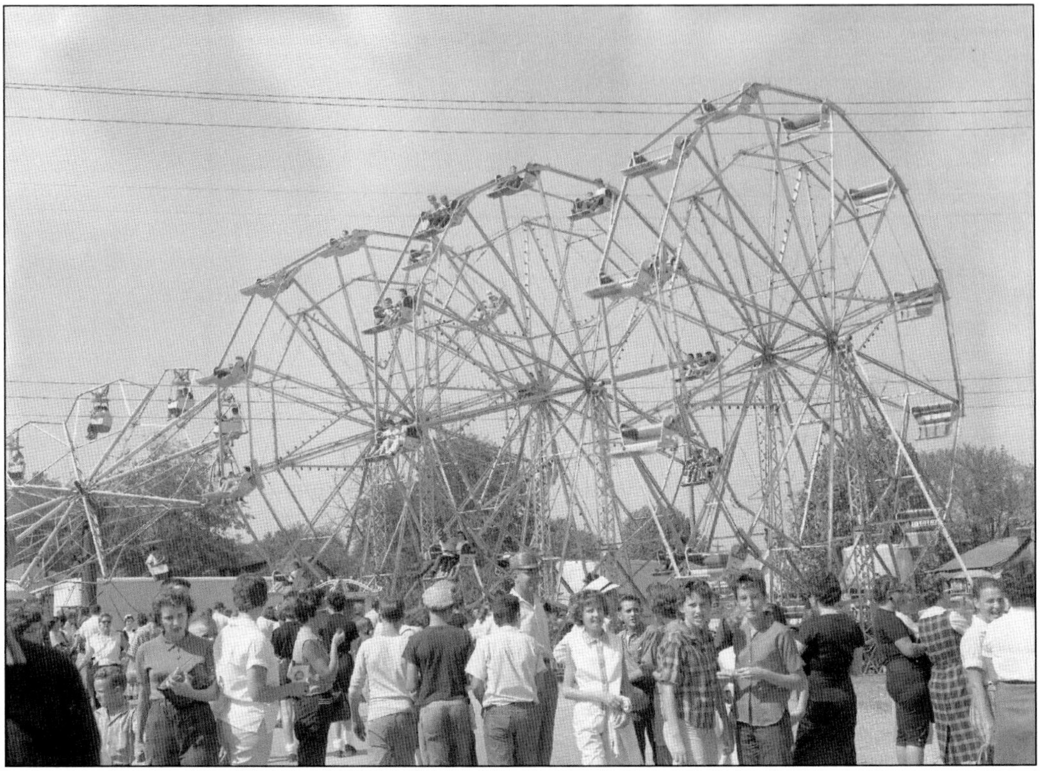

The Midway is a favorite part of the fair for many visitors. In the image below, four young girls eat popcorn as they enjoy the excitement. (Both, Nashville Public Library, Special Collections.)

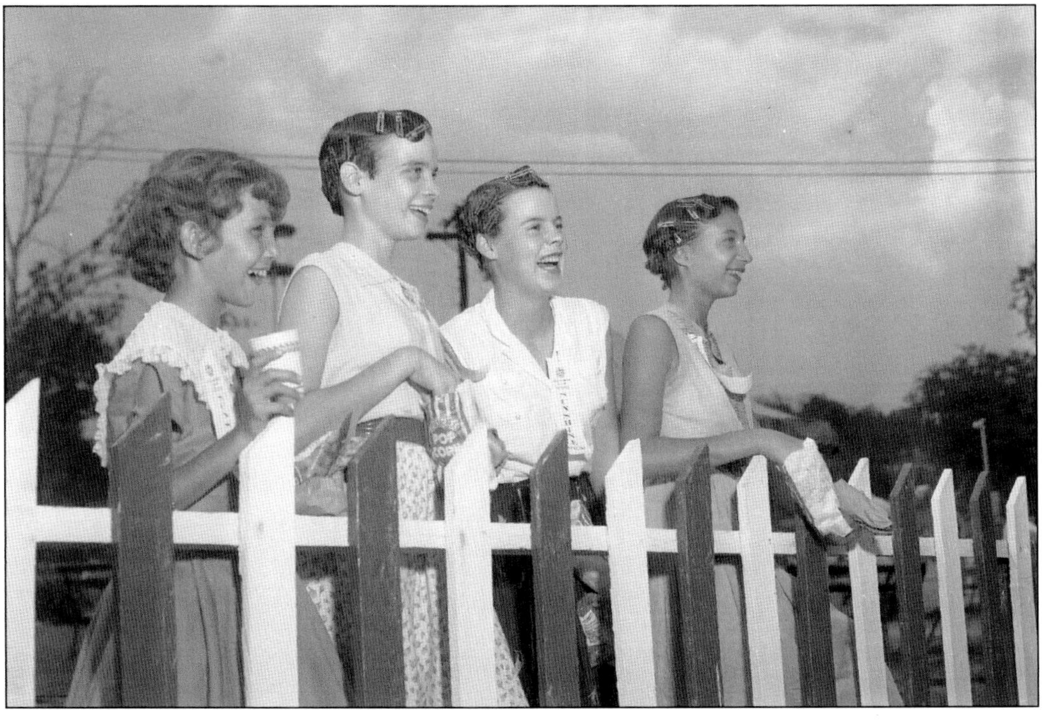

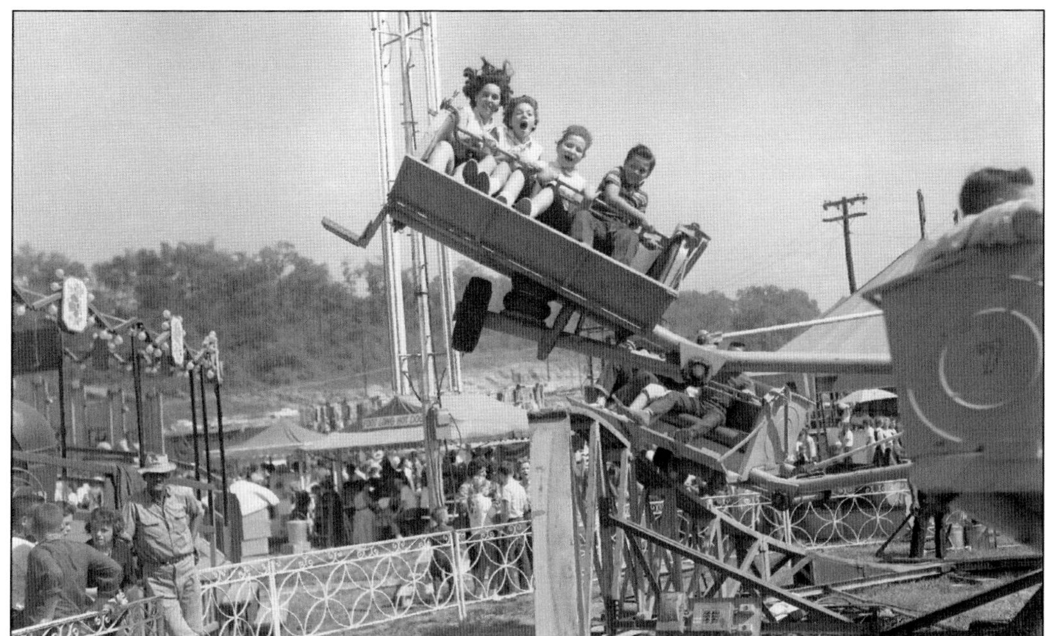

Whether it was the Tilt-a-Whirl, roller coaster, Ferris wheel or carousel, everyone had their favorite ride. The rides and concessions at the Midway provided entertainment for all ages. (Above, Nashville Public Library, Special Collections; below, Metro Nashville Archives.)

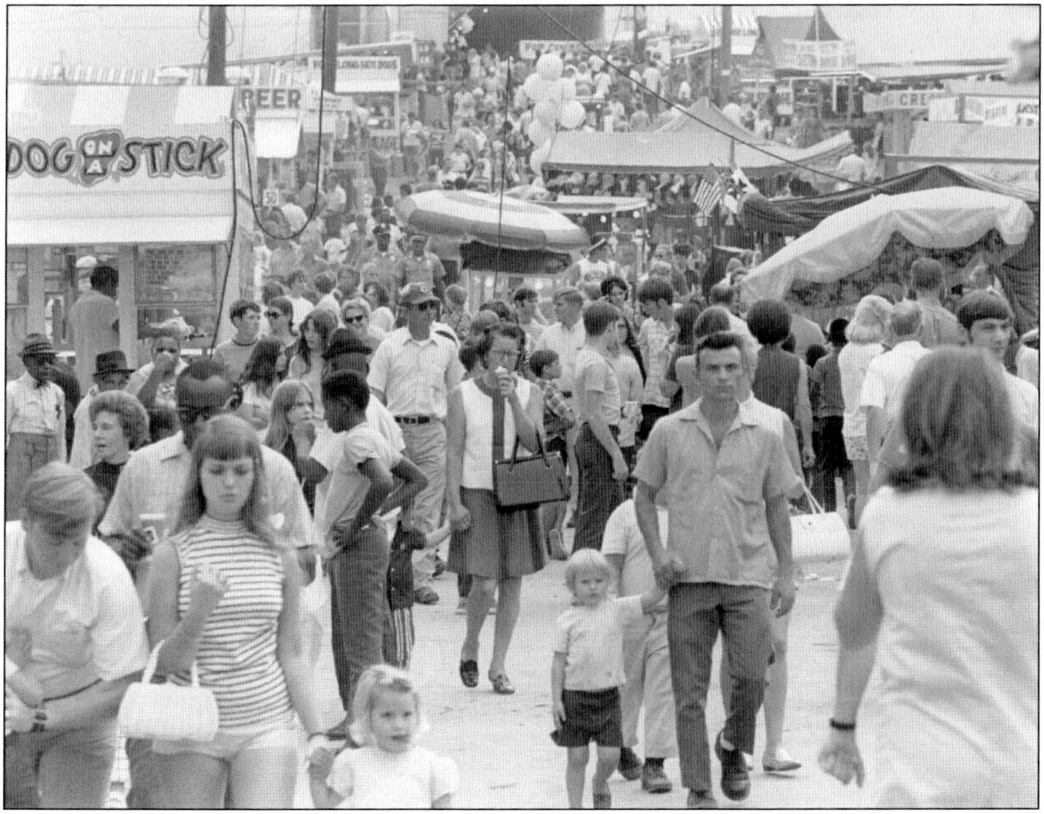

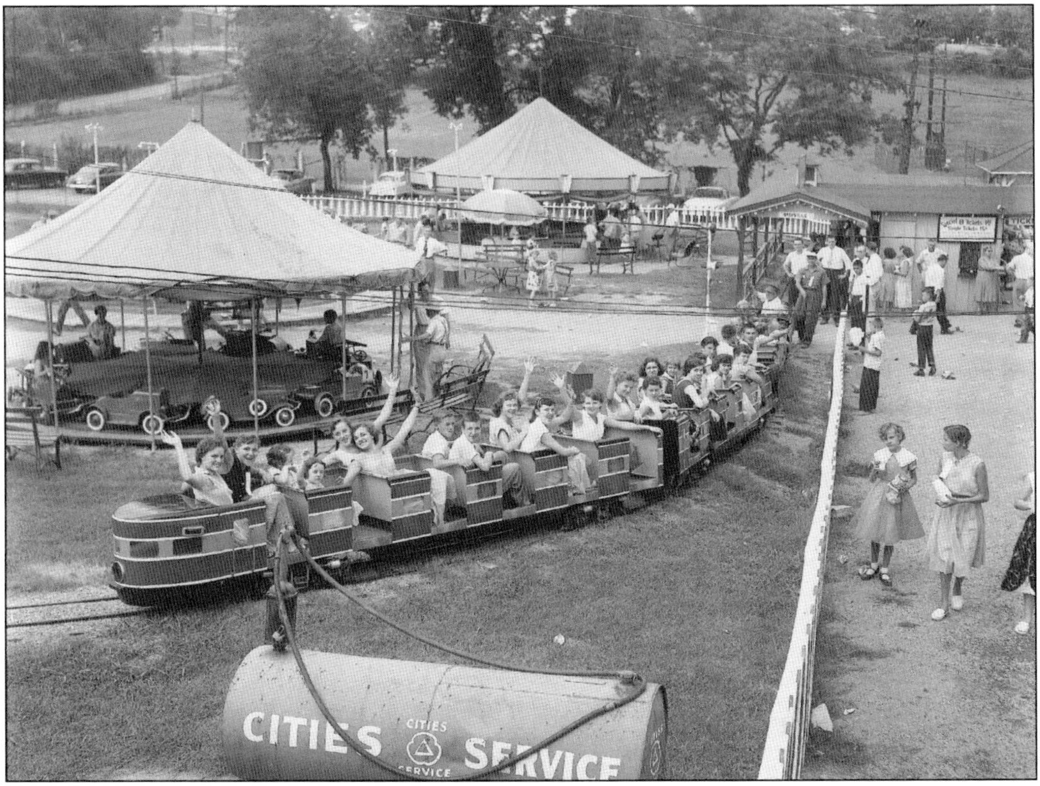

In addition to the carnival rides and booths that accompanied the state fair, the fairgrounds were also home to Fair Park, a permanent year-round attraction that featured numerous rides, including a miniature train ride and the impressive Skyliner roller coaster. (Both, Nashville Public Library., Special Collections.)

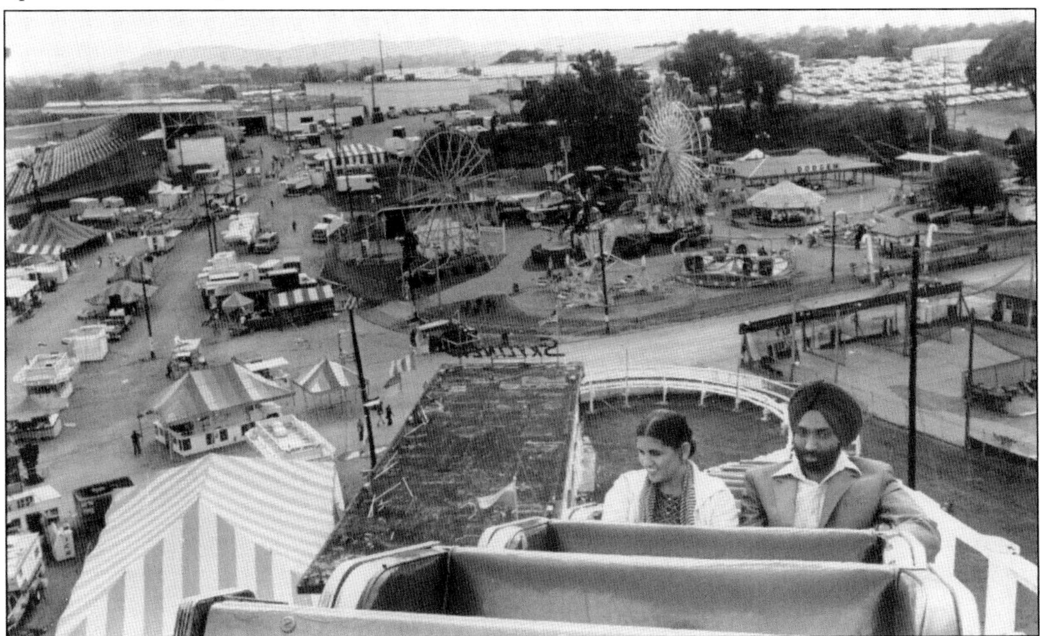

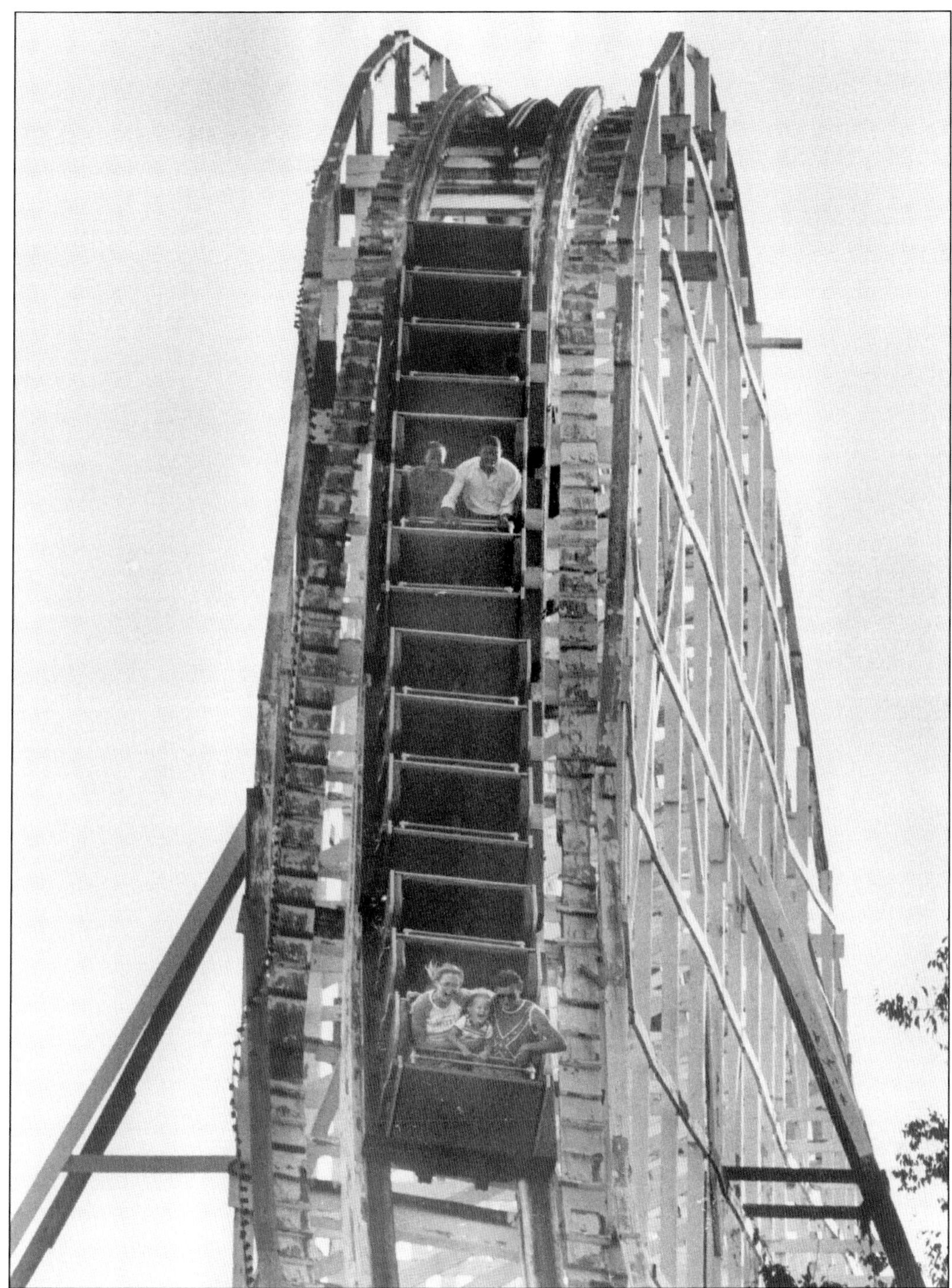

Opened in 1965 as a new addition to Nashville's Fair Park, the Skyliner was an impressive wood roller coaster that thrilled riders for more than 30 years. This view shows a small group of people enjoying it during the ride's last days. (Nashville Public Library, Special Collections.)

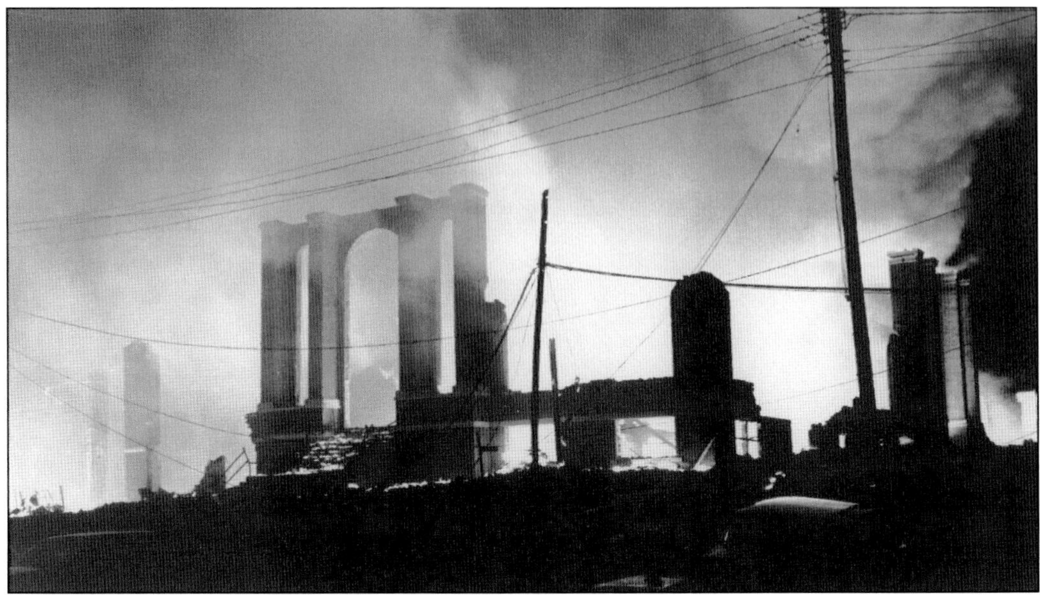

On September 20, 1965, at approximately 10:30 p.m. on the opening day of the Tennessee State Fair, a fire broke out behind the grandstand, quickly spreading to several adjacent buildings. By the time firefighters had contained the blaze, the Administration, Women's, Merchants, and 4-H Buildings, as well as the grandstand, were completely destroyed. The blaze, with flames as tall as 200 feet, could be seen from much of the South Nashville area. The massive fire caused $10 million in property damage, injuring 18 firefighters and fair patrons. Miraculously, there were no fatalities. (Both, Metro Nashville Archives.)

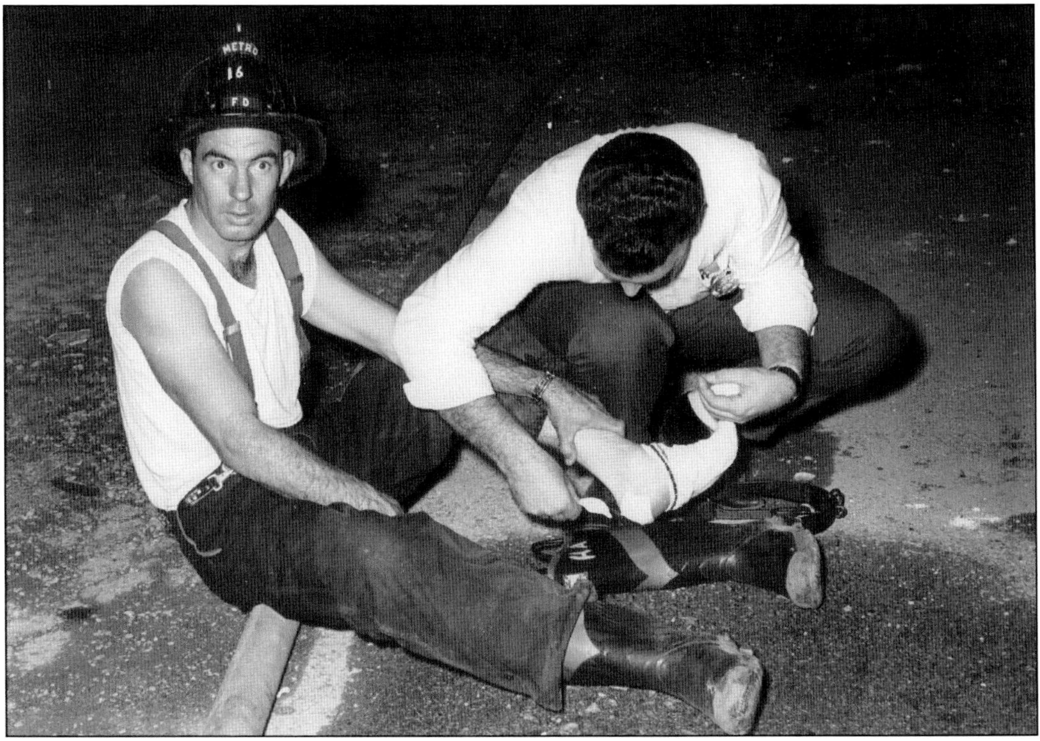

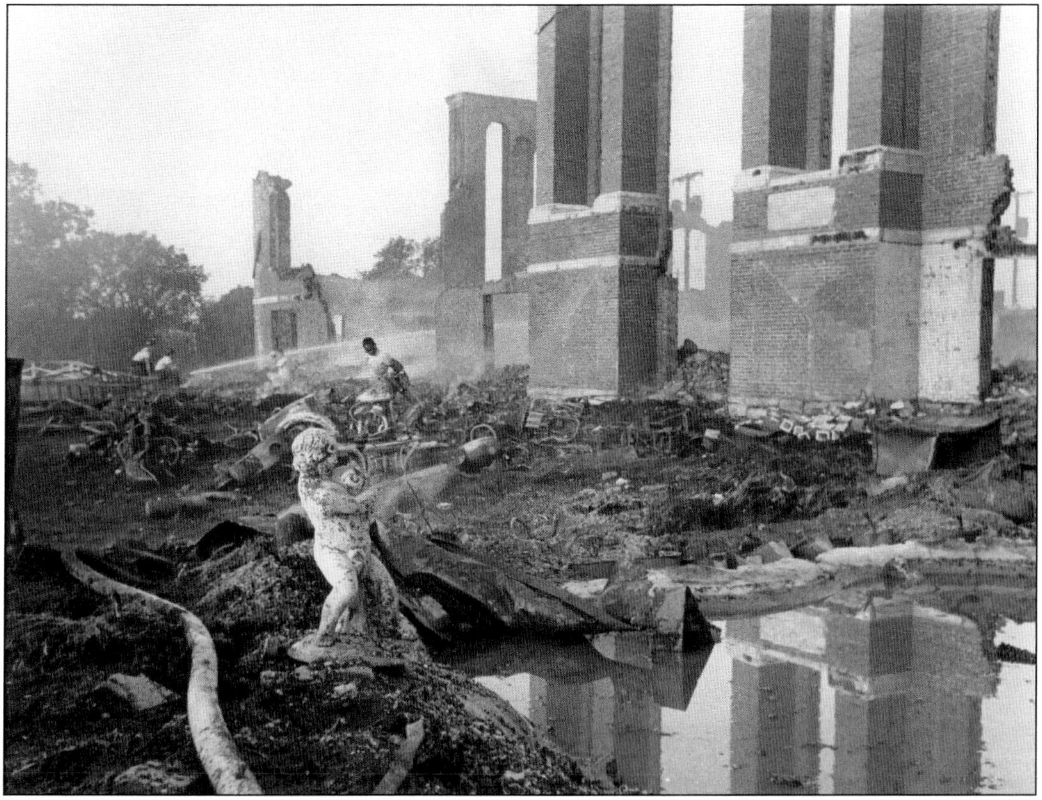

The following morning, the full extent of the damage could be seen. The four brick and wood buildings, more than 50 years old, were a total loss. Workers remove debris from the runs (top image) while a city official assesses the damage. (Above, Metro Nashville Archives; below, Nashville Public Library, Special Collections.)

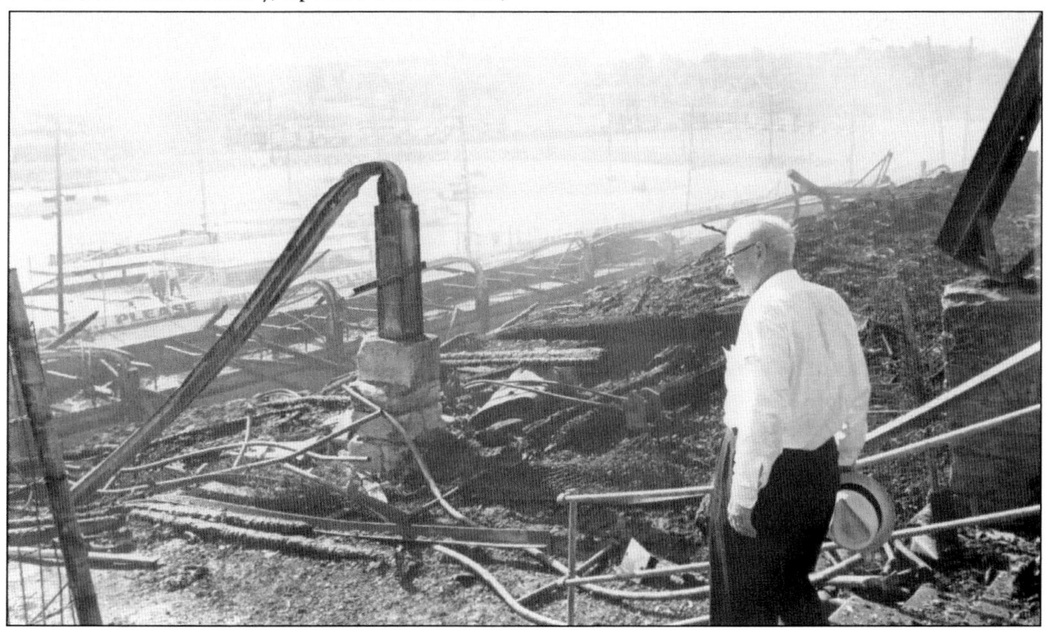

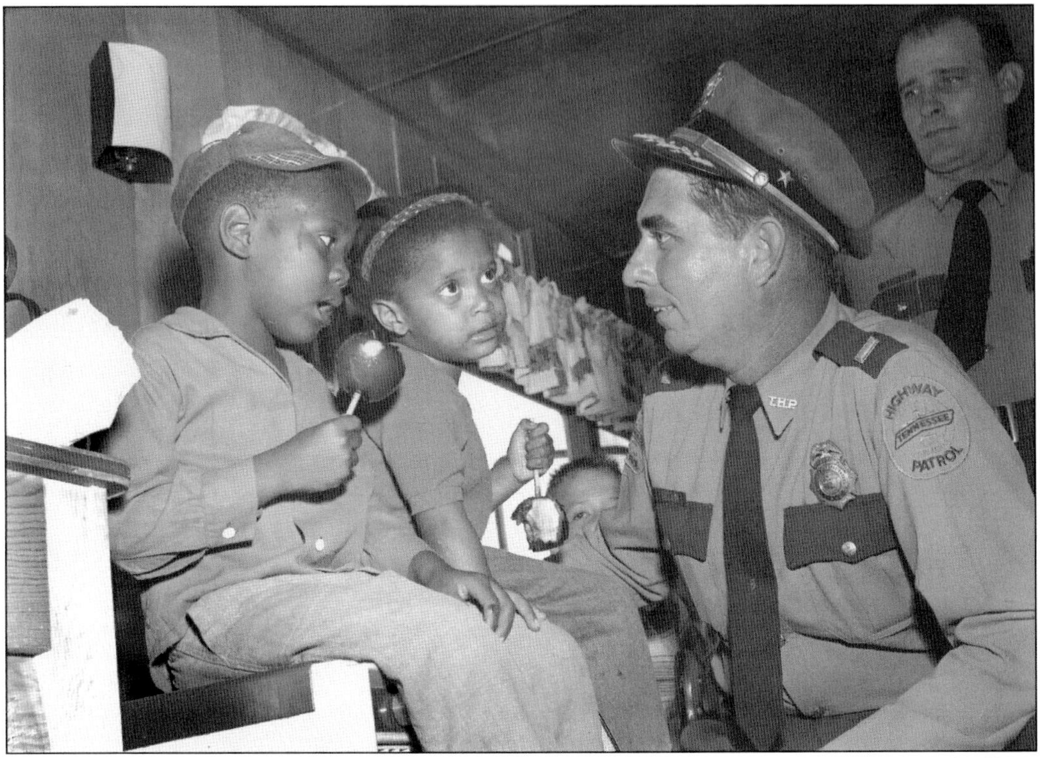

On a hot day during the fair, an unidentified Tennessee Highway Patrol lieutenant and officer give taffy apples to youngsters that became separated from their parents at one of the exhibitors' halls. (Nashville Public Library, Special Collections.)

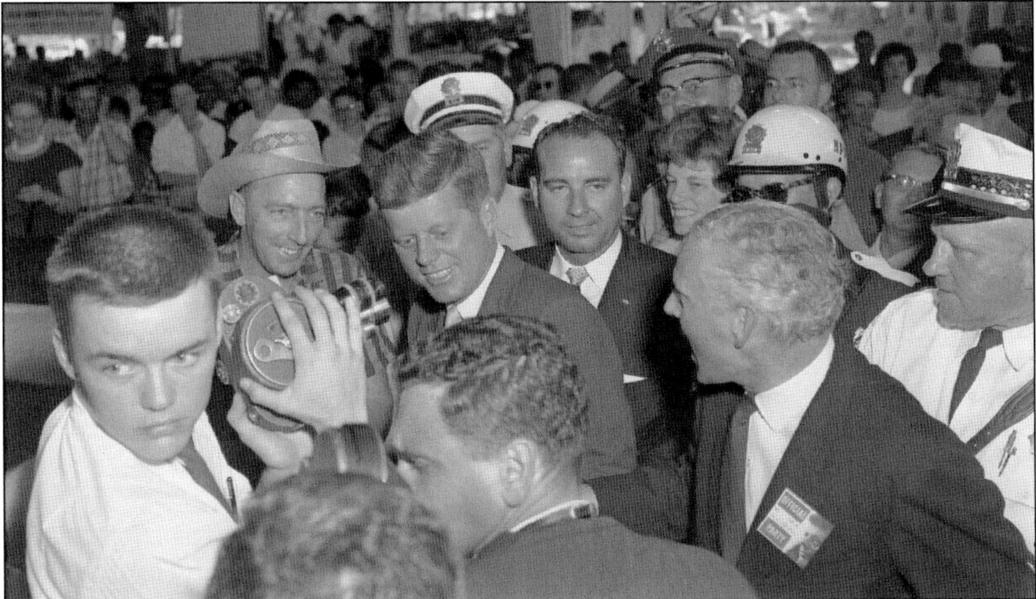

Massachusetts senator John F. Kennedy makes a brief appearance at the Tennessee State Fair during his presidential campaign stop in Nashville on September 21, 1960. (Nashville Public Library, Special Collections.)

Seven

Municipal Airport and Berry Field

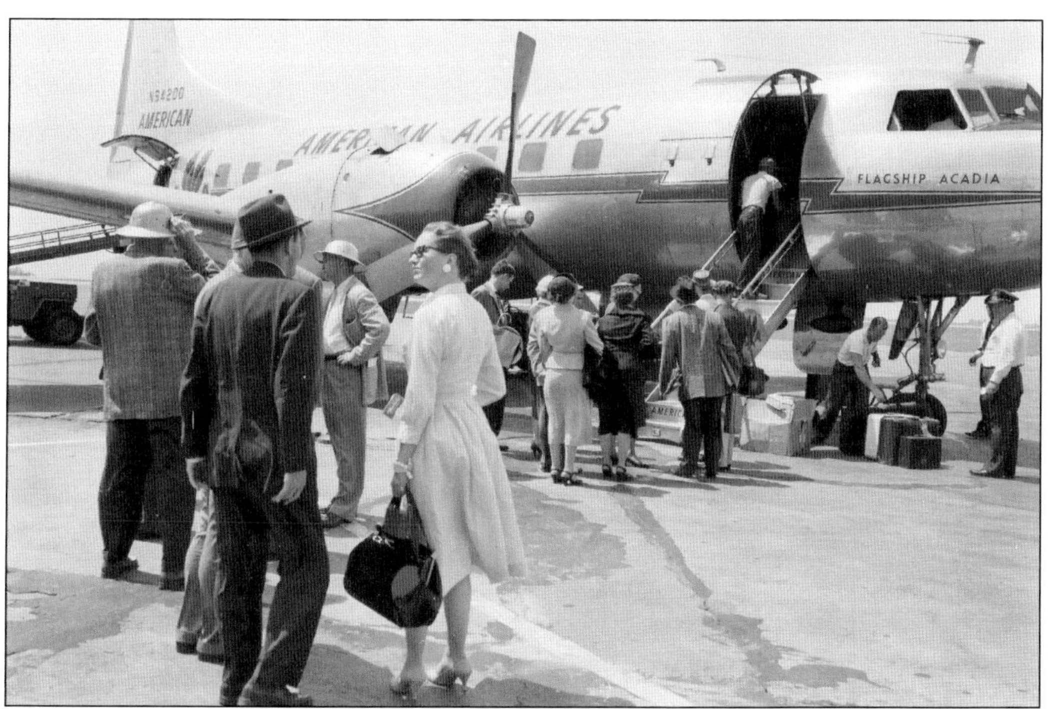

Nashville has long been regarded as a vital hub for passenger and commercial aviation. November 1, 1936, ushered in the era of modern air travel with the dedication of Nashville's Municipal Airport. The 1940s and 1950s was an era when passengers were pampered by airlines vying for their patronage, a time before jets when the Convair 240 and other models ruled the skies. (Tennessee State Library and Archives.)

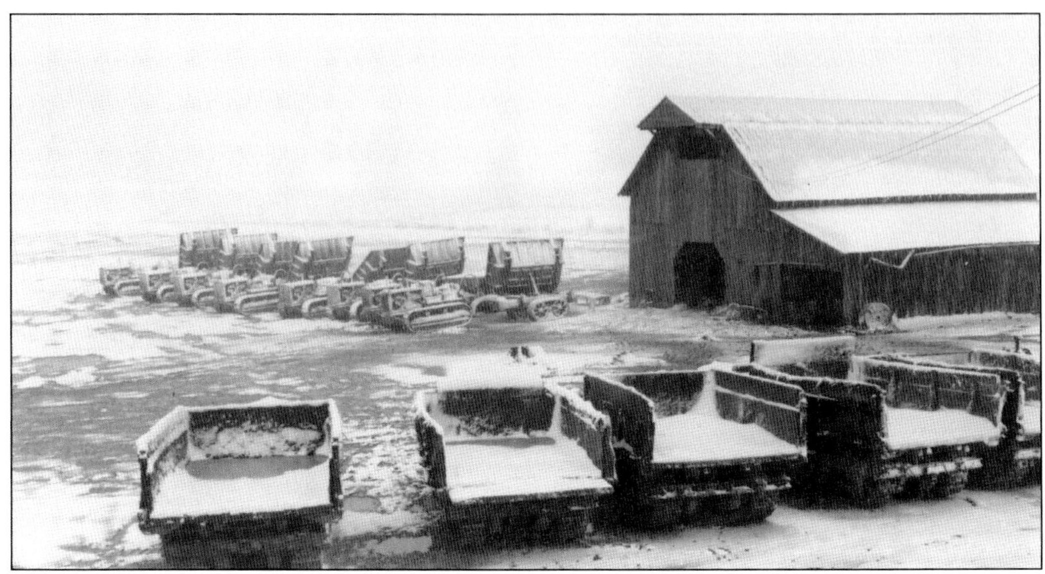

Heavy construction equipment is staged next to an abandoned barn on what had once been the Harris family farm in this early-1935 view. The property and adjacent parcels totaling 317 acres was purchased for construction of Nashville's municipal airport using government loans. Located about five miles southeast of the city, the site was the perfect location allowing ample room for future expansion. Later that same year (below), the grading of the field for runways and hangars has made considerable progress as the future airport takes shape. (Both, Tennessee State Library and Archives.)

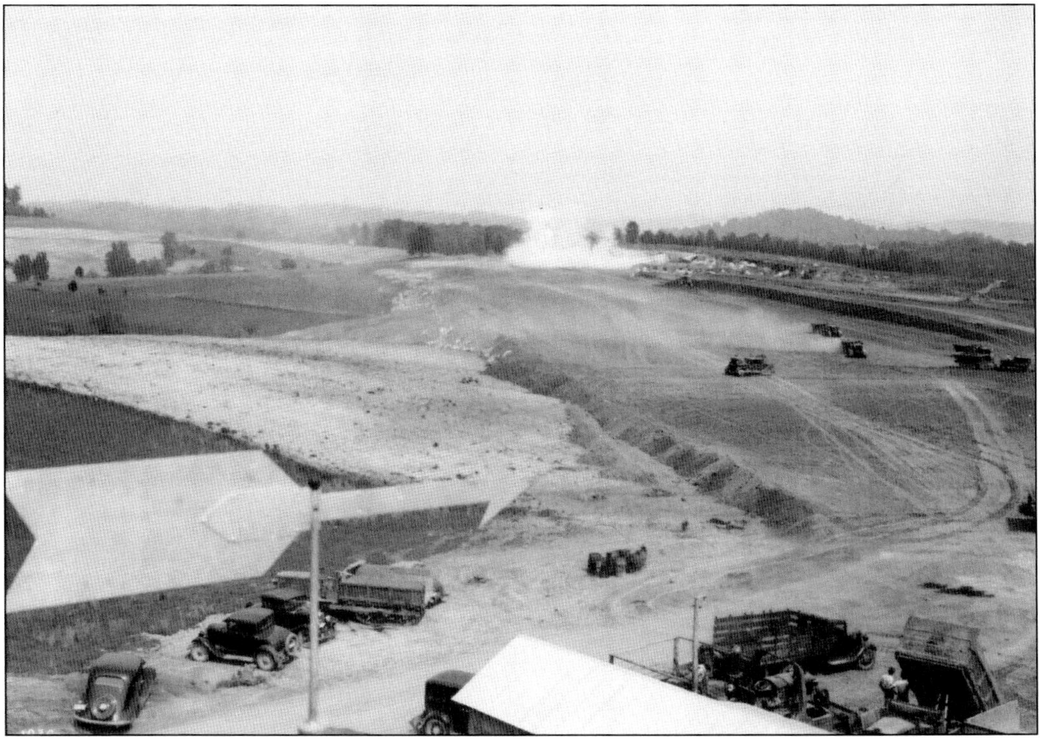

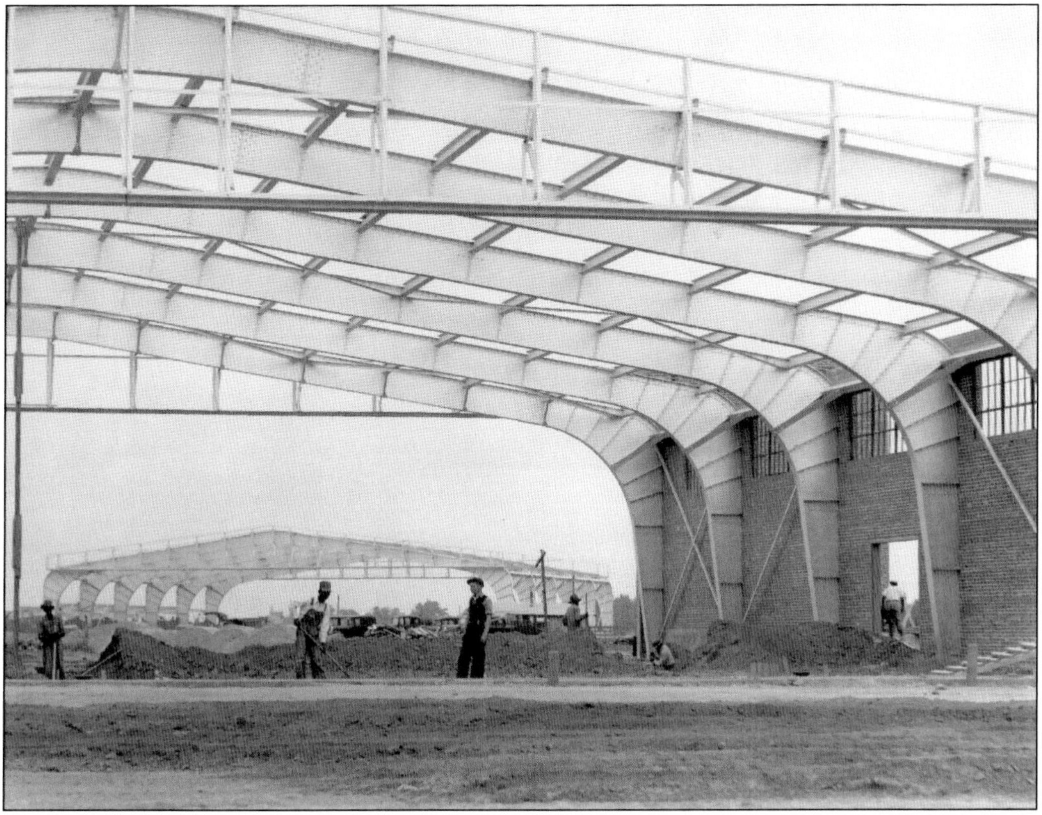

Steel work on the hangars at Nashville's airport is well underway in this scene from the summer of 1936. Several weeks later, below, the hangars and other structures are nearing completion. The entire facility will be pressed into service later that year. (Above, Nashville Public Library, Special Collections; below, Tennessee State Library and Archives.)

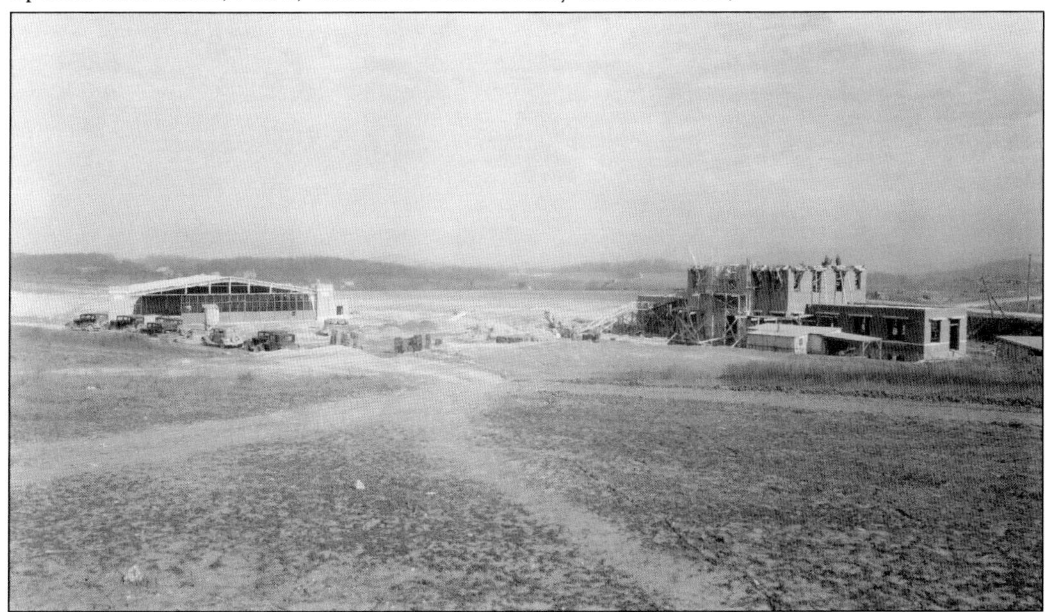

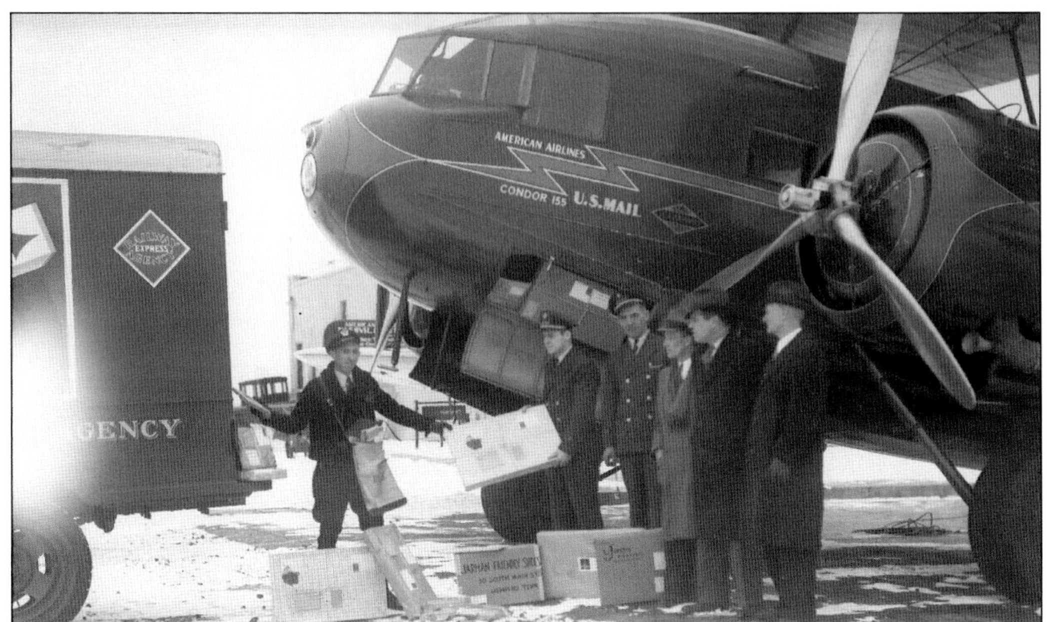

Beginning in 1936, America Airlines inaugurated new mail and express service from Nashville to Washington. All commercial flights were still using Sky Harbor Airport, near Murfreesboro. It would be nearly a year before Nashville's new airport was ready for business. E.B. Hoover of the Railway Express Agency transfers packages from his truck to D.D. Thomas of American Airlines while other officials look on. (Nashville Public Library, Special Collections.)

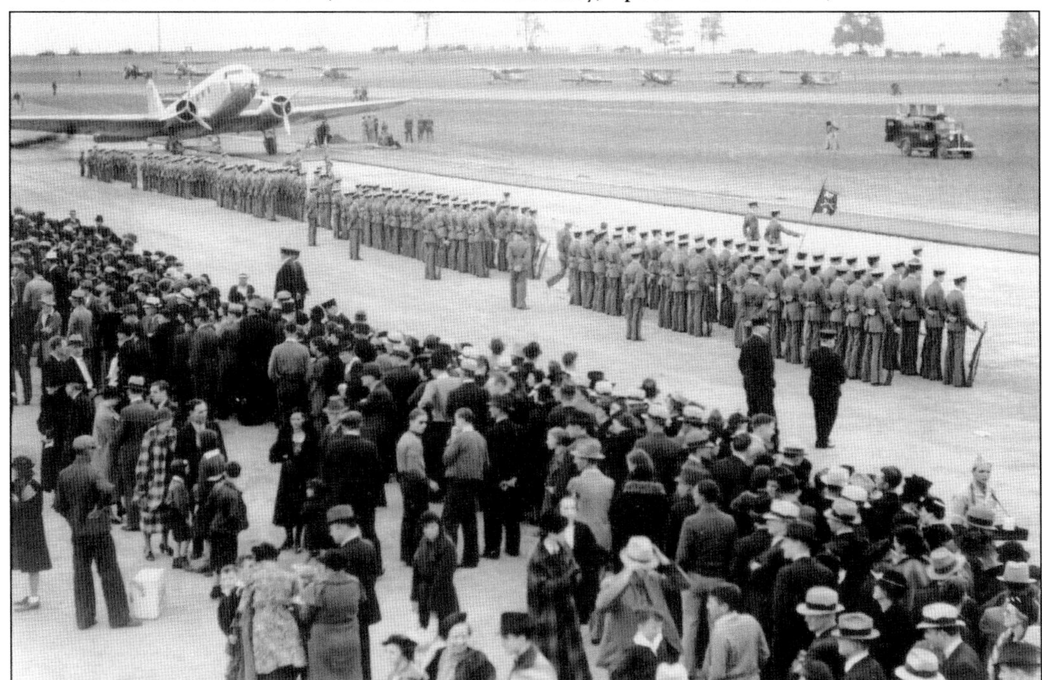

The opening of Nashville's municipal airport ushered in a new era in transportation for middle Tennessee. The crowd watches as the proceedings begin on a chilly November 1, 1936. (Metro Nashville Archives.)

First Lady Eleanor Roosevelt steps off a plane in Nashville on March 6, 1938, during refueling. In the early years of air travel, it was not unusual for celebrities to mingle with crowds during stops. (Nashville Public Library, Special Collections.)

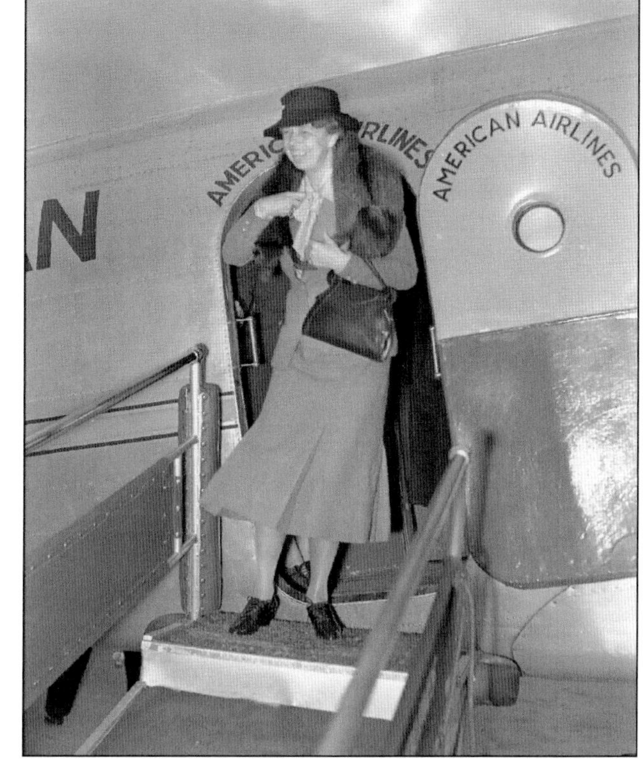

In a scene recorded at municipal airport in November 1938, a woman believed to be a stewardess holds Tennessee's state flag with an American Airlines DC-3 as a backdrop at an unknown celebration. (Tennessee State Library and Archives.)

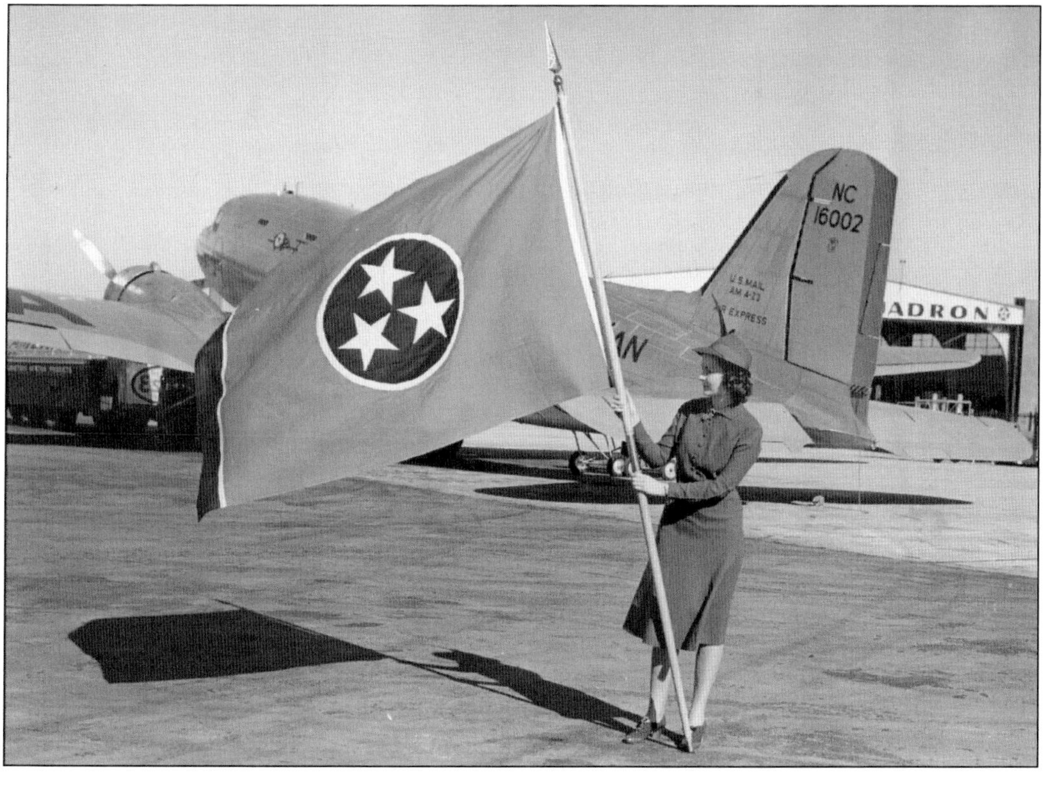

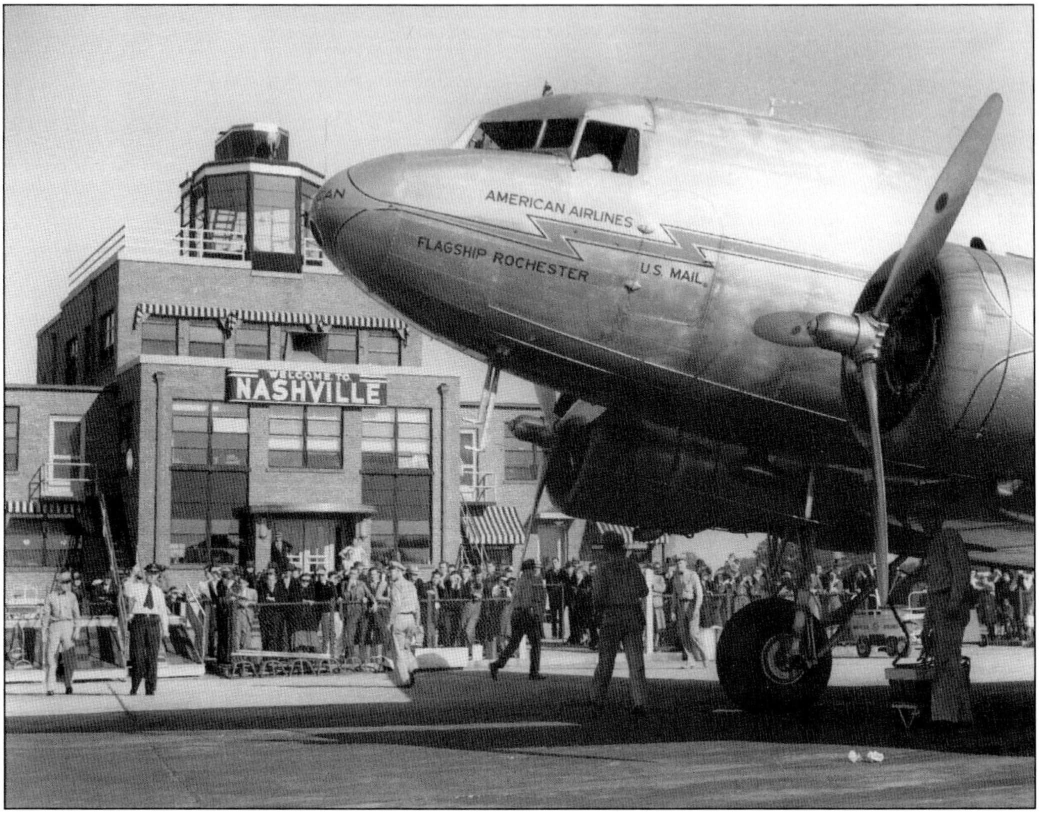

A crowd gathers at Nashville's passenger terminal to get a closer look at one of American Airlines' newest plane, the Flagship Rochester. The Douglas DC-3 protected the schedules of flights serving Nashville and other cities throughout the 1940s and attracted record-setting ridership for airlines at the time. (Tennessee State Library and Archives.)

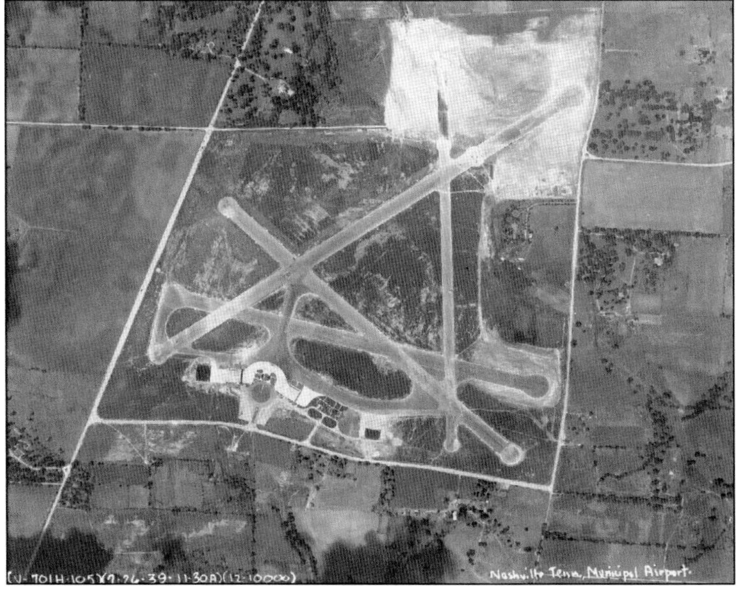

In this 1939 aerial view looking west, the runways are being extended to accommodate larger aircraft and additional flights. The expansion of the facility forced closures of McGavock and Couchville Pikes (upper right)—the first of many improvements over the next decade. The passenger terminal and hangars are at bottom of image. Murfreesboro Road is to the left of the airport. (Tennessee State Library and Archives.)

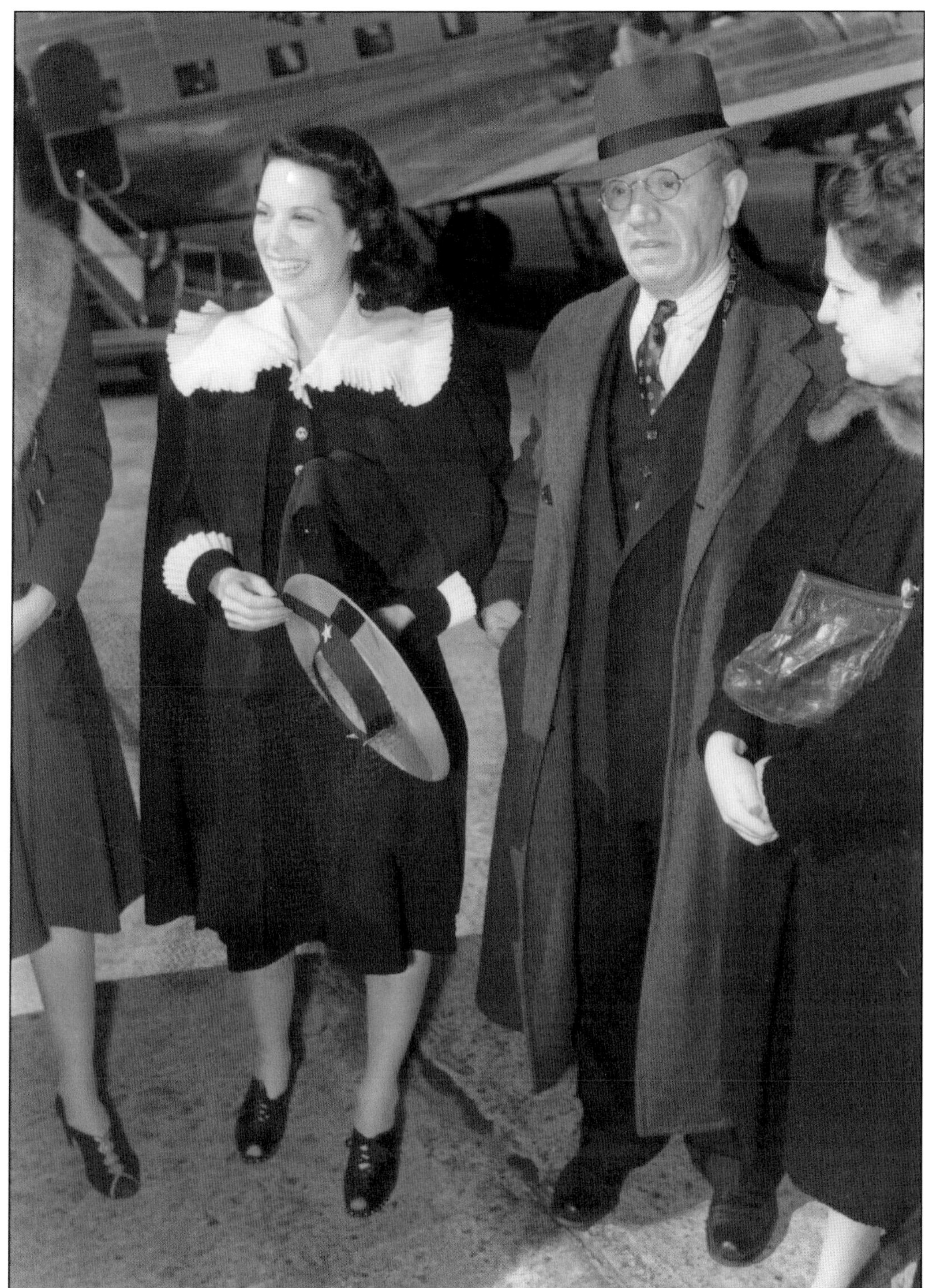

Radio singer Dinah Shore is seen in Nashville on March 14, 1941, when her flight made a brief refueling stop on its way from Los Angeles to Washington, DC. Shore graduated from Nashville's Hume-Fogg High School in 1934. (Metro Nashville Archives, Banner Collection.)

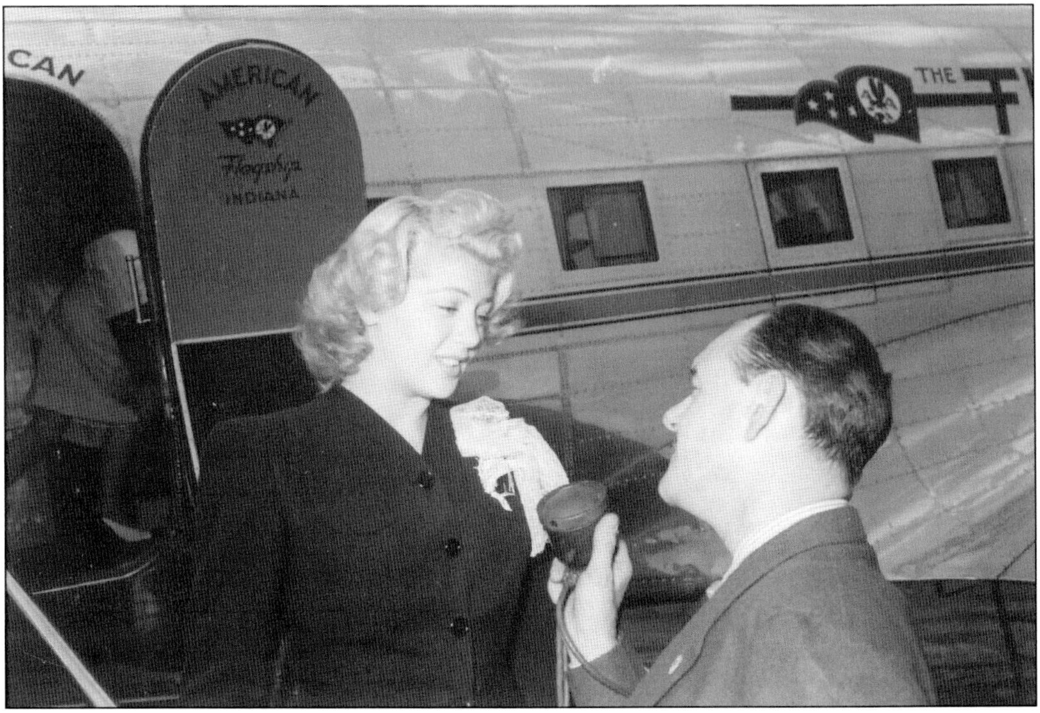

Glamorous movie star Lana Turner is interviewed by a local radio station as she disembarks from American Airlines' *Flagship Indiana* on May 1, 1941, during a refueling stop en route to Cincinnati. Like other stars landing in Nashville, Turner was besieged by autograph seekers. (Metro Nashville Archives, Banner Collection.)

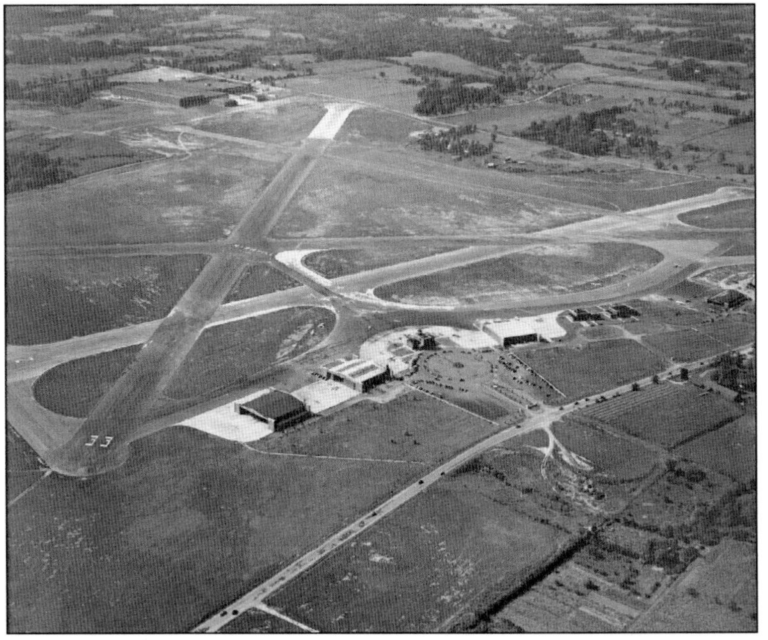

In just five years, many changes happened at Nashville Municipal Airport. The facility and field were renamed Berry Field in 1939, in honor of Col. Harry S. Berry, state WPA administrator; additional hangars were added; and a runway was extended. This 1941 view faces northwest. The passenger terminal and Bogle Road can be seen at in the center. (Tennessee State Library and Archives.)

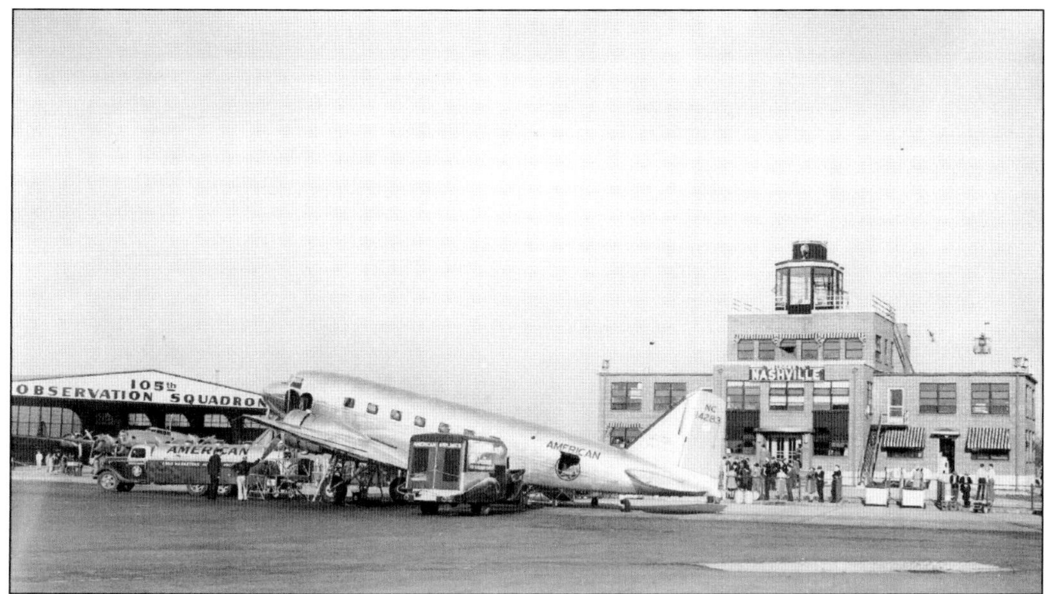

An American Airlines DC-2 makes a brief stop in Nashville to refuel around 1940. To the left are the planes and hangar of the Tennessee National Guard's 105th Observation Squadron. (Tennessee State Library and Archives.)

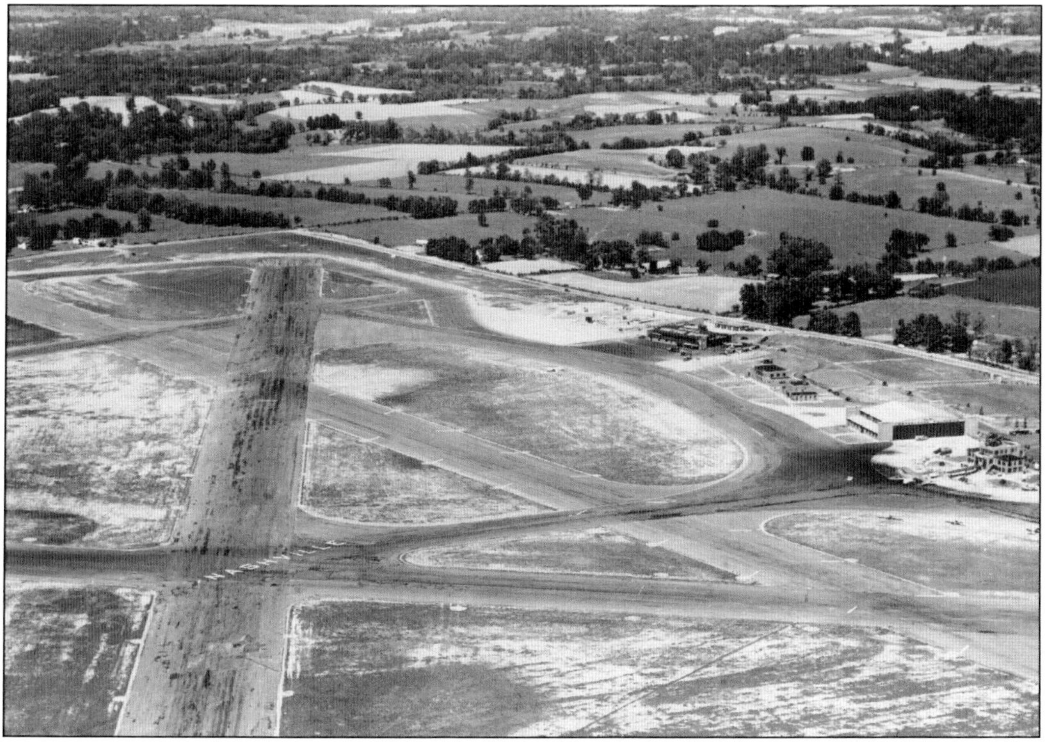

During the early years, Berry Field was surrounded by farmland offering unlimited opportunities for future expansion. In this 1941 scene, facing northeast, the passenger terminal can be seen at extreme right. Today, all the rural property visible at the top of this view is part of the current Nashville airport and crisscrossed by much longer runways. (Tennessee State Library and Archives.)

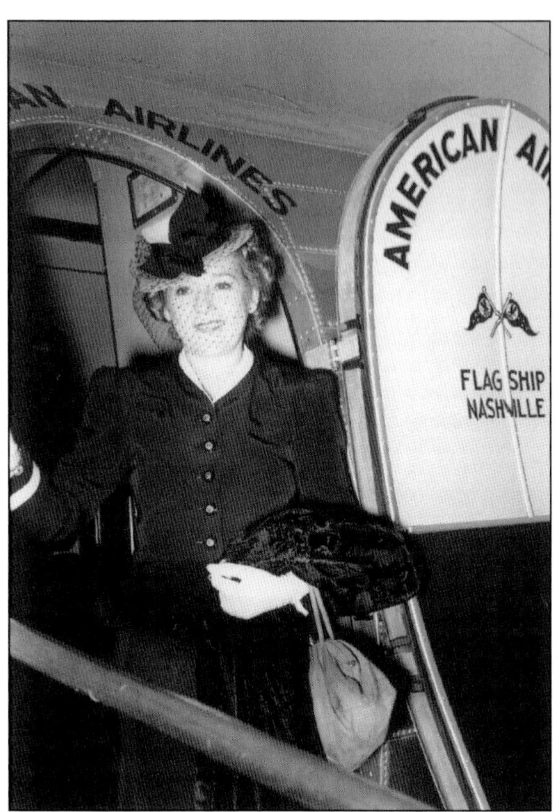

Film star Mary Pickford steps off American Airlines' *Flagship Nashville* in May 1940 during a routine stop on a New York–to–Los Angeles flight. The Douglas DC-3 had just begun service on the airline a few weeks earlier. (Metro Nashville Archives, Banner Collection.)

This view shows Berry Field's passenger terminal as it appeared in the late 1940s with new additions. In spite of efforts by the city to modernize and expand the facility to keep pace with increased traffic, it remained inadequate and outdated. (Metro Nashville Archives.)

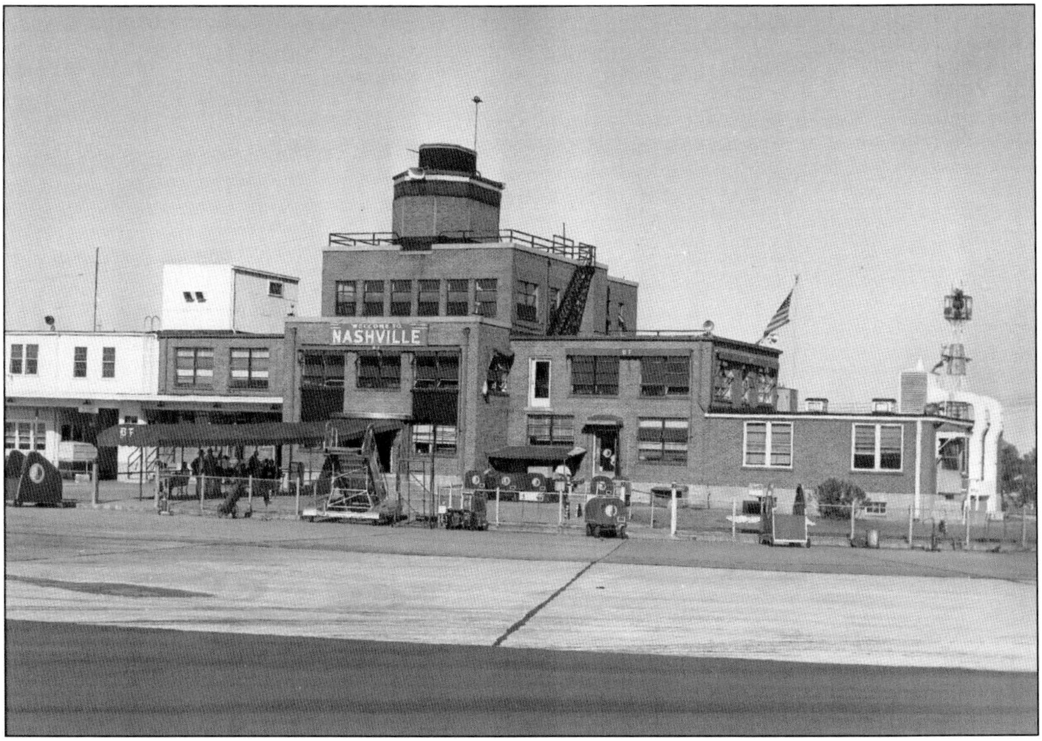

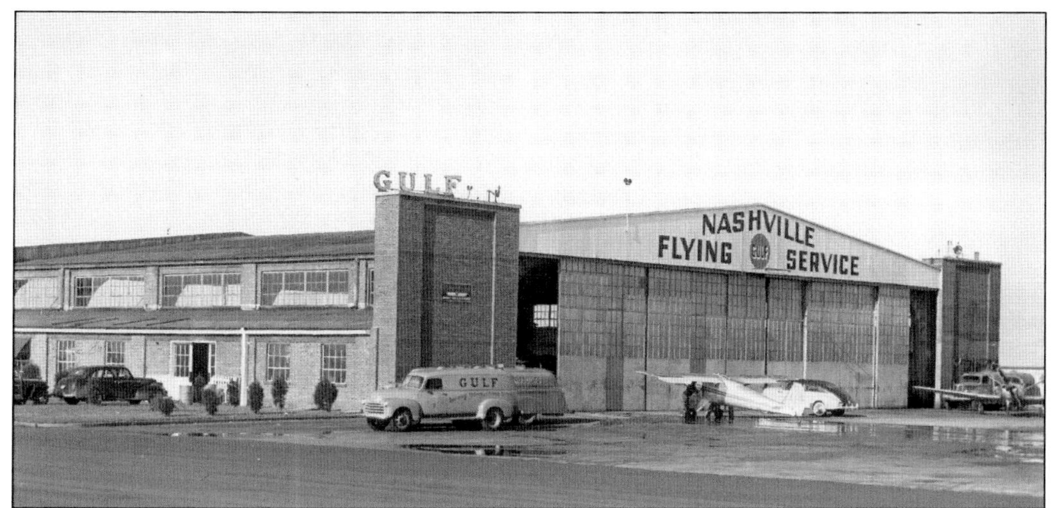

For decades, Nashville Flying Service provided many services at Berry Field including airplane sales and service, charter flights and flight instruction. It was one of several firms catering to both businesses and flyers. (Metro Nashville Archives.)

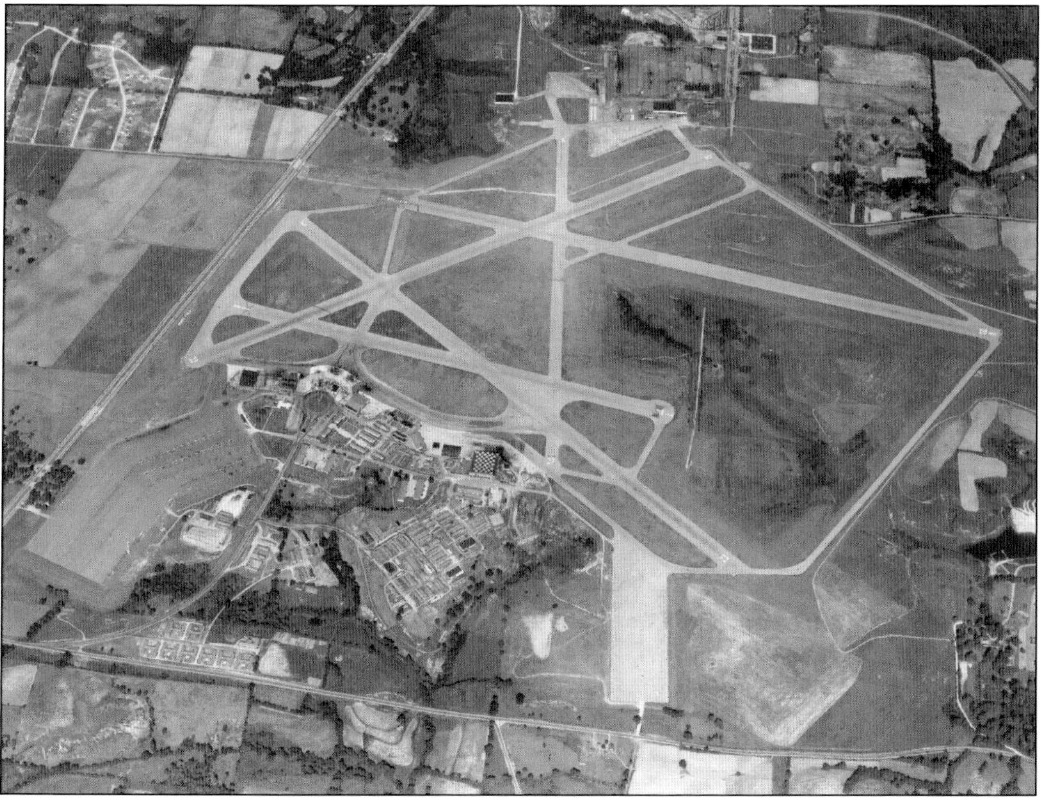

By 1948, Berry Field had gone through several changes. In this view, new runways have been added, existing ones lengthened, and scores of buildings have been added. An expanded military presence necessitated the closing of Bogle Road, the original entrance to the airport. The airport entrance was moved to the east requiring the extension of Donelson Pike, visible on the bottom. (Tennessee State Library and Archives.)

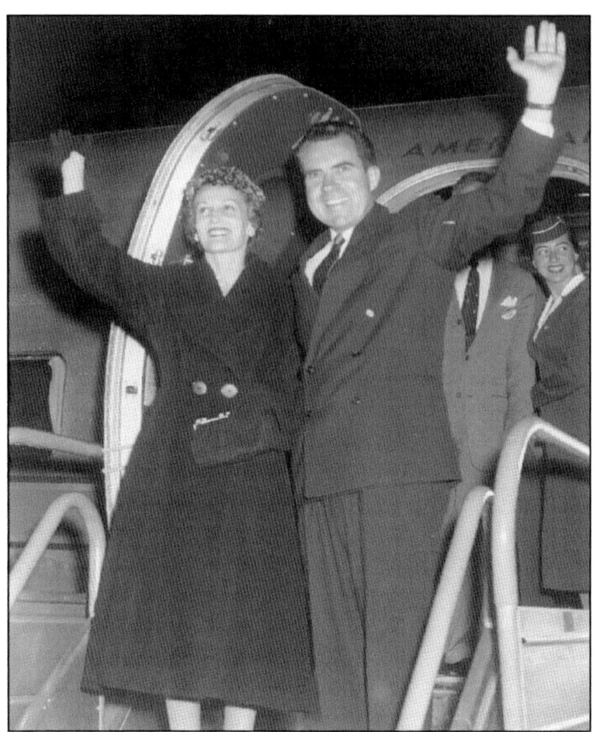

On September 27, 1952, Republican vice presidential candidate US senator Richard Nixon and his wife, Patricia, wave to a crowd before boarding a chartered airliner at Nashville's Berry Field. Nixon had been in Nashville to attend a political rally. (Nashville Public Library, Special Collections.)

Passengers board Eastern Airlines' *Silver Falcon* at Nashville's Berry Field in August 1954. Unlike other aircraft models of the day, the Martin-built 404 boarded from the rear rather than the side. (Tennessee State Library and Archives.)

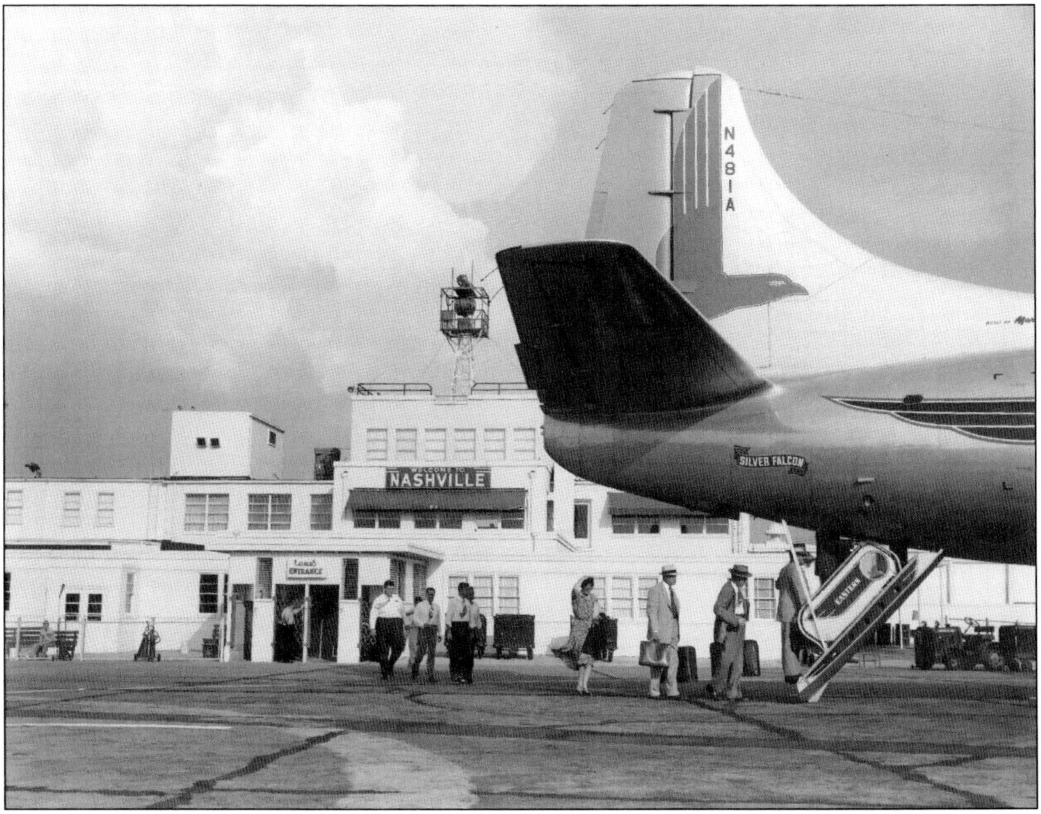

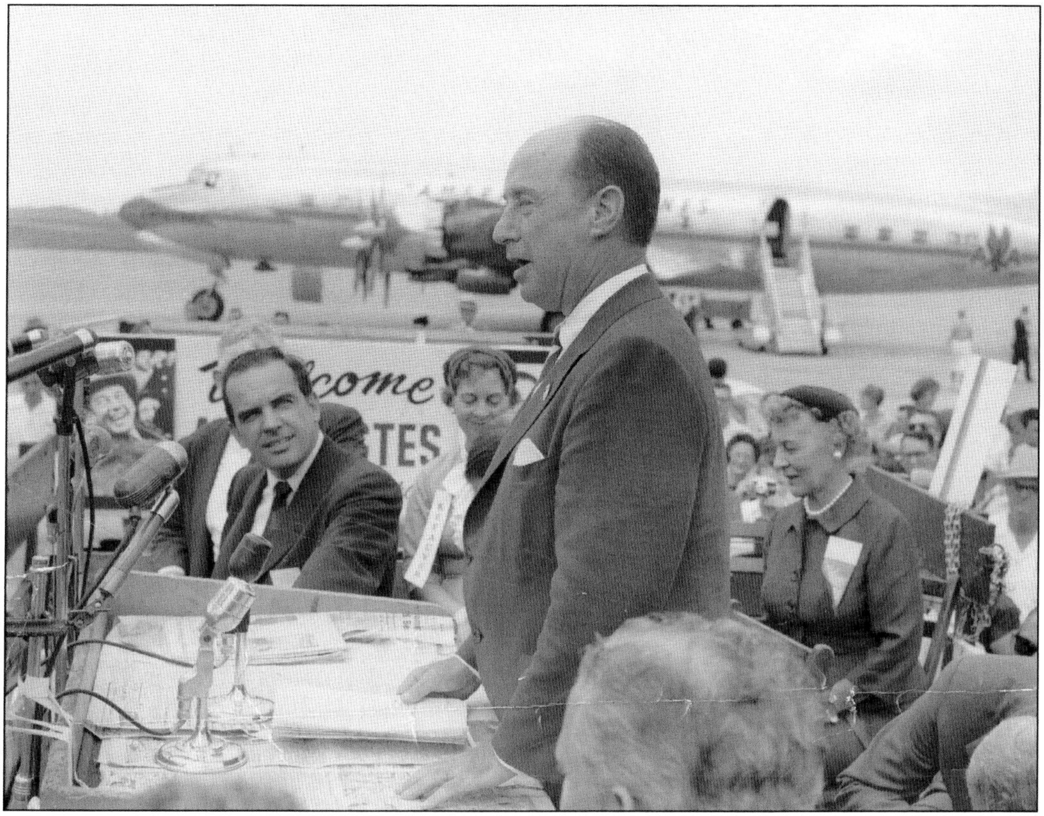

By the mid-1950s, it had become commonplace for presidential candidates to campaign by air. During his 1956 presidential campaign swing through Tennessee, presidential candidate Adlai Stevenson delivers a speech during a quick stopover in Nashville. Tennessee governor Frank Clement, at left, listens attentively. (Tennessee State Library and Archives.)

This aerial view of the passenger terminal at Berry Field recorded during the late 1950s gives an idea how many times the facility had been added onto during the 25 years it had been in use. With the dramatic increase of flights into Nashville, plans had been in the works for many years to move to a new terminal on the opposite side of Berry Field. (Nashville Public Library, Special Collections.)

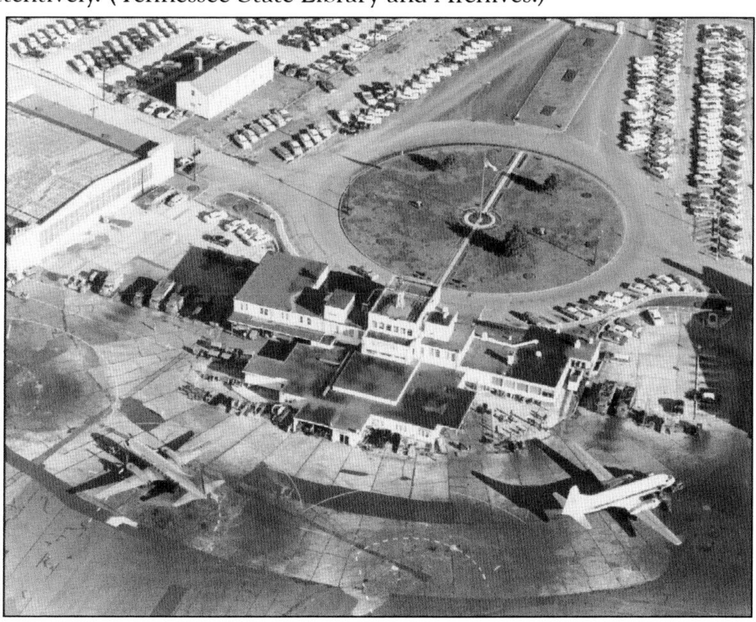

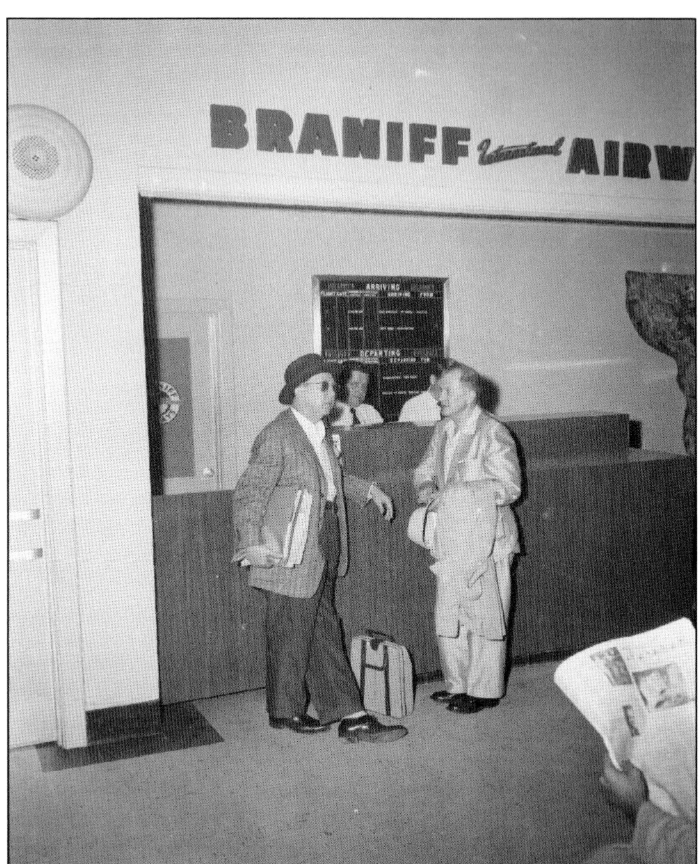

Passengers check in at the Braniff Airways ticket counter shortly before boarding their flight in 1957. Until the late 1960s, visitors were free to view departing planes from outdoor viewing areas and even accompany passengers to the boarding gates. (Tennessee State Library and Archives.)

Planes from both American and Eastern Airlines take on luggage and supplies simultaneously in front of the aging passenger terminal in 1960. The following year, a new and much-larger facility on the opposite side of Berry Field will replace it. (Tennessee State Library and Archives.)

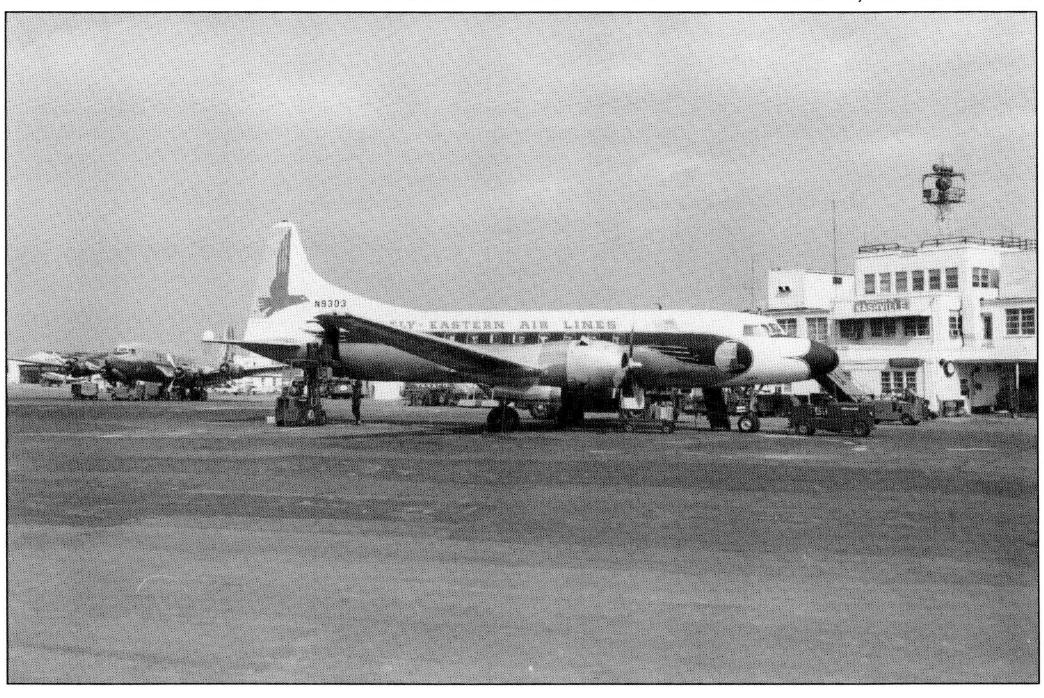

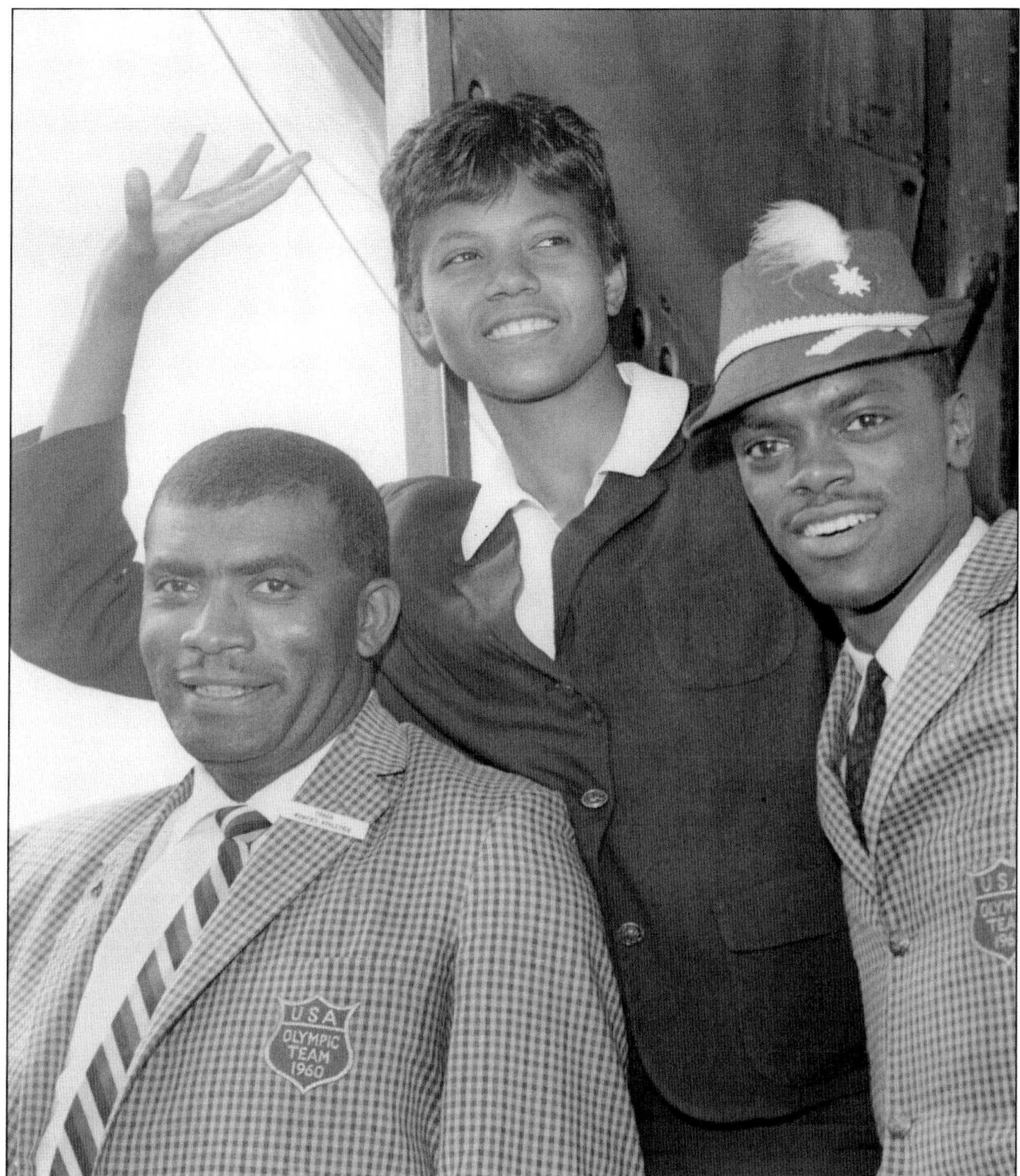

On September 29, 1960, from left to right, Tennessee State University coach Ed Temple, three-time Olympic gold medal winner Wilma Rudolph, and broad-jump ace Ralph Boston disembark from a plane at Nashville. Hundreds of TSU students and well-wishers welcomed the triumphant team back home from the 1960 Summer Olympics in Rome, Italy. (Nashville Public Library, Special Collections.)

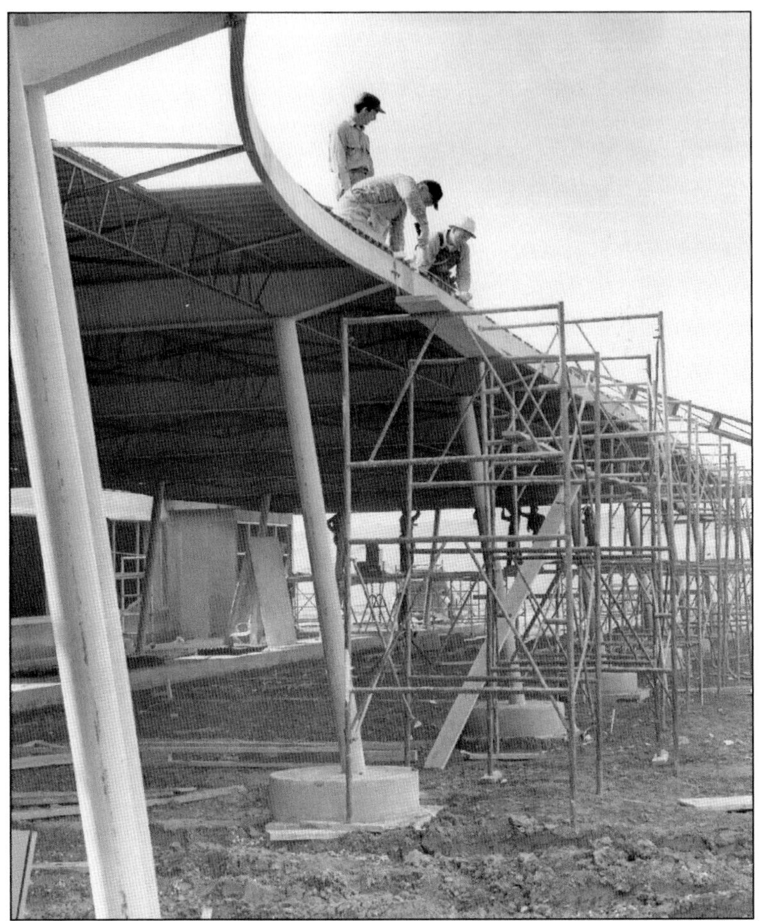

Construction on Nashville's new terminal building is well underway in these images from 1959 as workers put finishing touches on the front canopy (left) and the administration building rises. The state-of-the art facility will usher in the jet age for Nashville. (Both, Nashville Public Library, Special Collections.)

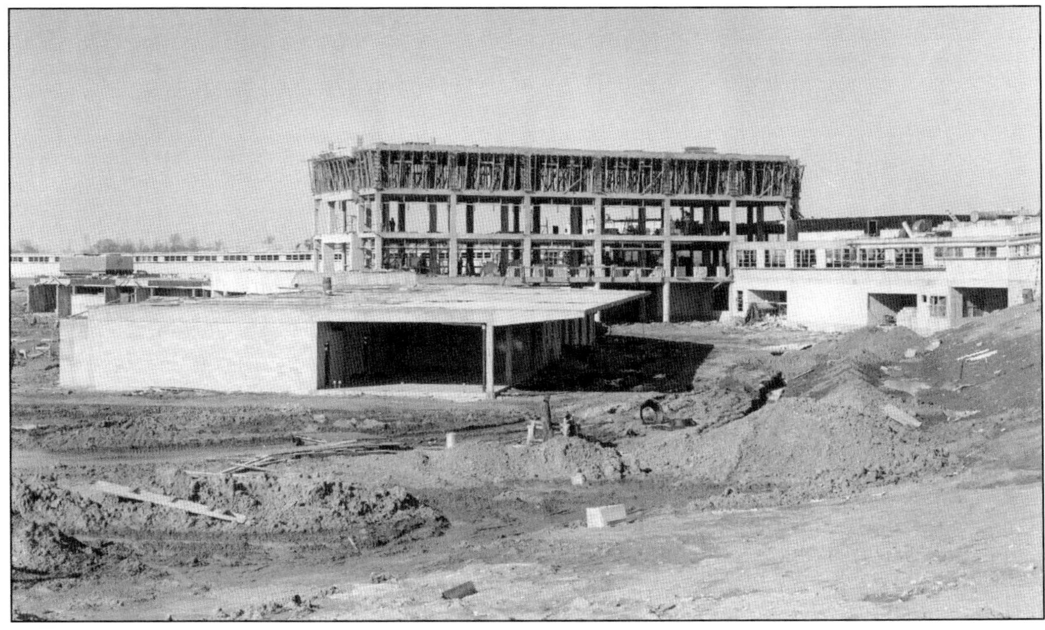

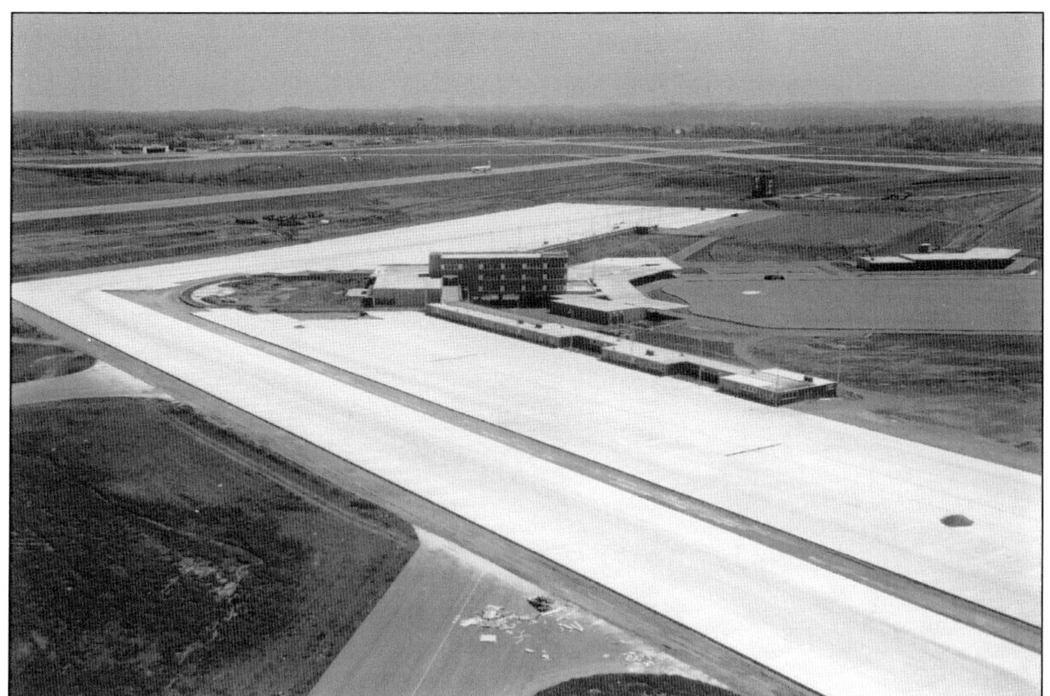

With only months before the opening of the new Doyle Terminal, much work remains to be done, including completion of the parking lot and additional work on the sprawling concrete apron. Across the airfield, pictured above upper right, the old terminal is visible. Below, the modern facility is shown several weeks after its dedication on November 1, 1961. (Both, Tennessee State Library and Archives.)

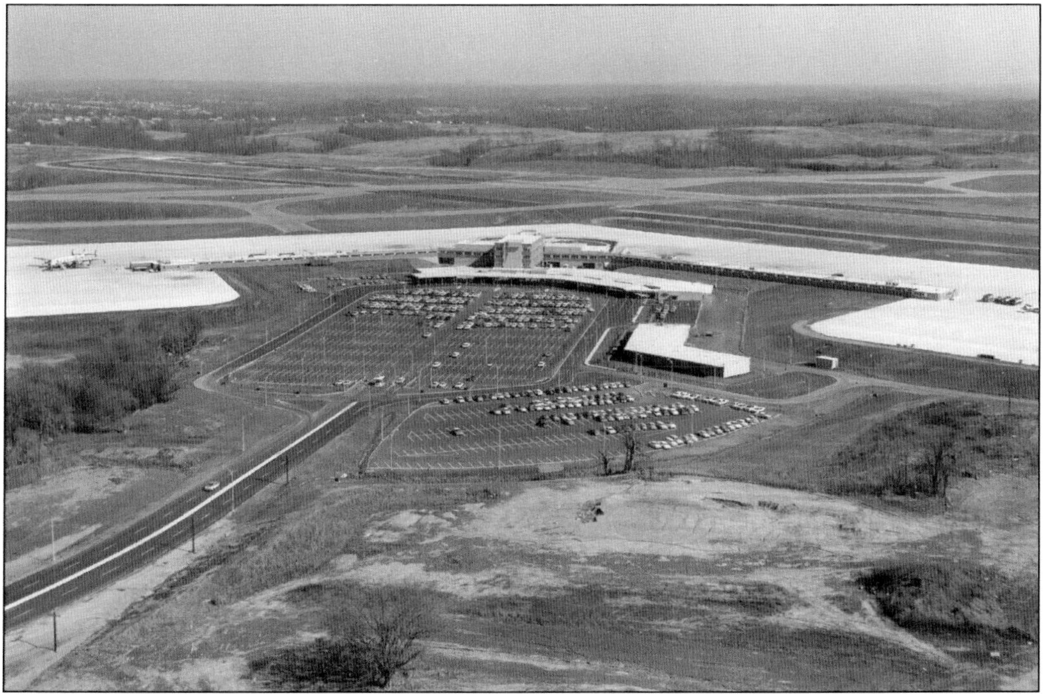

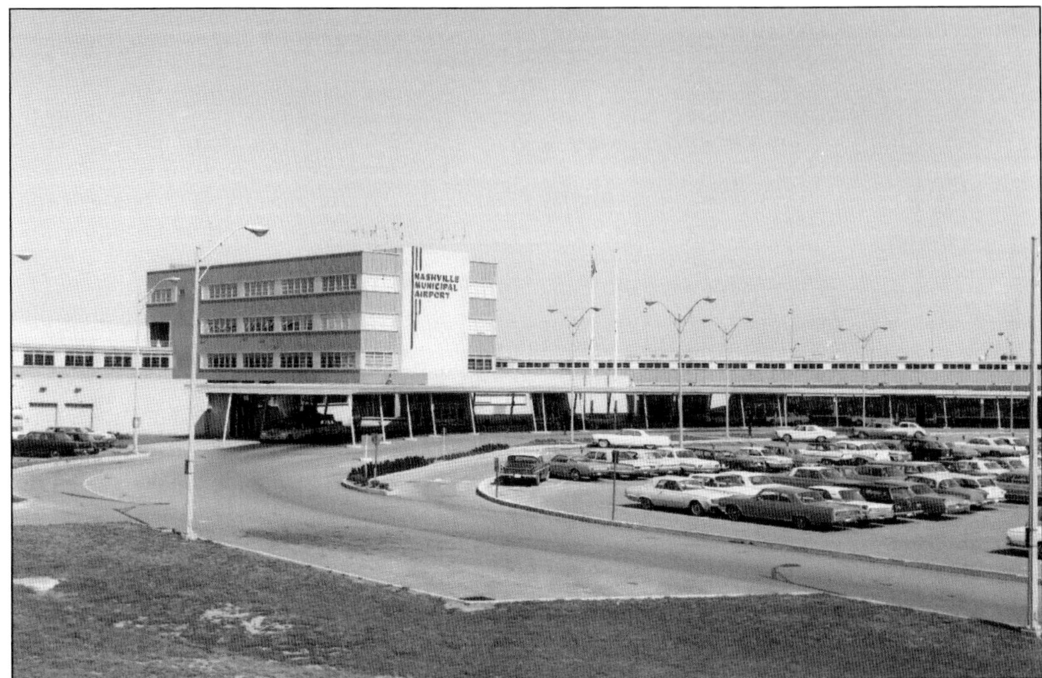

By the time this 1967 view was made, Nashville's airport boasted several additional airlines, a restaurant, post office, a reading room and library, a nursery and full service bank. Increasing air traffic would necessitate moving to a newer and larger facility 20 years later. (Tennessee State Library and Archives.)

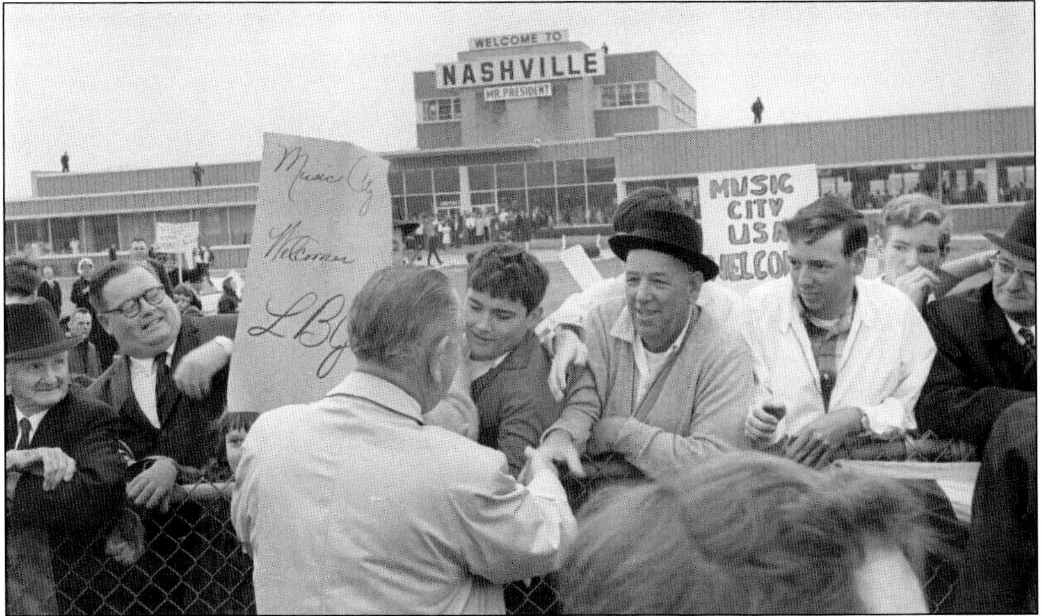

Pres. Lyndon B. Johnson shakes hands with part of the large crowd on hand to greet him at the municipal airport in March 1967. The president was in Nashville to participate in ceremonies honoring Pres. Andrew Jackson at the Hermitage plantation and to address the state legislature at the state capitol. (Tennessee State Library and Archives.)

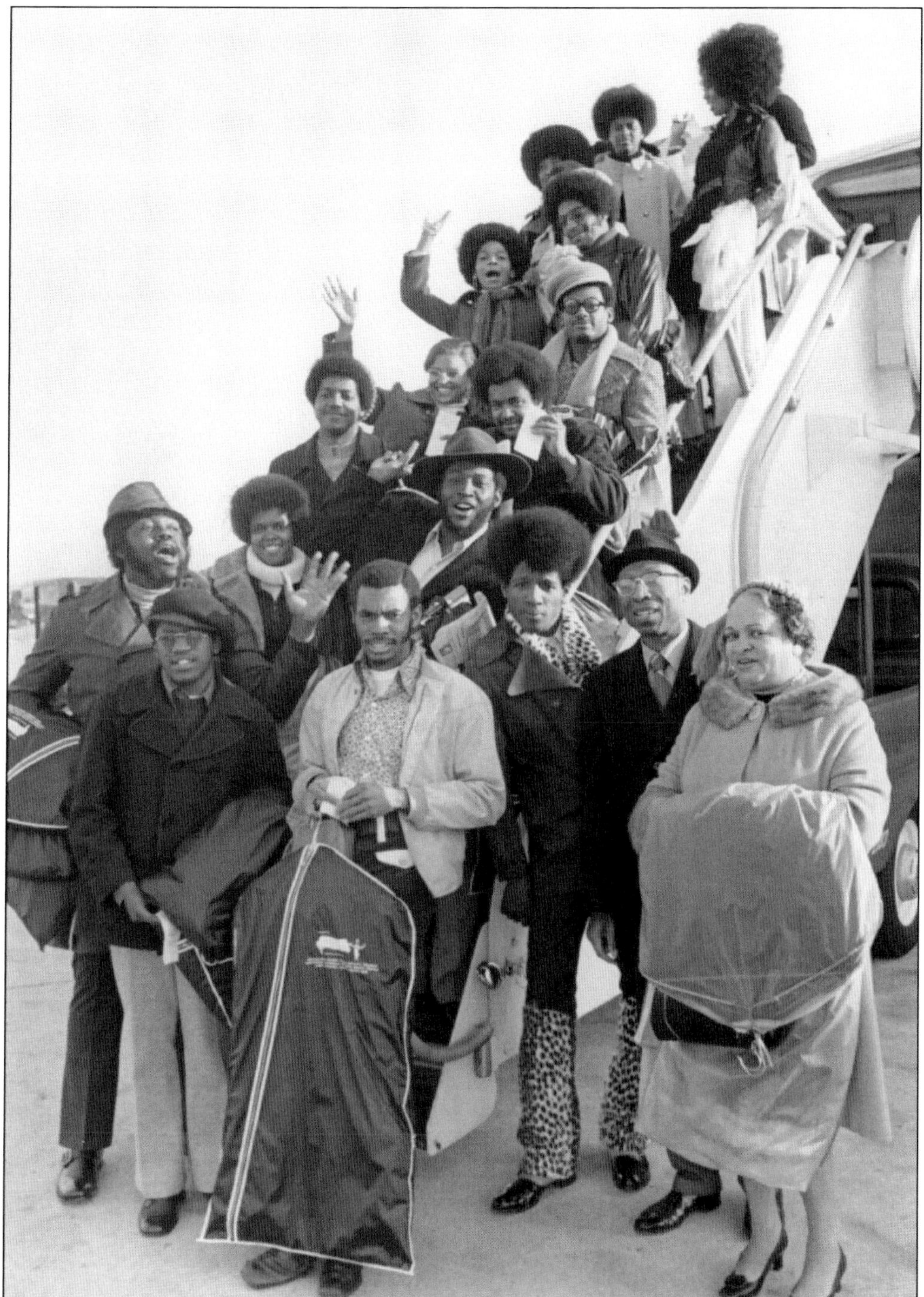

The Fisk Jubilee Singers strike a pose in December 1971 as they board a plane at Nashville's Metro Airport for Washington, DC, where they are scheduled to appear in concert at the John F. Kennedy Center for the Performing Arts. The concert was one of several events in the year-long centennial celebration of the founding of the a cappella ensemble. (Nashville Public Library, Special Collections.)

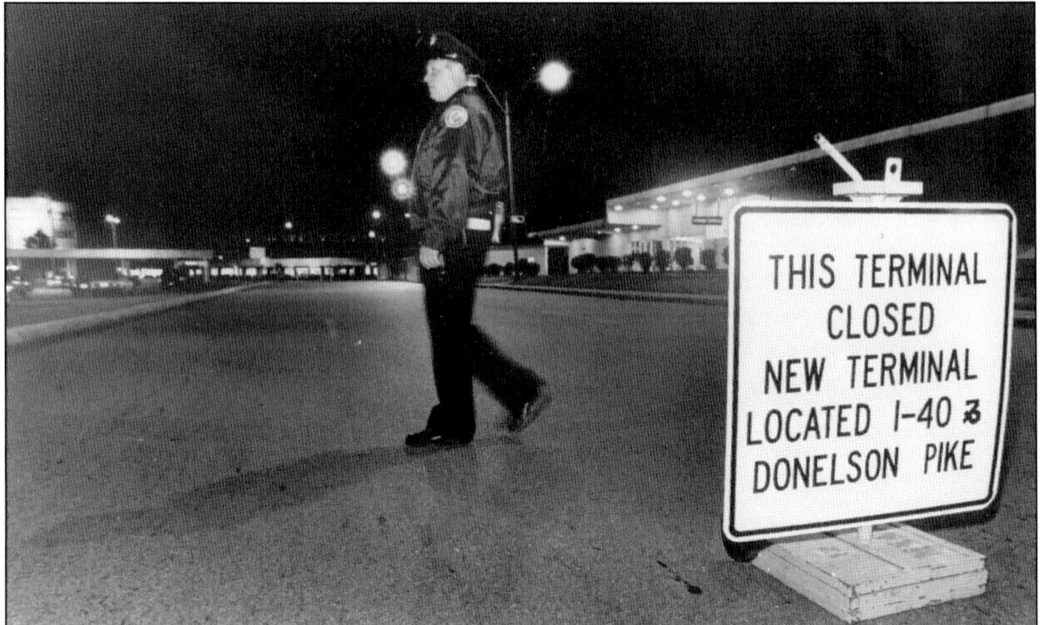

On September 14, 1987, Nashville's new Metro Airport opened for business with great fanfare, replacing a 25-year-old building that was outdated and inadequate. The $200 million facility contained more than 15 retail shops, various restaurants, bars, and snack bars. The new airport also had 46 boarding gates and a dual-level parking garage. In the image below, the 750,000-square-foot terminal is already crowded with passengers during the holiday season later that year. (Both, Nashville Public Library, Special Collections.)

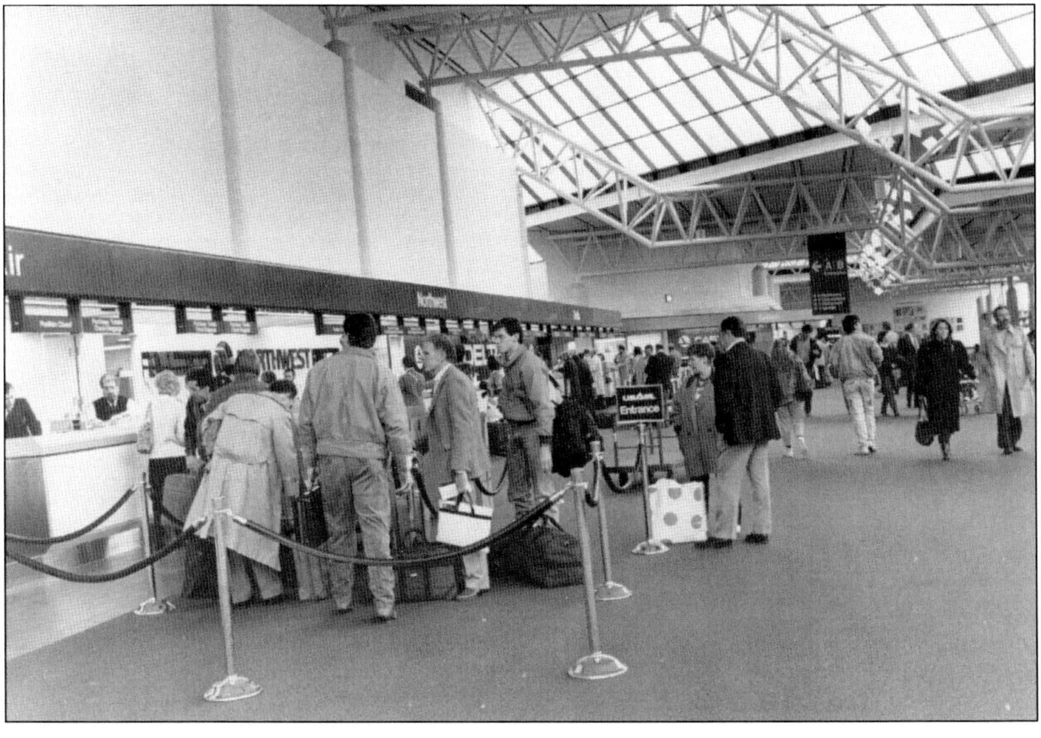

Eight

Interstates and Urban Renewal

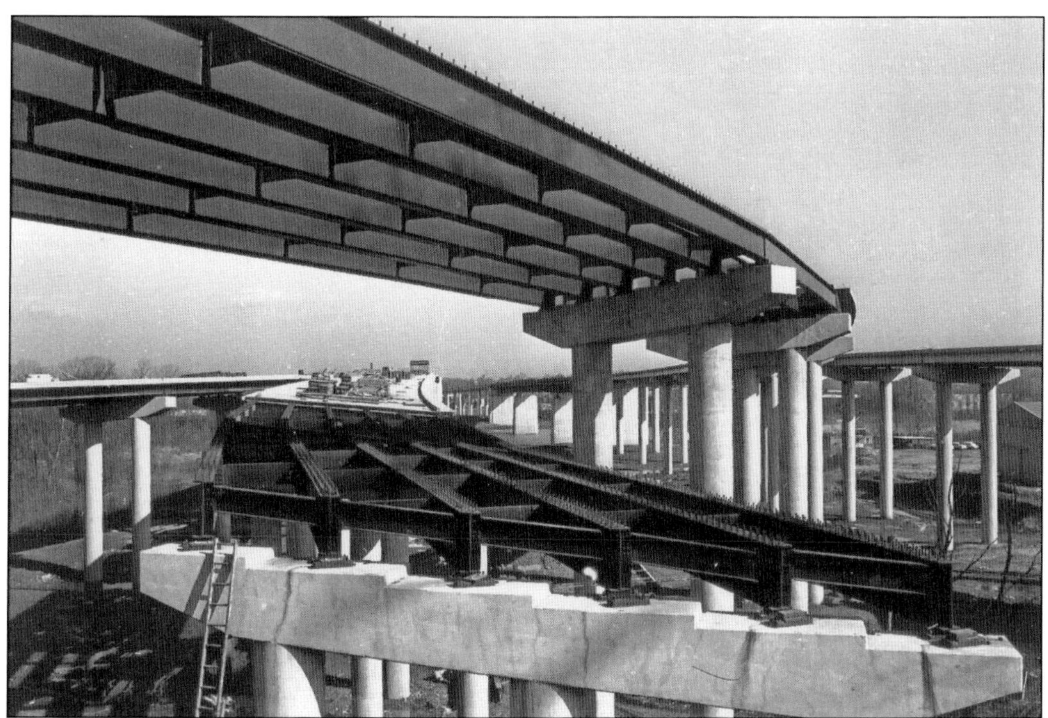

The steel beams on the diverging bridges of the Silliman Evans Memorial Bridge are symbolic of the road to the future South Nashville will experience in the years after World War II. During the next 30 years, the region would be transformed with new neighborhoods, widened thoroughfares, a new airport, shopping centers, and suburban sprawl. Today, South Nashville continues to evolve. (Metro Nashville Archives, MDHA Collection.)

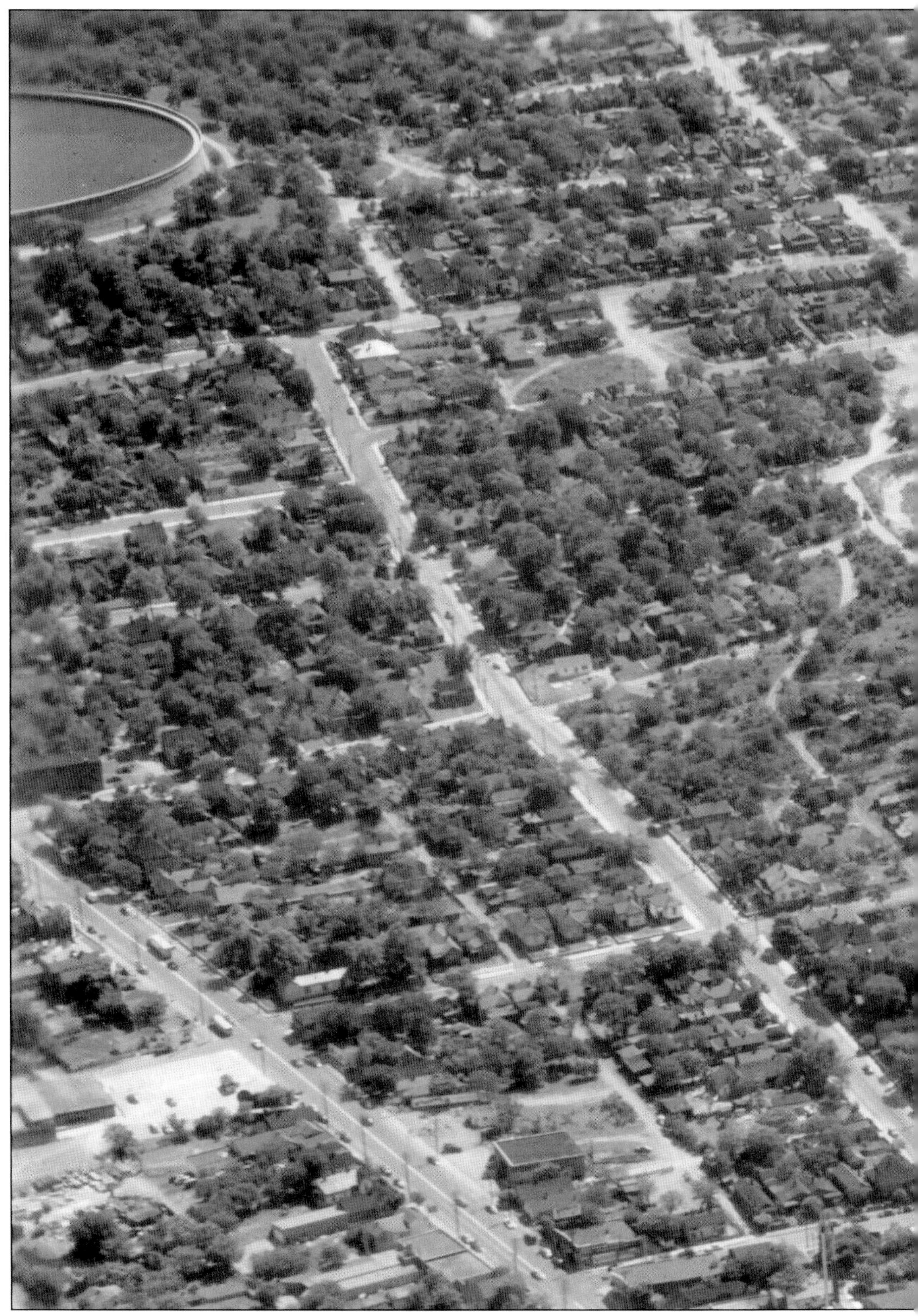

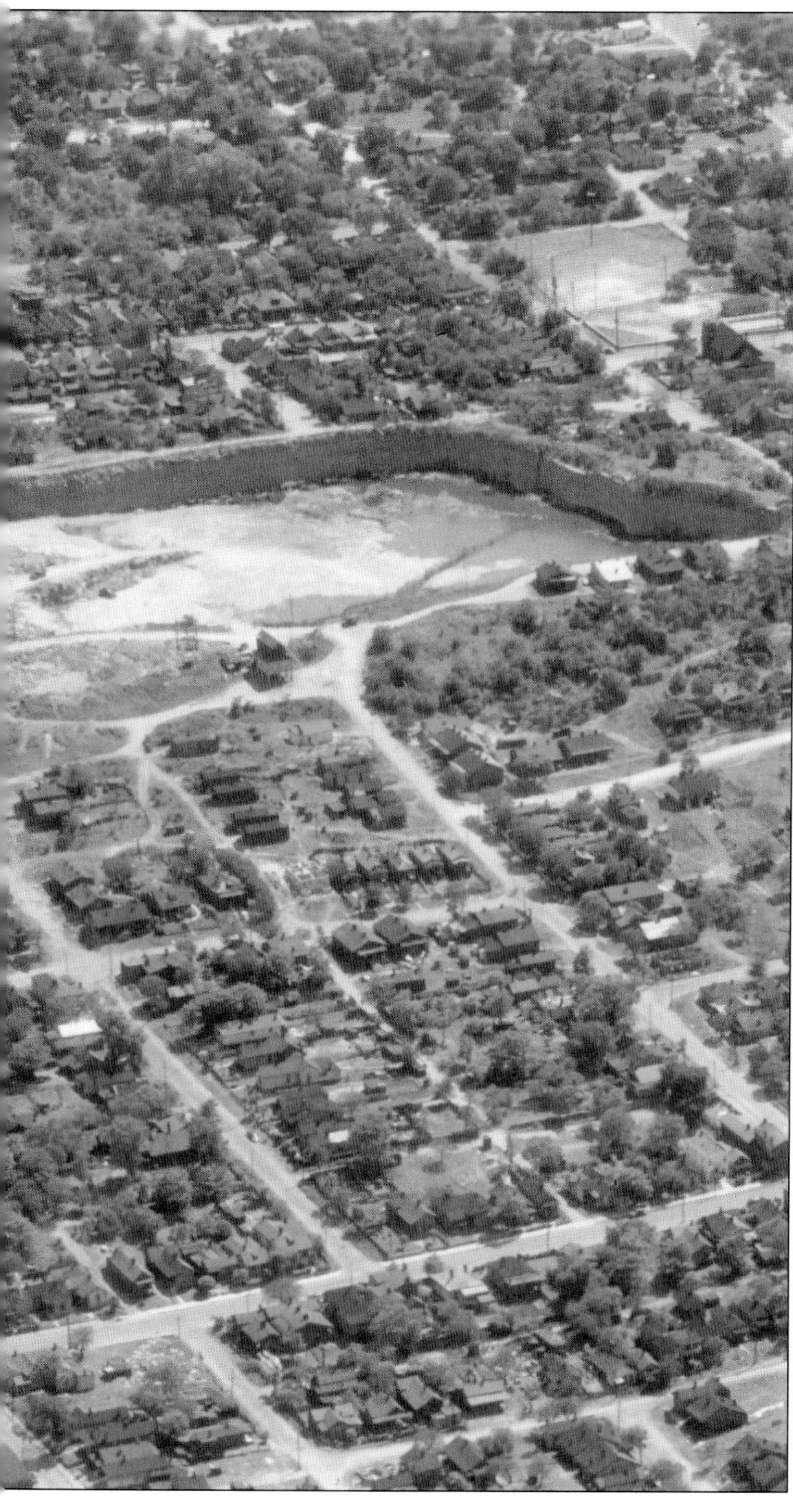

No community in South Nashville has changed more drastically over the years than the Edgehill area. The large quarry in the center was called Rock Crusher Hill. Located near Twelfth Avenue South and Edgehill Avenue, the giant pit, which measured 600 feet long, 400 feet wide, and 40 feet deep was the result of a stone crushing operation once operated by the city. It ceased operations in the early 1940s. For years, the area was covered with shacks, outdoor toilets and neglected streets. In 1961, Nashville turned the quarry and surrounding property over to the parks board, which began filling in the 70-year-old pit. During the early1960s an attractive city park, community center and new middle school were constructed on the property. This 1949 view looks southwest, with the City Reservoir visible at left. (Metro Nashville Archives, MDHA Collection.)

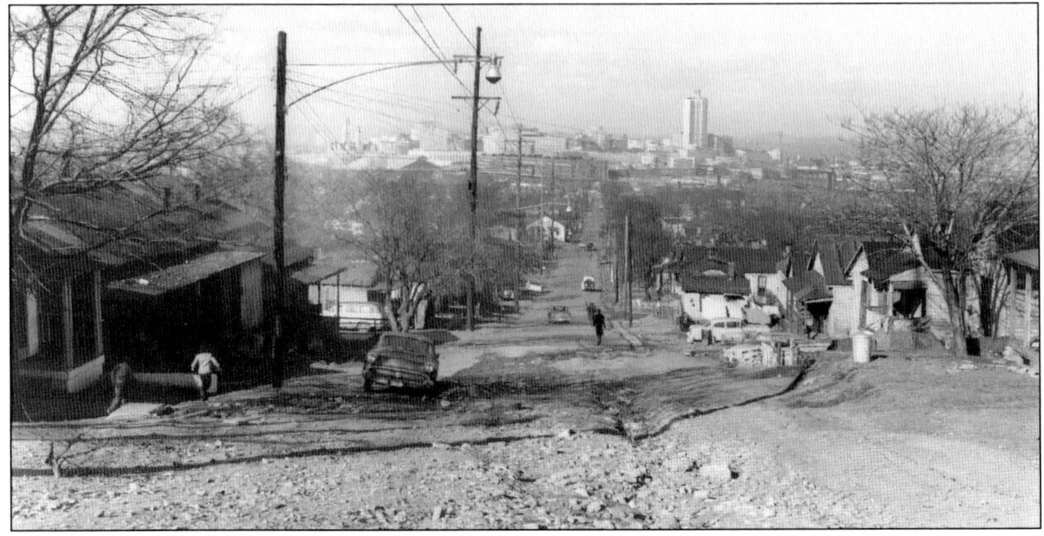

In this image recorded by a city photographer near Rock Crusher Hill, Tenth Avenue South is visible, looking north toward downtown Nashville around 1960, illustrating the deplorable condition of some city streets in this Edgehill neighborhood. Today, the street in this scene no longer exists; the construction of Interstate 40 and a 1960s urban renewal project obliterated most traces of it. (Metro Nashville Archives, MDHA Collection.)

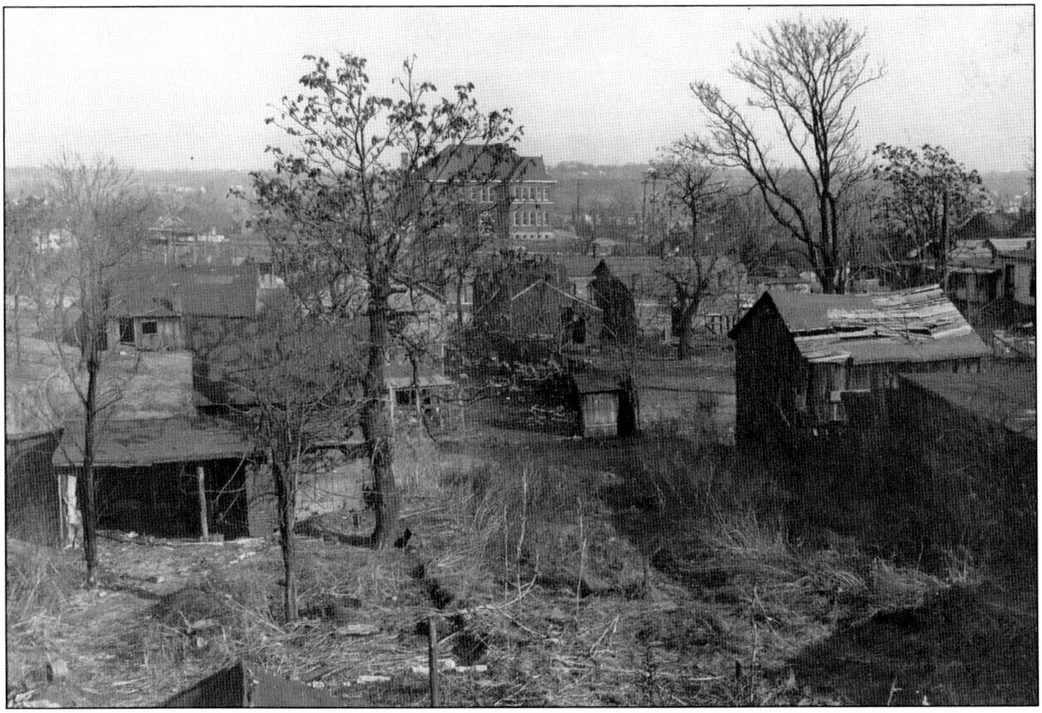

In 1939, the Nashville Housing Authority and city officials announced the construction of Nashville's largest public housing development to provide affordable housing to those with low incomes. This view looks east from Maury and Cannon Streets toward Napier Elementary School, seen in the distance behind the houses, before slum clearance began a few weeks later for the future site of the J.C. Napier Homes. (Metro Nashville Archives, MDHA Collection.)

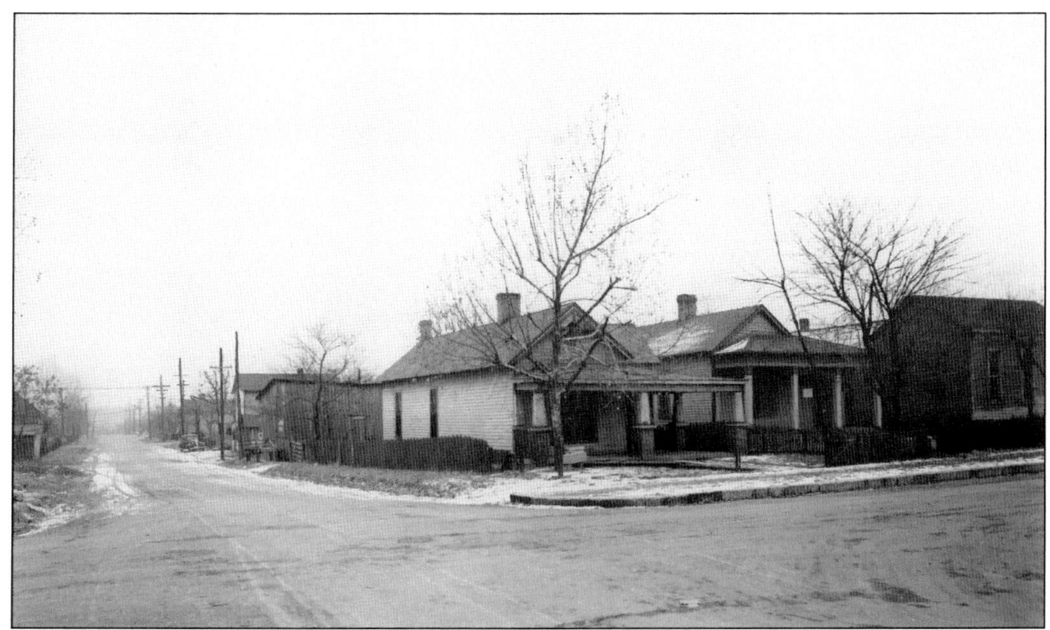

Before the demolition of the project site, a photographer from the housing authority took photographs of the neighborhood to assess property values. The view above was taken from Cannon and Claiborne Streets in early 1940. Abandoned dilapidated houses slated for slum clearance will soon be replaced by two-story brick apartments. These neglected buildings were less than two miles southeast of downtown Nashville. (Both, Metro Nashville Archives, MDHA Collection.)

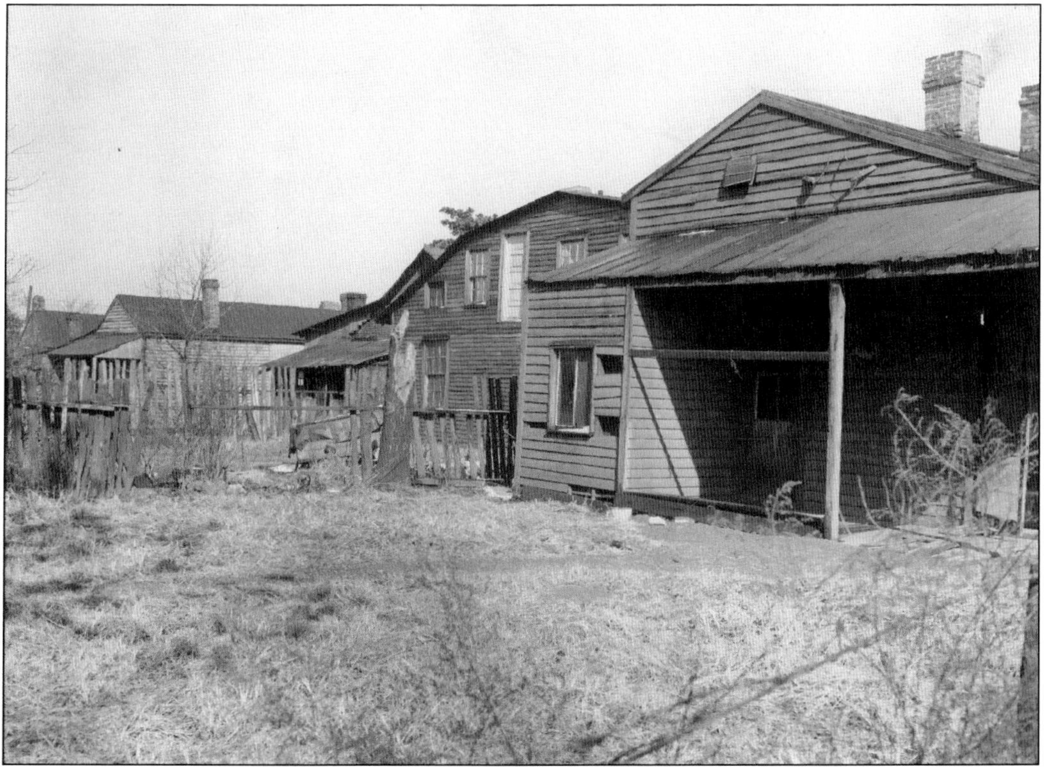

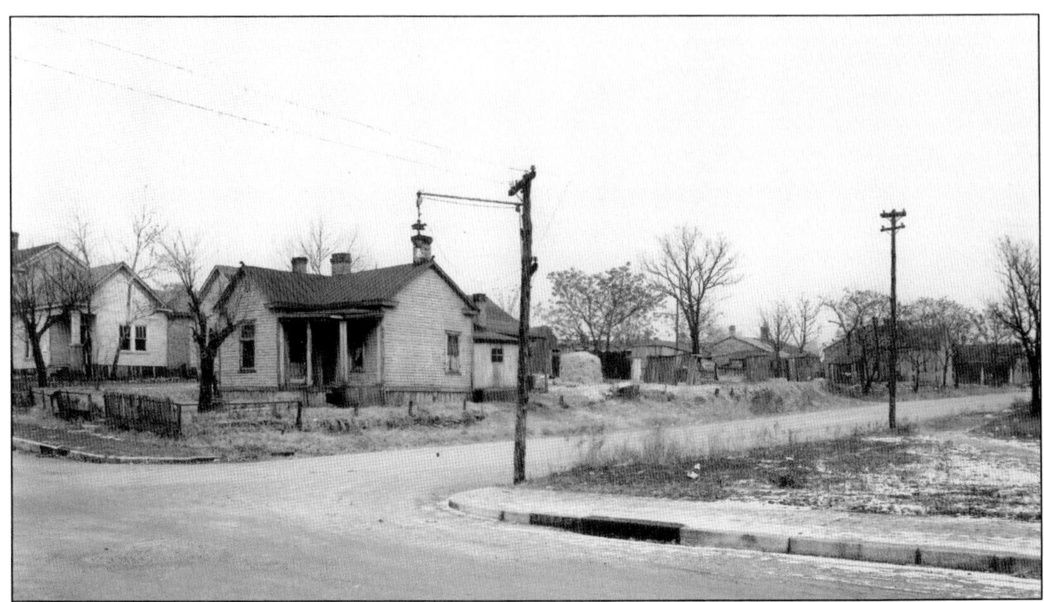

While clearing the area for the J.C. Napier Homes 114 substandard houses and businesses along Cannon, Claiborne, Lewis, Maury and Robertson Streets were quickly razed before construction could begin. The view above looks northeast from Claiborne and Robertson Streets in 1940. As part of the new development, several cross streets were also removed to create a more open environment for residents. Many backyard properties in the condemnation zone were rocky, uneven and often included an outdoor privy. (Both, Metro Nashville Archives, MDHA Collection.)

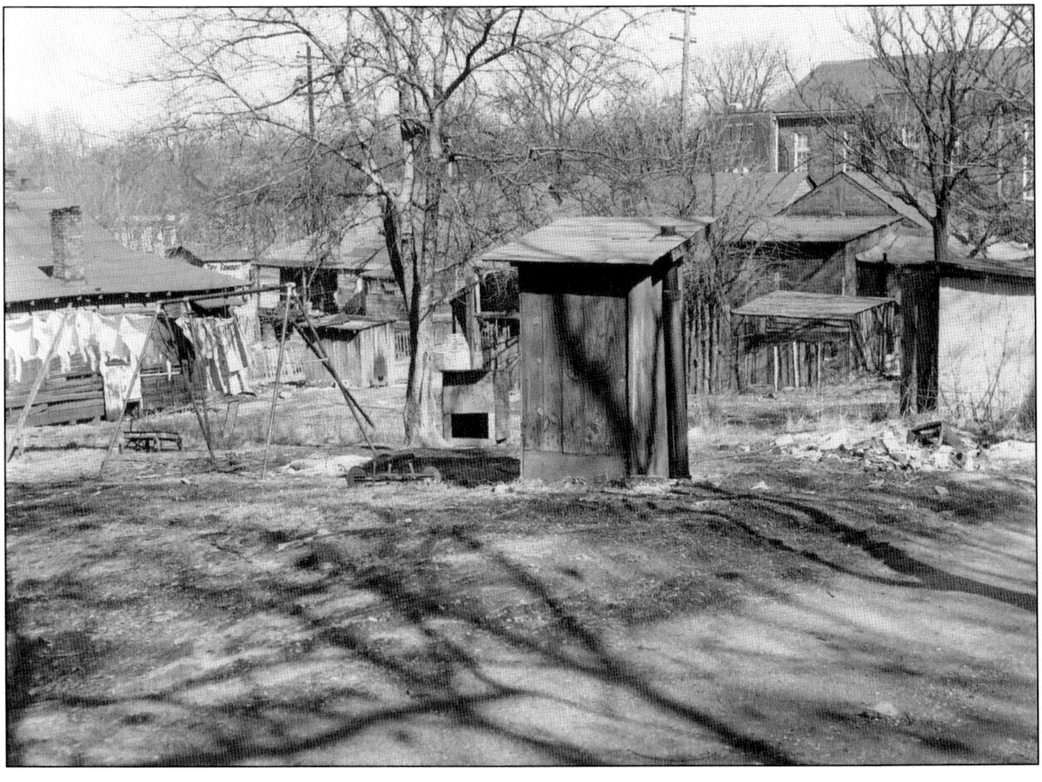

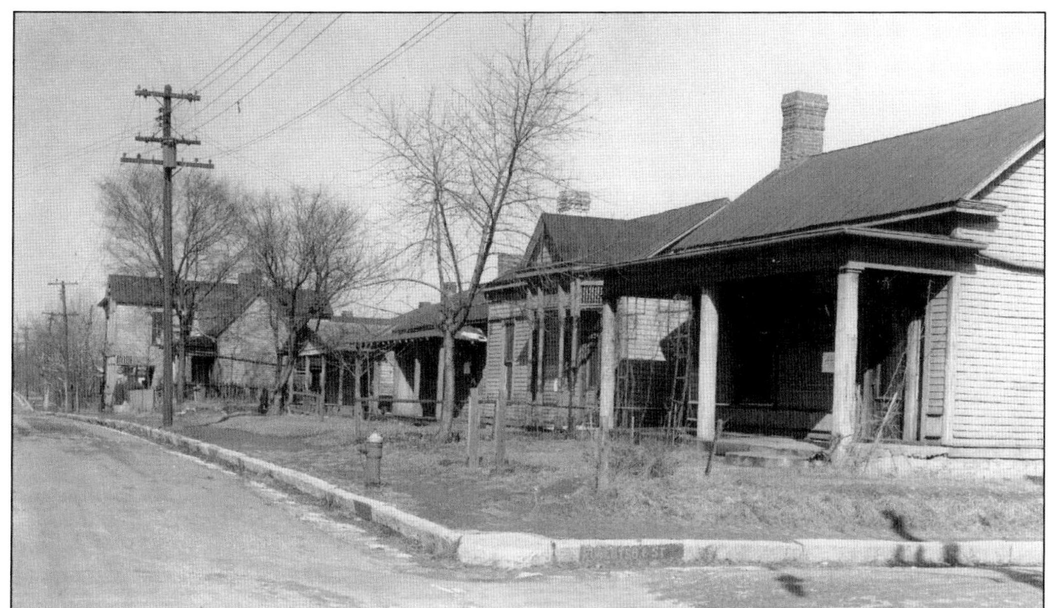

A row of condemned houses awaits demolition in this 1940 view facing north on Maury Street at Robertson. After closer examination, condemnation signs can be seen posted on the doors. The brick sidewalks that once adorned the streets have been removed but the cut-stone curbs remain. Today, this intersection does not exist but is now part of the common area in the center of the J.C. Napier Homes. (Metro Nashville Archives, MDHA Collection.)

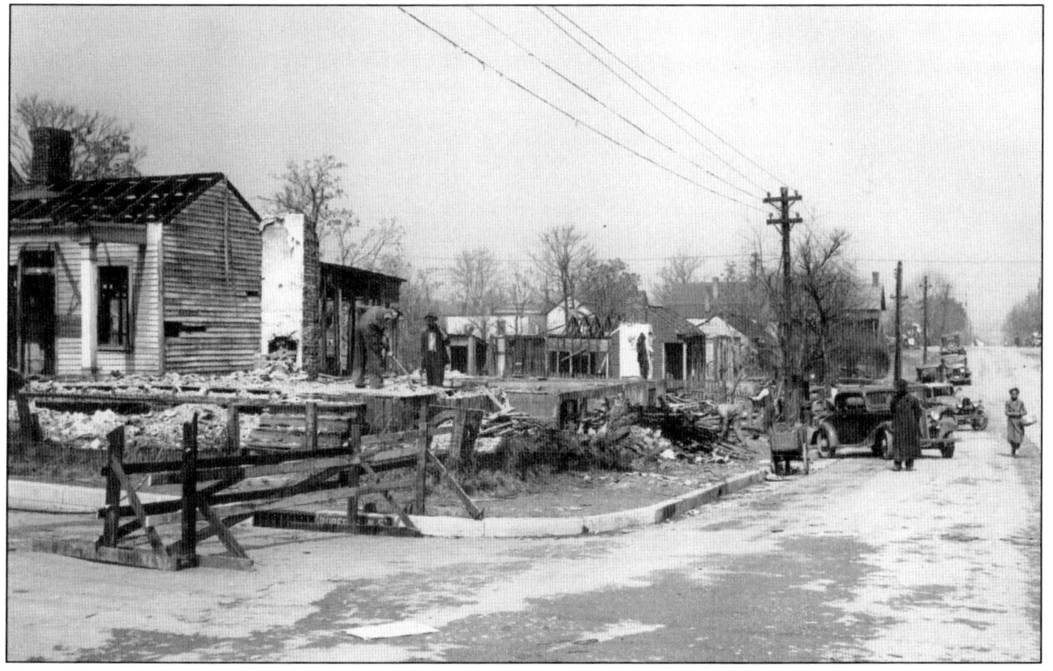

Demolition has started on the first of the 114 houses to be cleared, beginning at the corner of Robertson and Lewis Streets. In the background, residents can be seen packing their cars. Within a few weeks, construction will begin on the new Napier development. (Metro Nashville Archives, MDHA Collection.)

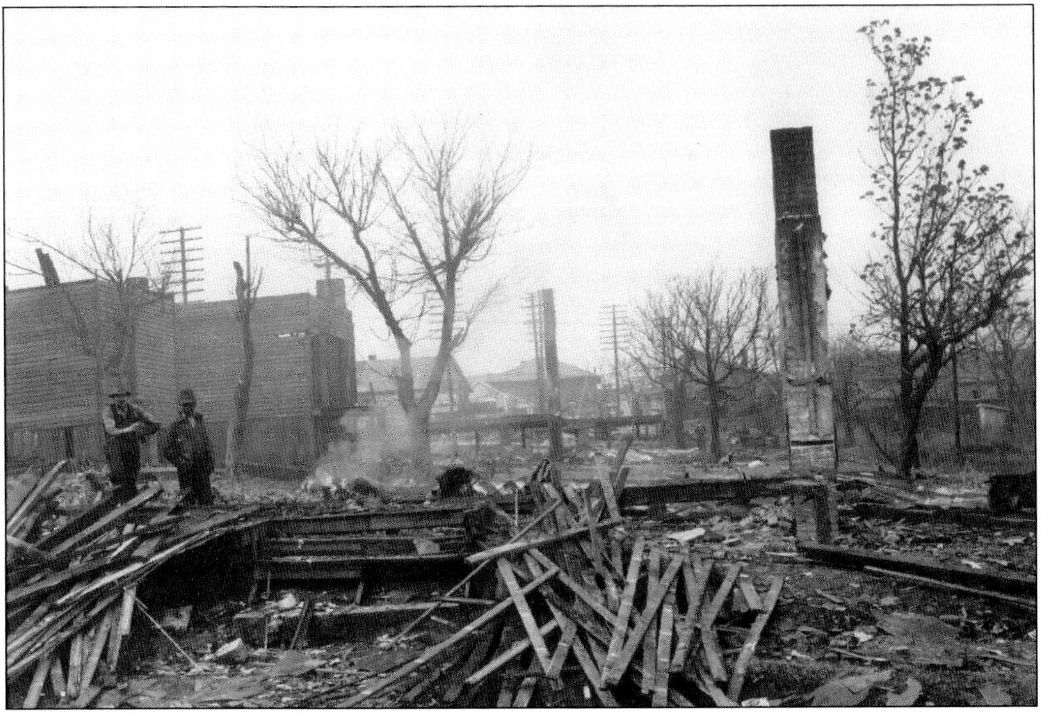

Demolition of the buildings on the Napier project site continues into the spring of 1940. While much of the wood and debris is either hauled to the dump or recycled, the remainder is burned on site. Below, with the exception of a few remaining structures and scattered chimneys, the six-block project site is nearly cleared. Soon, new roads will be graded, and streets will be reconfigured for the public housing development. (Both, Metro Nashville Archives, MDHA Collection.)

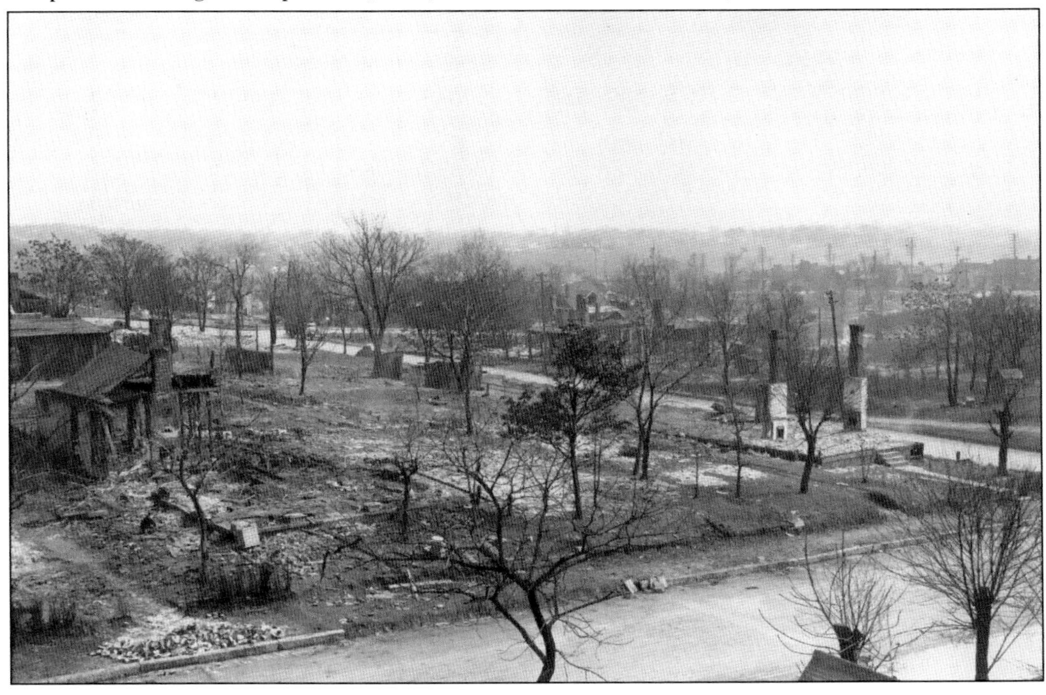

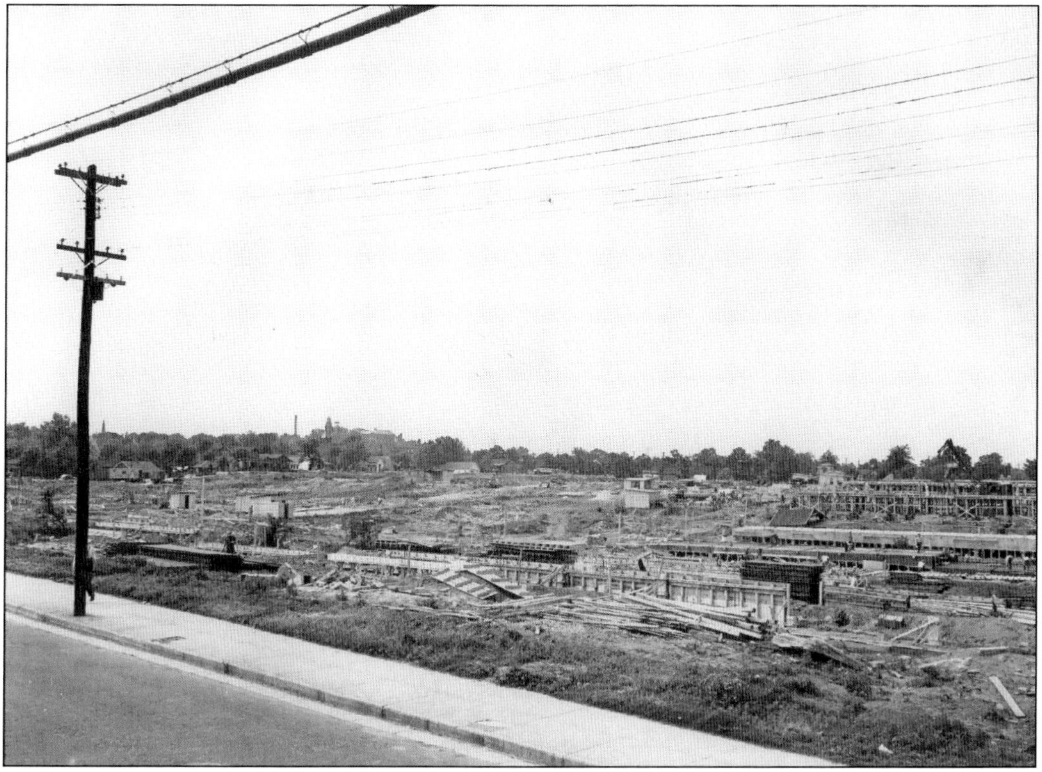

Once all demolition and grading of the site was completed, construction of the foundations for the 35 buildings began immediately. The image above, looking north, shows the progress from Lafayette Street near Lewis in 1940. In a view that faces east toward Lewis Street, carpenters cut up lumber for forms and framing. Napier Elementary School is visible at left in the background. (Both, Metro Nashville Archives, MDHA Collection.)

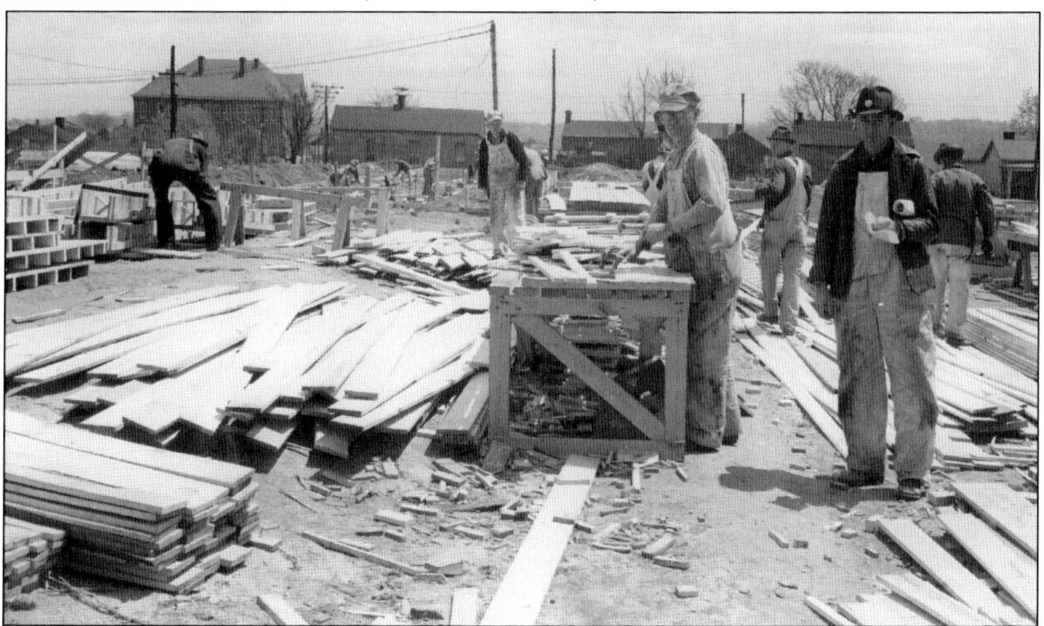

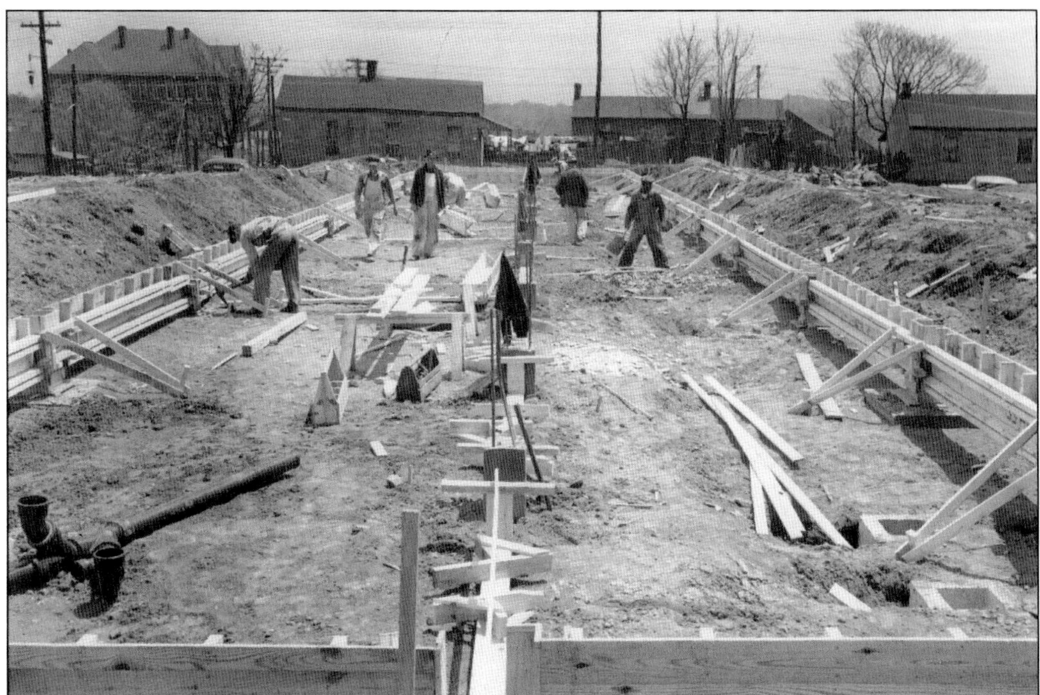

The city of Nashville was a pioneer in public housing, with the first two projects constructed during the 1930s. When the J.C. Napier Homes opened in 1941, it was the largest public housing development in the city, containing 332 units. Construction workers build forms for the foundation of one of the 35 buildings that are part of the project. Below, progress continues as floors are built for the apartments. (Both, Metro Nashville Archives, MDHA Collection.)

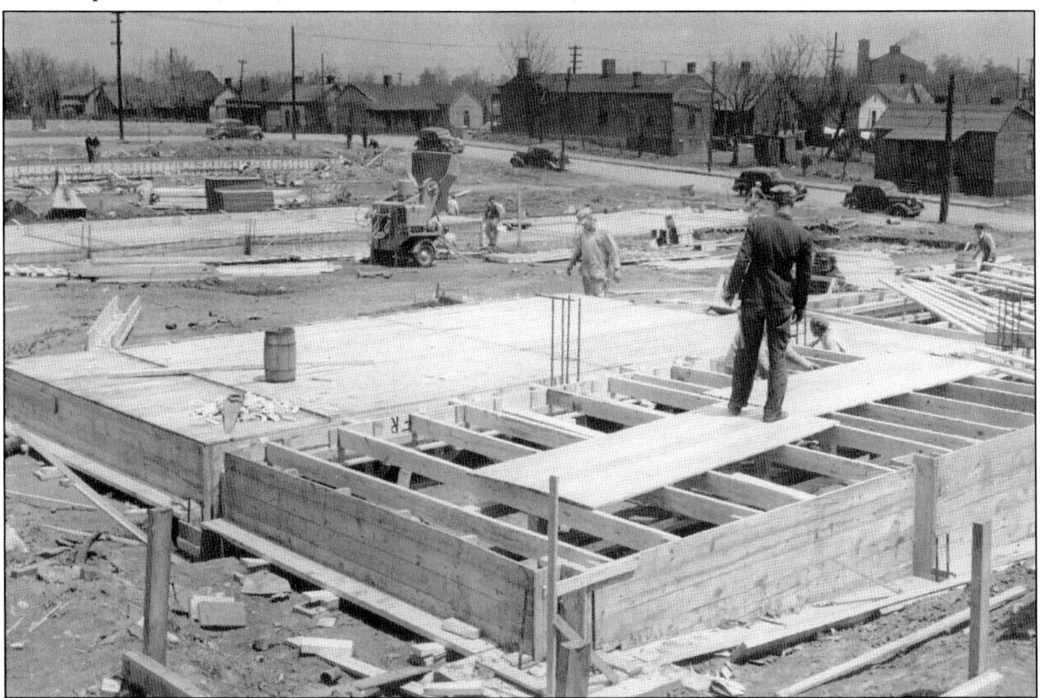

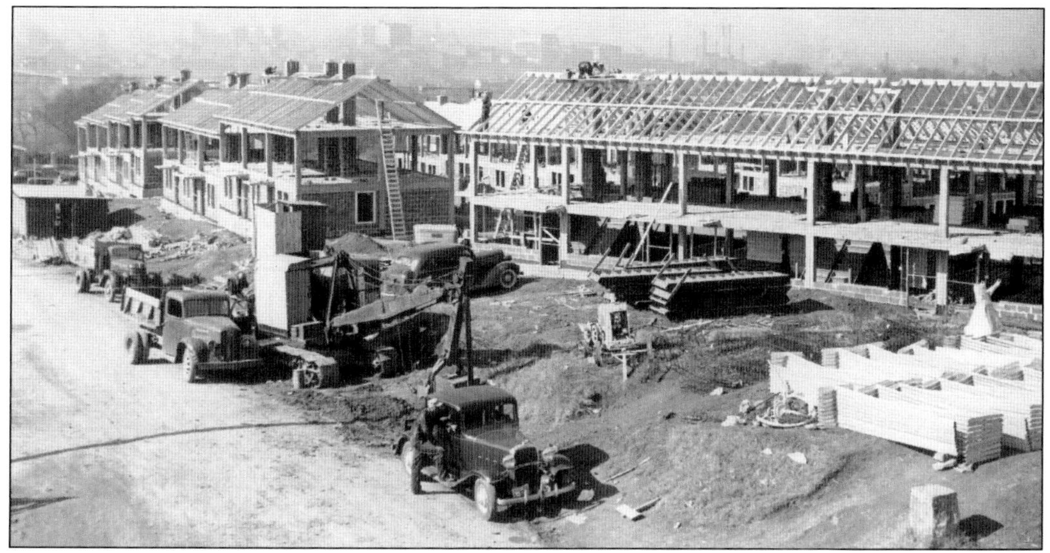

Initially, the J.C. Napier Homes were bordered by Lafayette, Claiborne, Cannon and Lewis Streets. In August 1940, additional federal funding was made available to the Nashville Housing Authority for increasing the size of the Napier Homes. As a result, the development was extended a block west from Claiborne Street to Wharf Avenue adding 148 more dwelling units. Work is progressing on the buildings as framing for the roofs has begun. The Nashville skyline is visible in the background. Below, brickwork has started on some of the buildings. When completed, the site area will have playgrounds, tenant yards, and landscaped areas. The project will also include a community house with space for meetings and administrative offices. (Both, Metro Nashville Archives, MDHA Collection.)

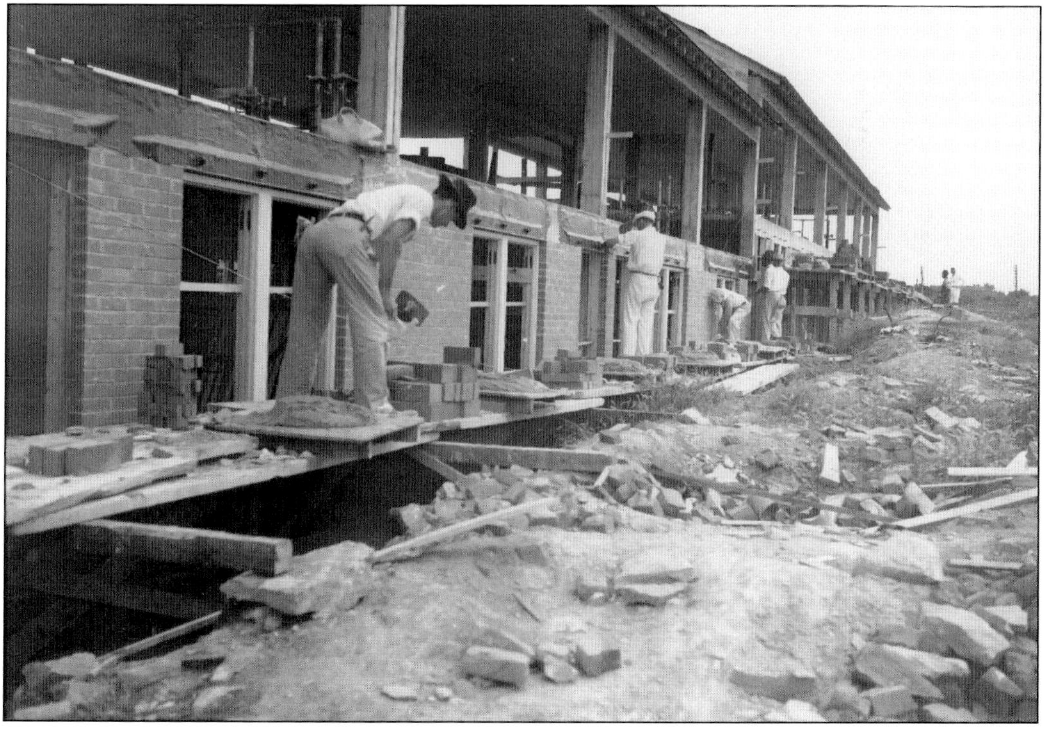

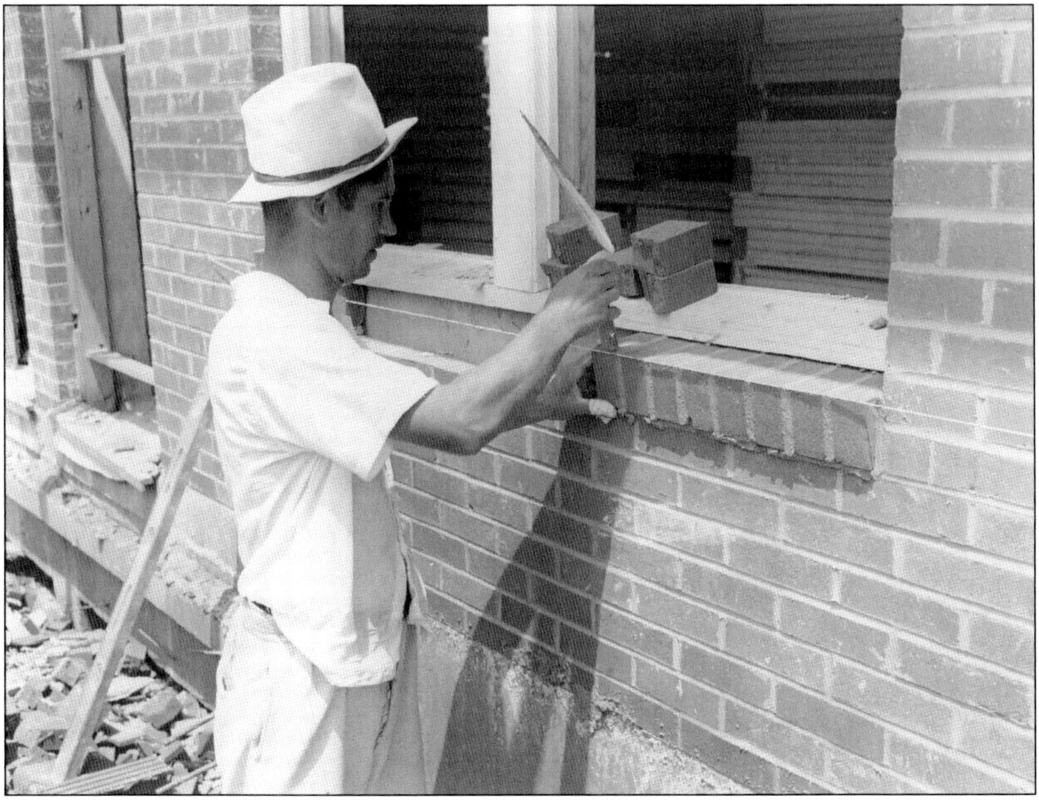

It took hundreds of construction workers made up of various trades more than 14 months to build and complete the Napier Homes. A bricklayer puts the finishing touches on one of the buildings. The development opened to tenants in April 1941. (Metro Nashville Archives, MDHA Collection.)

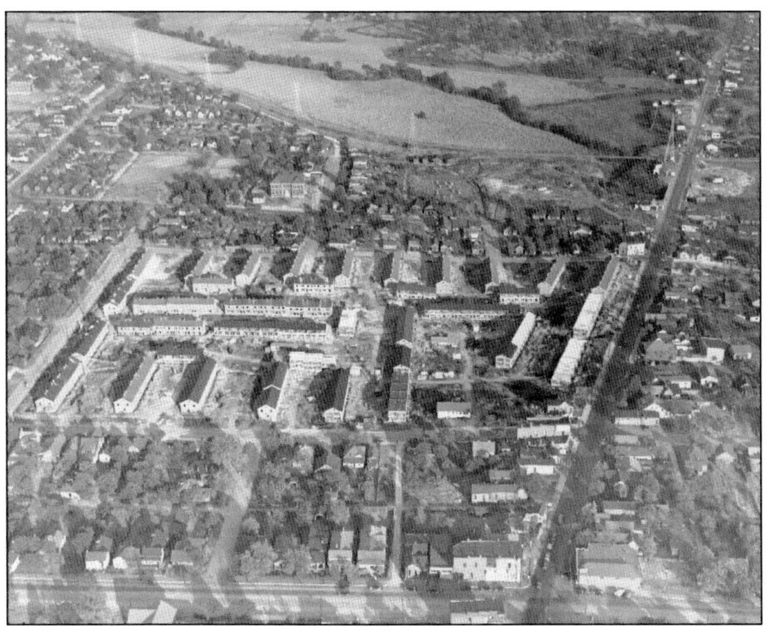

A bird's-eye view of the J.C. Napier Homes depicts how extensive the project was as the development nears completion in 1940. In this scene, facing east, the 1898 Napier Elementary School is visible beyond the project. Farther east is the Tennessee Central Railway track, Brown's Creek, and the city limit. To the right is Lafayette Street, and Wharf Avenue is below. (Metro Nashville Archives, MDHA Collection.)

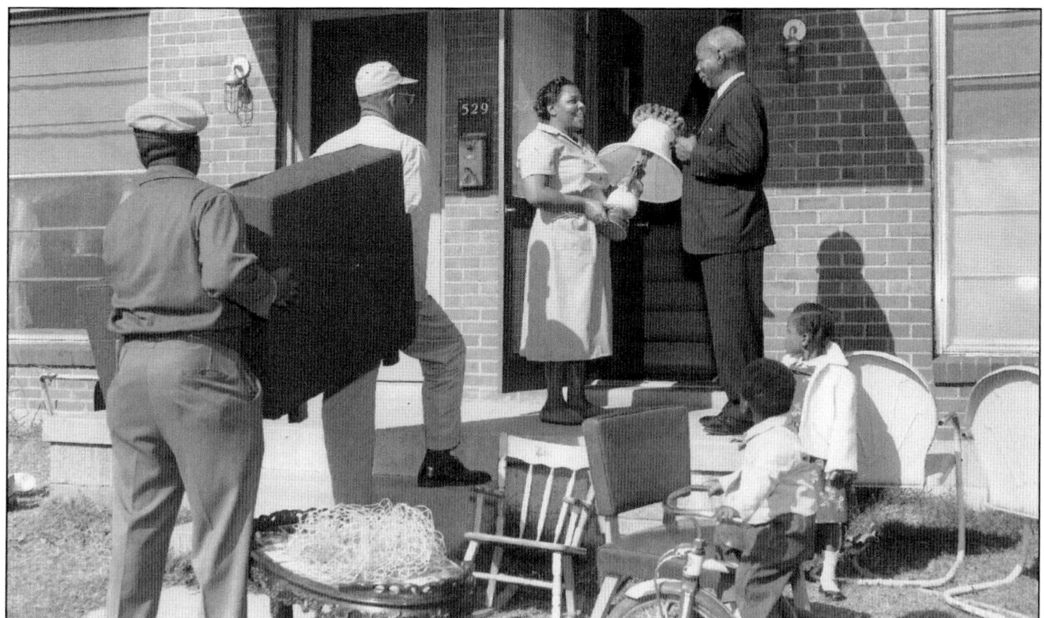

From 1940 through the 1970s public housing developments such as the Vine Hill, J.C. Napier, Tony Sudekum, and Edgehill Homes and other developments were constructed across South Nashville and other parts of the region, providing affordable housing for many residents. In this 1950s image, a family is welcomed into their new home by an unidentified housing authority official. (Metro Nashville Archives, MDHA Collection.)

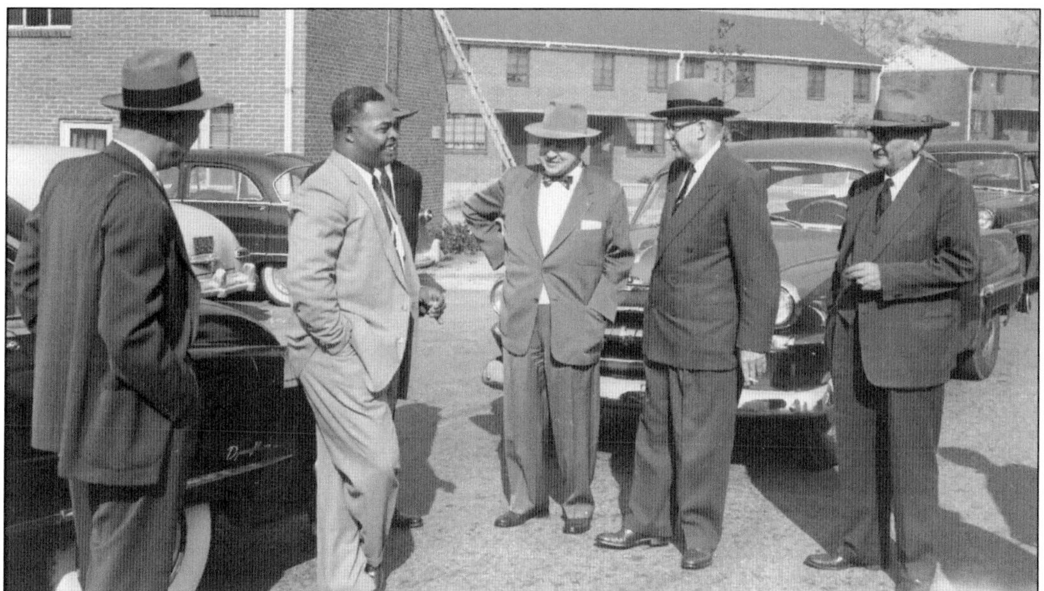

During Nashville mayor Ben West's tenure, much had been accomplished toward the construction of affordable housing. Officials take a tour of the Edgehill Homes Project during the dedication of the project in 1953. From left to right are unidentified; Deerwood McCord, project manager; Mayor Ben West; Charles Slusser, commissioner of the US Public Housing Administration; Director A.R. Hanson of PHA's Atlanta office; and Will Cheek. (Metro Nashville Archives, MDHA Collection.)

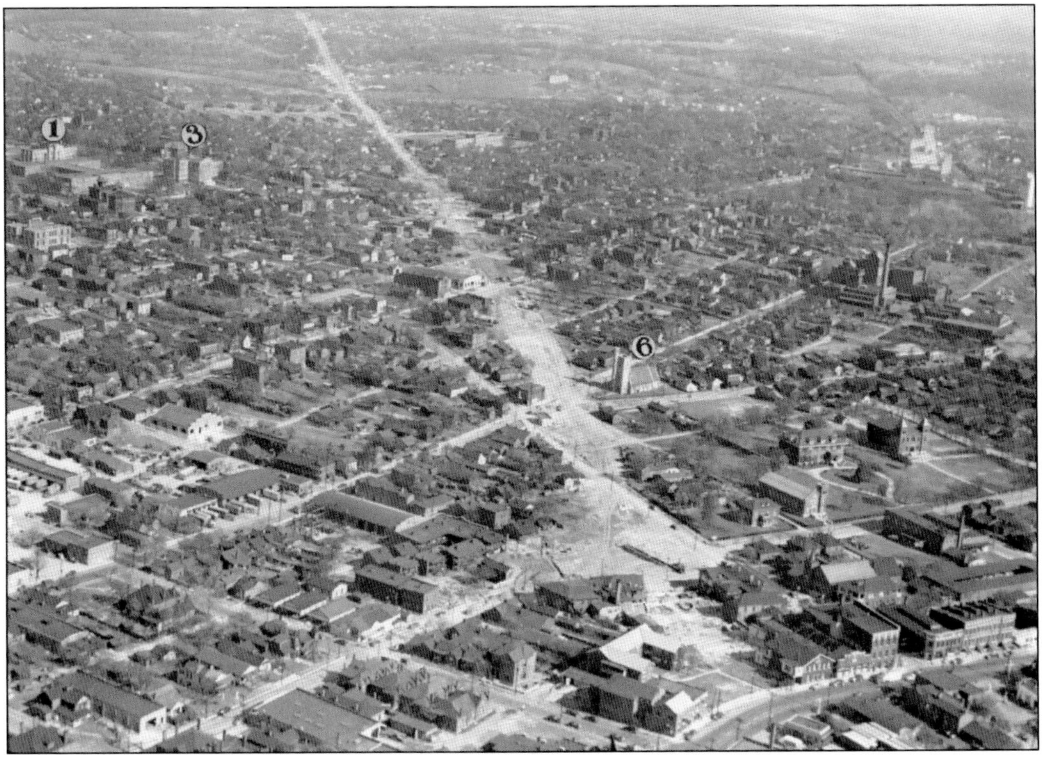

A major urban renewal project that affected South Nashville was the Lafayette Street extension project that involved the widening of Lafayette Street between city limits and downtown, extending it west from Second to Eighth Avenue South. Landmarks visible in this 1946 view, facing southeast, include the Children's Museum and Howard School (at left), Holy Trinity Episcopal Church (center), and the William Gerst Brewery (at right). (Nashville Public Library, Special Collections.)

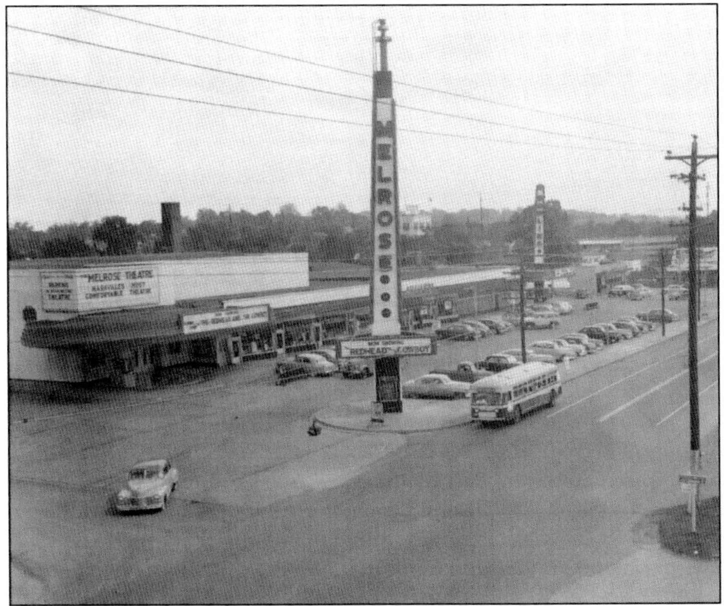

After the 1940s, suburban living became popular with a growing population. Soon, restaurants and shopping centers followed to serve the new communities. One of the first of these to open was Melrose Center, located on Franklin Road in the city of Berry Hill. Opened in 1942, the development boasted a movie theater, bowling alley, and 10 retail stores. Soon, additional businesses had moved into the area. (Metro Nashville Archives, MDHA Collection.)

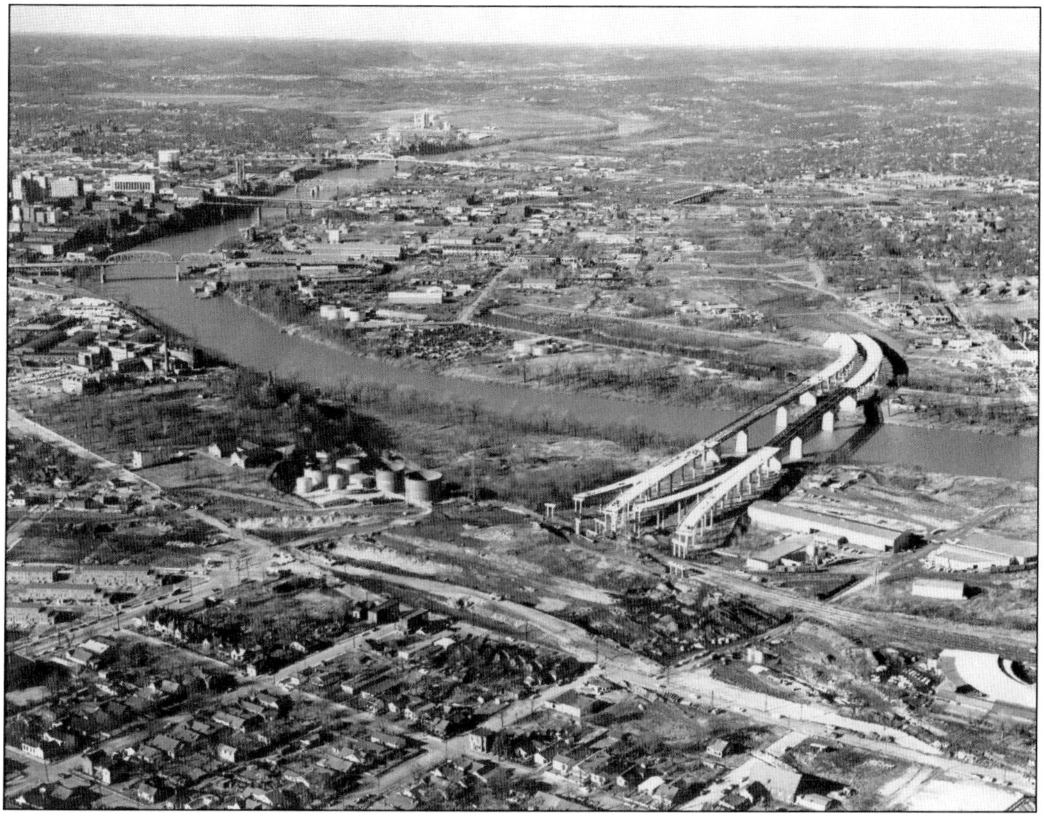

Construction progresses on the magnificent Silliman Evans Memorial Bridge in this 1961 scene. When completed three years later, the span will take Interstates 65 and 24 across the Cumberland River, connecting East and South Nashville, allowing heavy traffic to bypass downtown congestion. This short superhighway segment was the first to be completed in the city, eventually connecting to six diverging legs of the national interstate highway system. (Metro Nashville Archives, MDHA Collection.)

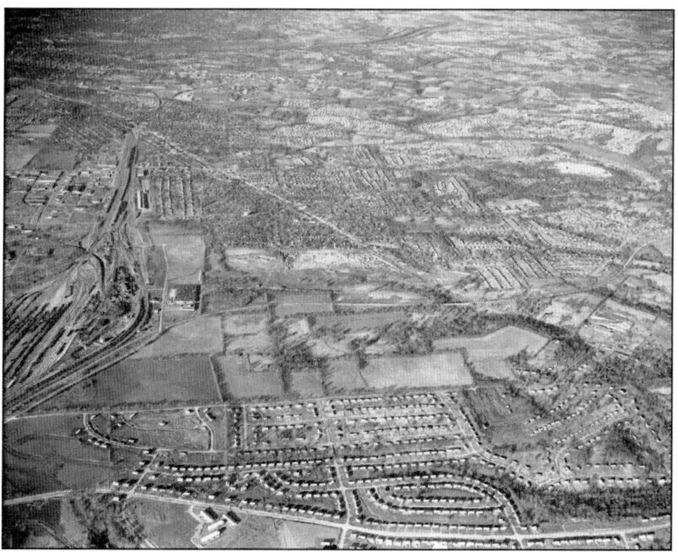

After the late 1950s, residential subdivisions were emerging everywhere around Nashville. This 1961 view looks north toward Nolensville Road and the Woodbine community. At left is the Louisville & Nashville Railroad's Radnor Yard. The 300-acre Croft family farm, at center, is now the site of the Nashville Zoo at Grassmere. (Metro Nashville Archives, MDHA Collection.)

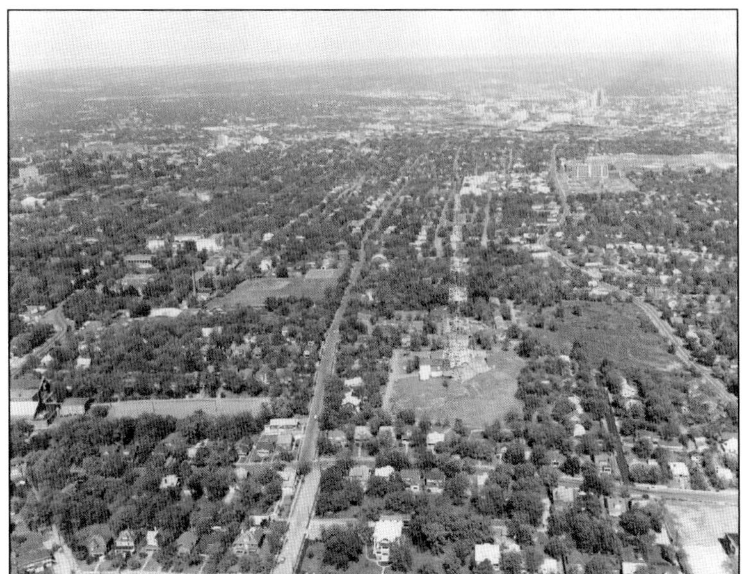

South Nashville is comprised of many neighborhoods. One of those is the Belmont-Hillsboro section, shown here during the mid-1960s. The expansion of Belmont College, the white buildings at left, and gentrification of the district has vastly changed the appearance of this region since this scene was recorded. Downtown Nashville can be seen in the distance. (Metro Nashville Archives, MDHA Collection.)

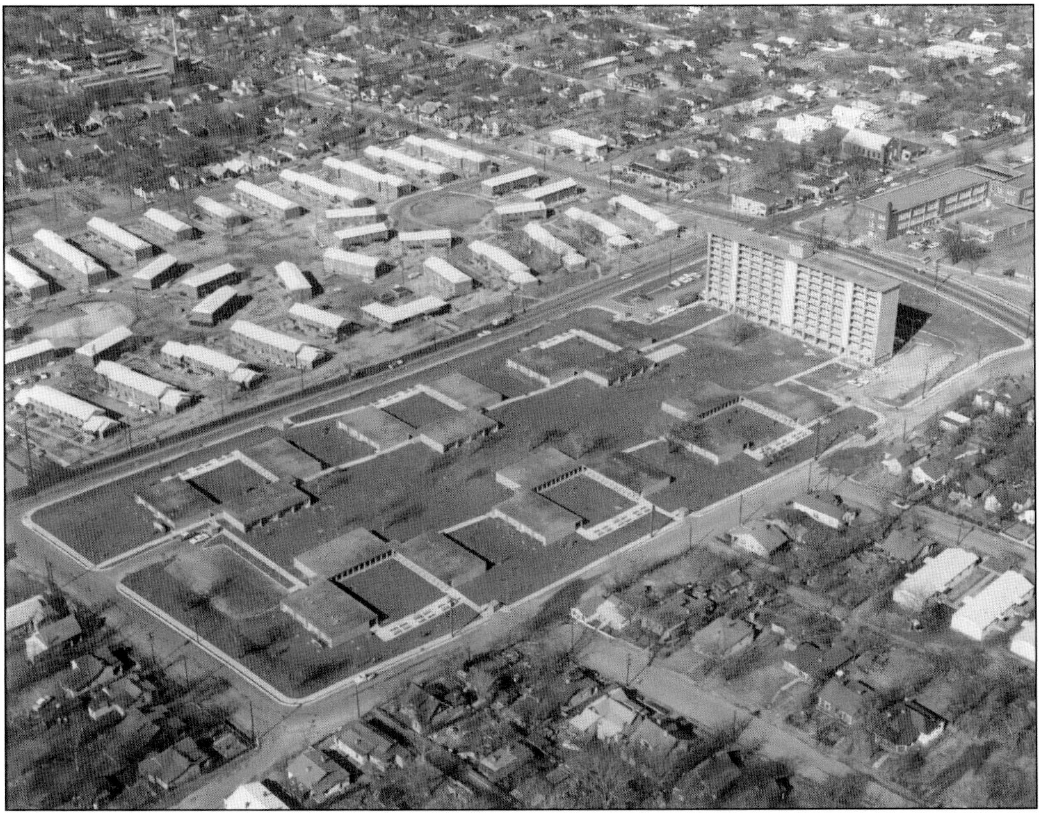

As part of the Edgehill Urban Renewal Project, the I.W. Gernert Homes were opened in 1965. The land was acquired by the Nashville Housing Authority to provide affordable housing for those displaced from urban renewal projects. At the time, it was the city's first low-rent development for the elderly. The 10-story tower and 18 single-story units are located at Twelfth Avenue South and Edgehill Avenue. (Metro Nashville Archives, MDHA Collection.)

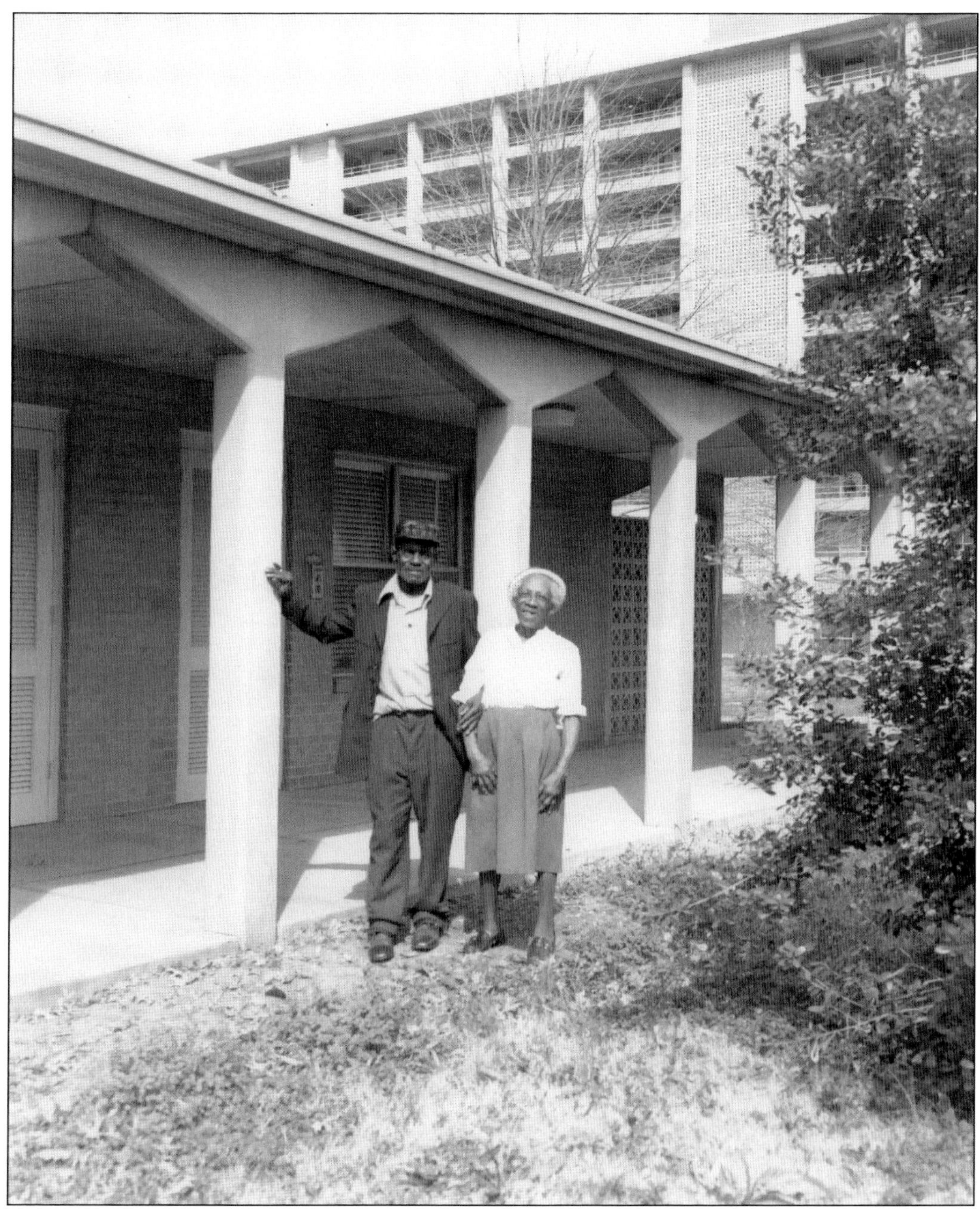

An unidentified husband and wife proudly stand in front of their new home at the I.W. Gernert Homes in the Edgehill community. The elderly couple was one of the first to move in to the low-rent development after its 1965 opening. The 18 single-floor apartment buildings and adjoining 10-story tower are constructed of concrete and brick, a vast improvement over the wood-frame buildings that had previously occupied the location. For many of the new occupants the rent was lower and offered hot-water and laundry facilities that their previous homes did not. The Gernert housing development occupies three city blocks near Twelfth Avenue South and Edgehill Avenue. It was the first of several urban renewal projects that would transform the South Nashville neighborhood during the 1960s and 1970s. (Metro Nashville Archives, MDHA Collection.)

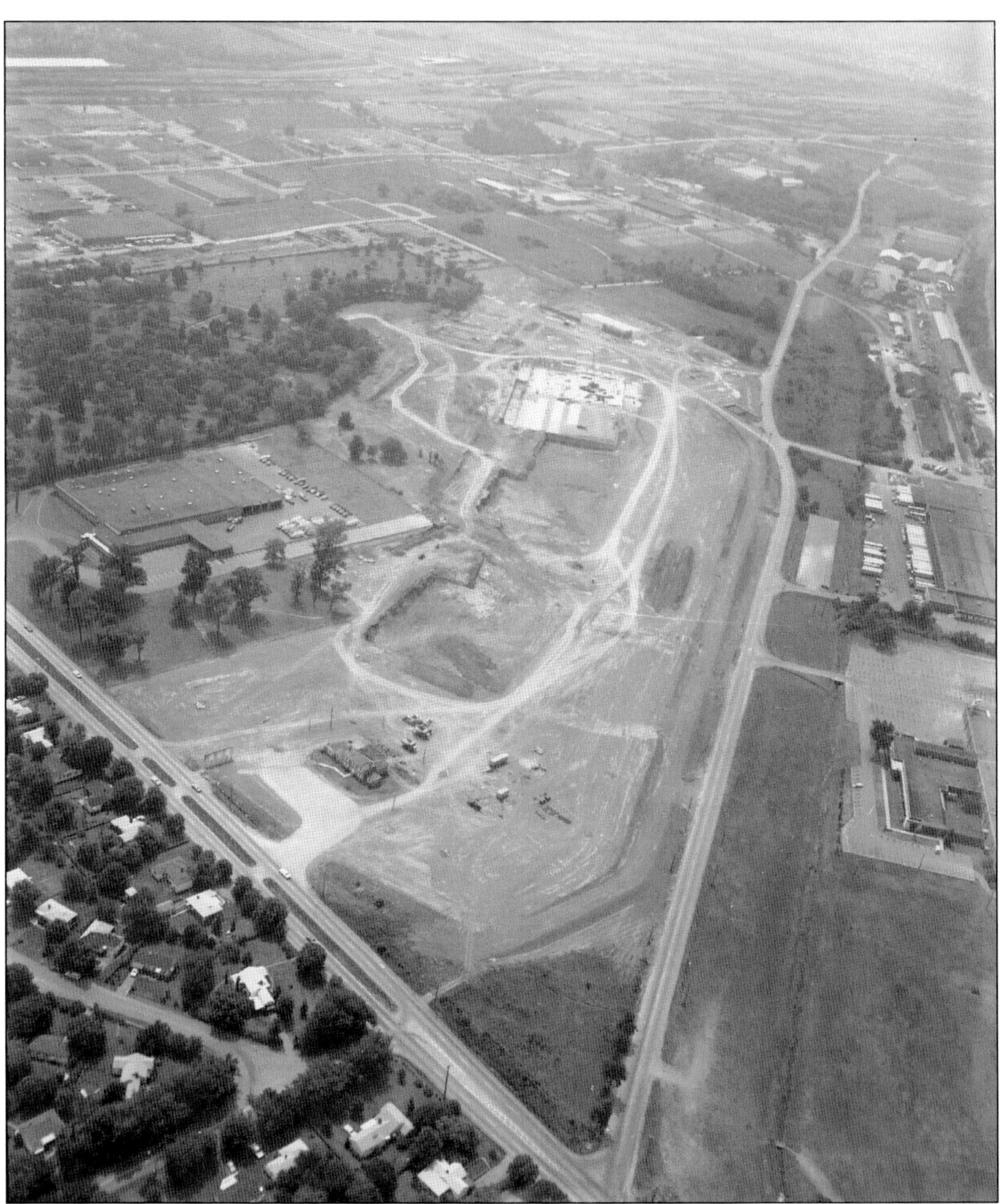

Construction has begun on Nashville's new Hundred Oaks Shopping Center in this 1966 view. Located at Thompson Lane, left, and Powell Avenue in the city of Berry Hill, the indoor mall would be one of the largest retail centers in the Southeast. The development took its name from a picturesque log home, shown at the bottom of the image, which had been on the site since the 1930s. The property surrounding the house was reportedly once surrounded by 100 oak trees. Over time, locals referred to the structure and land as "Hundred Oaks." It would be nearly two years after the ground breaking before the shopping center's completion in late 1967. Since the photograph was made, the area around the development has changed dramatically with big-box stores, restaurants, and commercial property replacing the residential areas and open land on the opposite sides of both streets. (Nashville Public Library, Special Collections.)

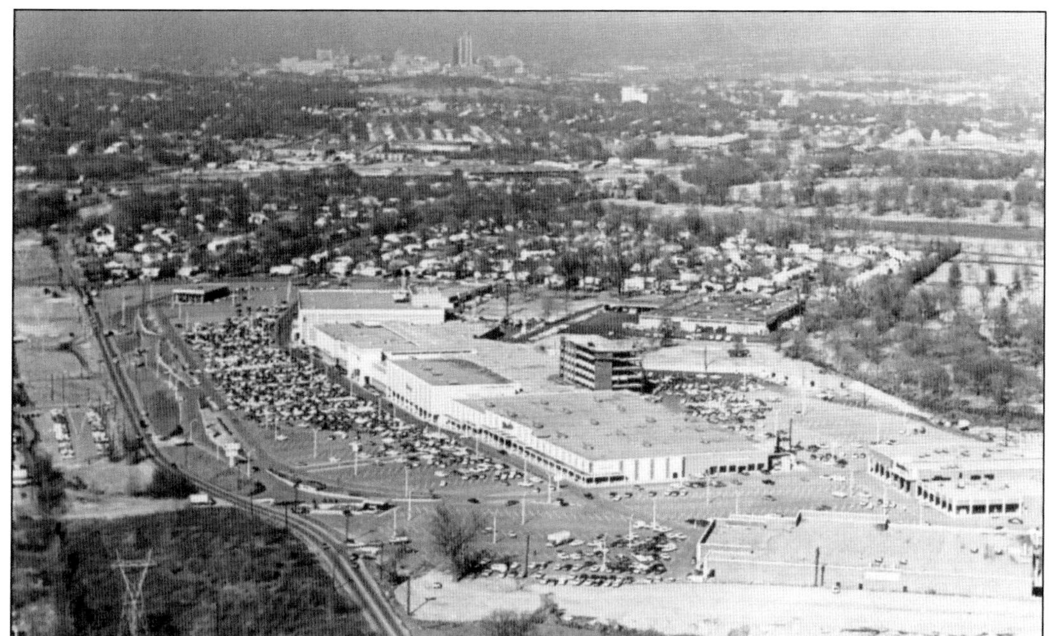

It was with great fanfare when Hundred Oaks Shopping Center opened to the public in late 1967. Located in South Nashville near Berry Hill, the 42-acre facility included a six-story office building, three major department stores, movie theater, 24-hour grocery store, and approximately 46 shops and restaurants. At the time of its opening, it was considered to be one of the largest retail shopping centers in the Southeast. Below, officials gather to plant a symbolic oak tree sapling at the sprawling shopping center during the October 26, 1967, dedication. Pictured from left to right are Secretary of State Joe Carr; Jack Belz, vice president of Belz Investment Company; Jewell Fulton, representing her husband, US representative Richard Fulton; Nashville mayor Beverly Briley; and Roy Shainberg, leasing agent for the center. (Above, Metro Nashville Archives; below, Nashville Public Library, Special Collections.)

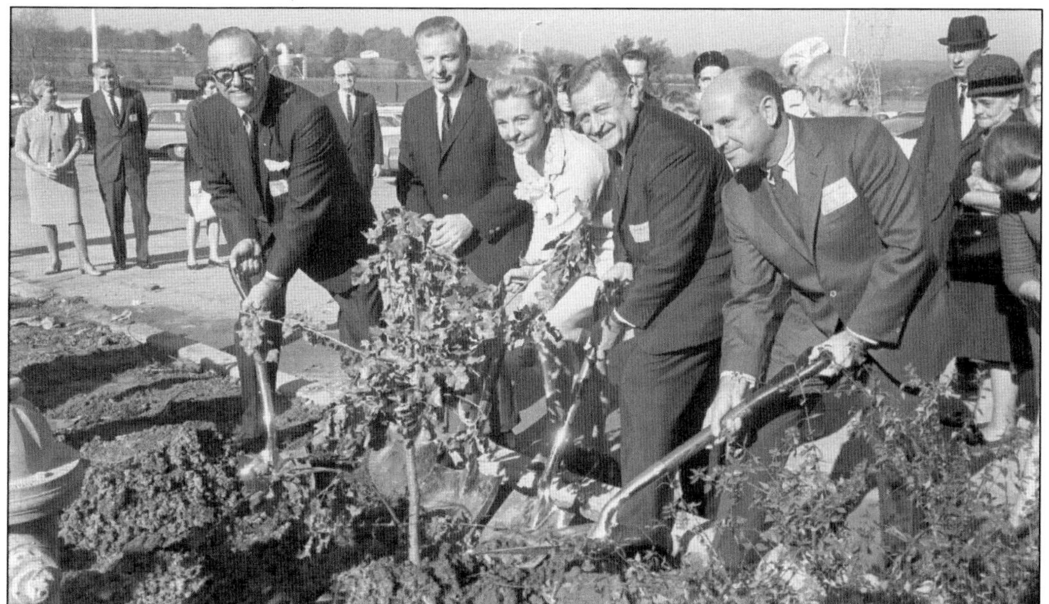

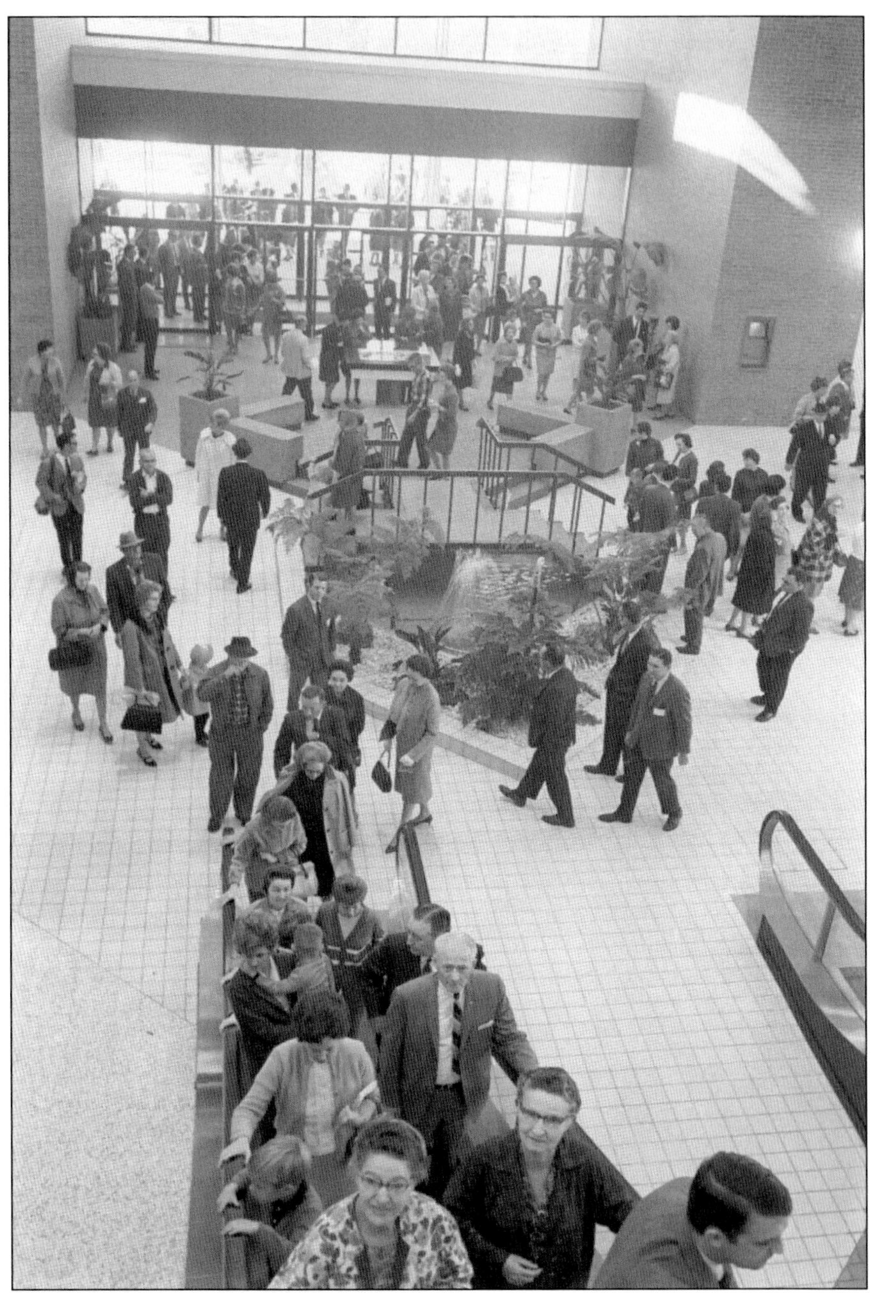

Hundreds of shoppers stream into the spacious lobby of Hundred Oaks Shopping Center as the mall officially opens on October 26, 1967. Although the two-level facility was not Nashville's first indoor mall, it was arguably the most impressive, offering three major department stores, numerous shops and restaurants, movie theater, drive-in banks and the city's first 24-hour super market. The appeal of a spacious parking lot and proximity to major highways gave the center an advantage to shopping downtown adding to the 1960s exodus to the suburbs. Ironically, decades later, Hundred Oaks Shopping Center fell out of favor with customers who preferred to patronize larger and more modern malls farther out of town. In recent years, the former mall property has been redeveloped into a medical center. (Nashville Public Library, Special Collections.)

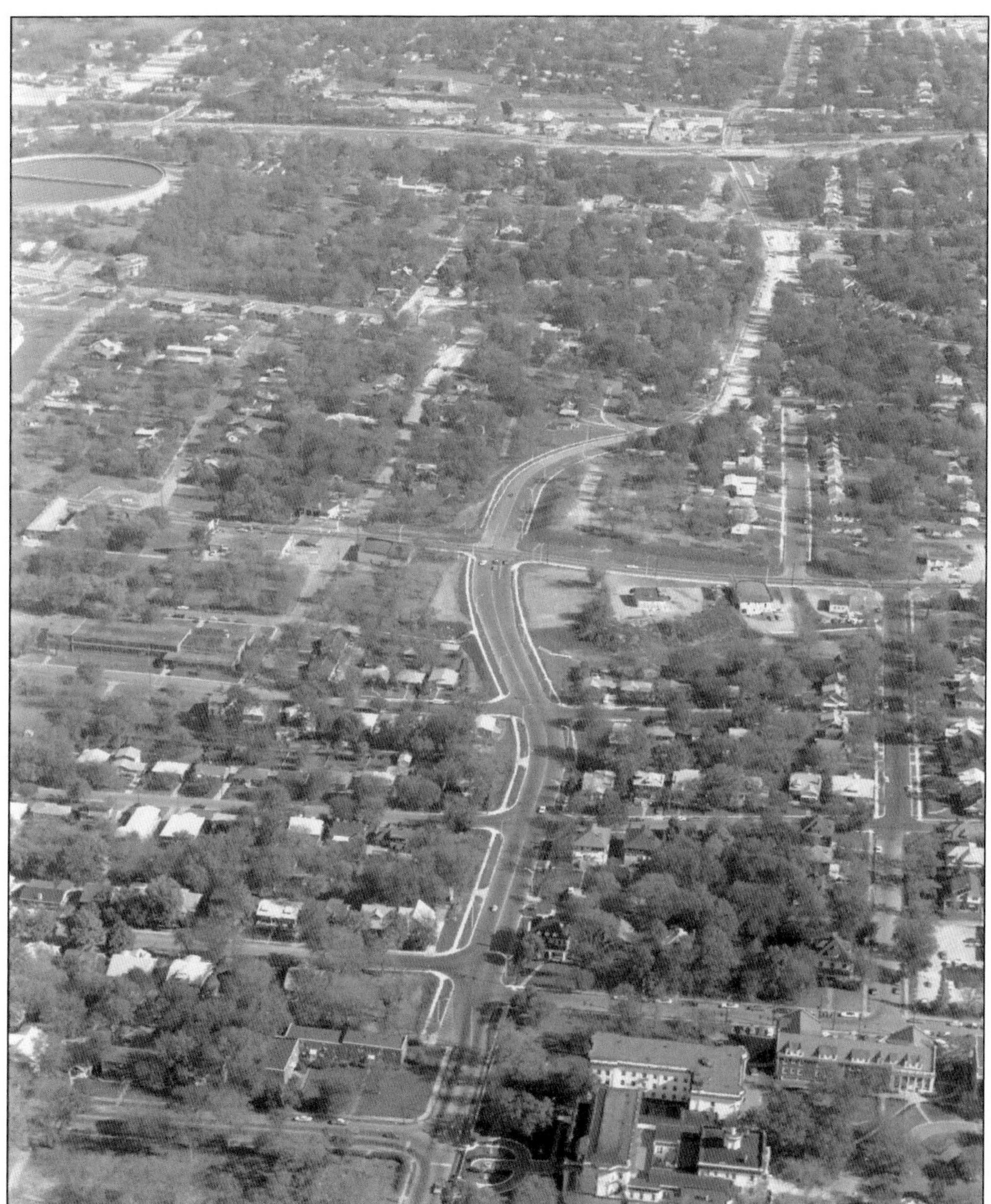

As part of the ongoing urban renewal projects in South Nashville during the 1960s and 1970s, new cross-town arterial streets were constructed to improve the flow of traffic. Often referred to as "belt connection roads," these new thoroughfares were designed by extending an existing street by realigning and widening it, resulting in the razing of many homes and businesses within the new right-of-way. In the early 1970s Wedgewood Avenue was extended west from Eighth Avenue to Twenty-First Avenue South to create a four-lane east-west boulevard using portions of Acklen, Grove, and Belcourt Avenues. This attractive new street gave improved access to the universities in the area, the interstate and the state fair grounds. Facing east, the completed Wedgwood Avenue, with its new curbs and sidewalks, is clearly visible in this image from about 1972. Belmont College can be seen near lower right corner. The City Reservoir and Interstate 65 are at the top. (Metro Nashville Archives, MDHA Collection.)

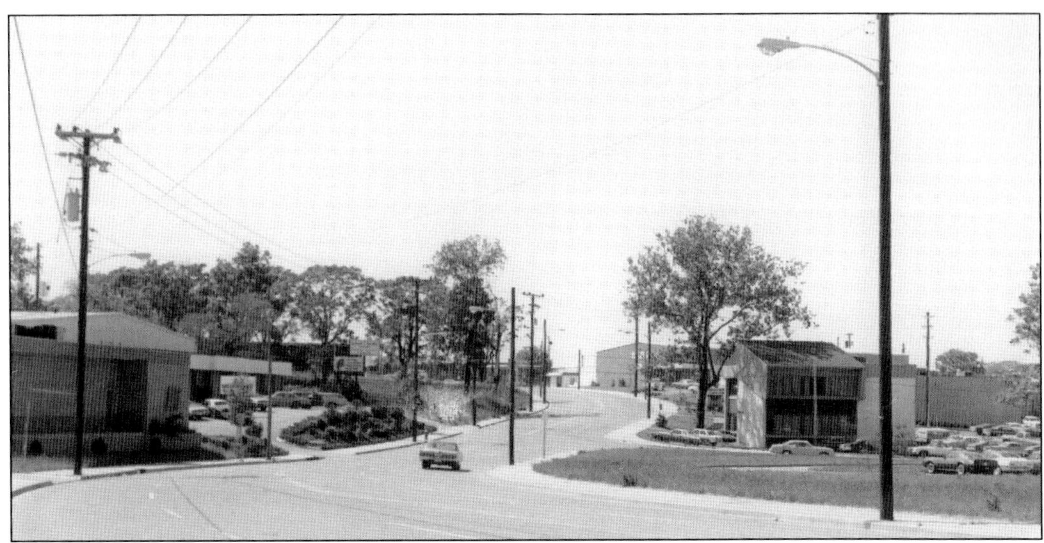

During the early 1970s, Division Street was realigned between Eighth and Twelfth Avenues as part of the continued modernization of the Edgehill neighborhood. This was done to create a new east-west artery and also to commercially redevelop the area. This view, made around 1974, faces west down Division from Eighth Avenue South. The street was extended east to Lafayette Street in 2017. (Metro Nashville Archives, MDHA Collection.)

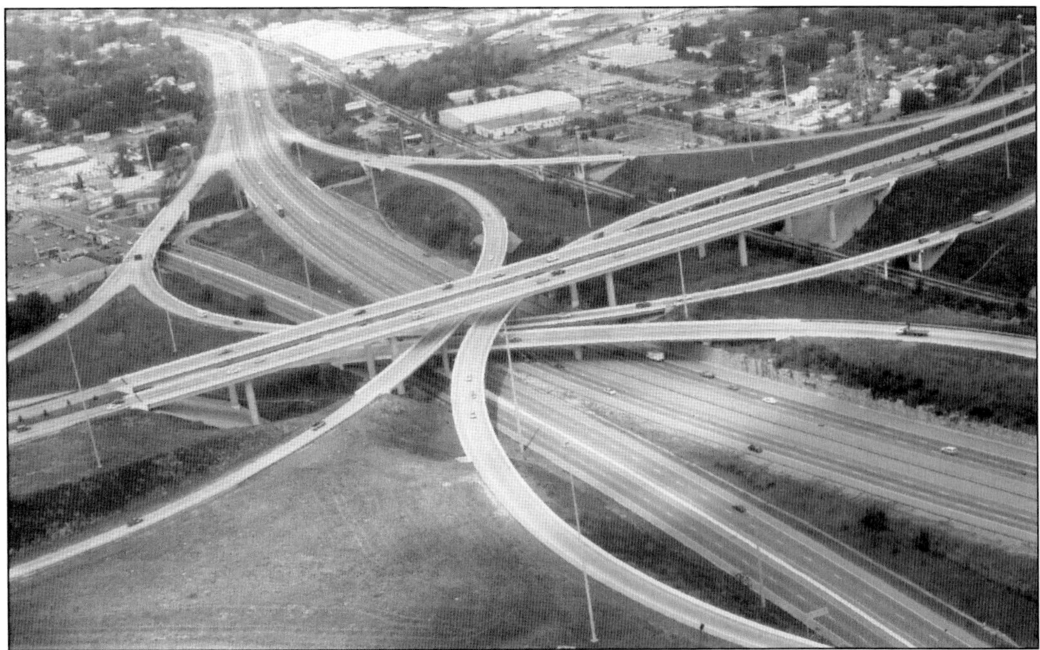

Wide-scale removal of residential and commercial buildings continued into the 1980s with construction of Interstate 440, also known as the city's Outer Loop, connecting all three of the city's interstate highways. The path of Interstate 440 was built over the right of way of the former Tennessee Central Railway and designed to allow traffic to bypass the downtown area. This view faces northeast of the Interstates 65 and 440 interchange near the city of Berry Hill. Since being opened to traffic in 1987, it remains the only four-level interchange in Tennessee. (Ralcon Wagner collection.)

Bibliography

Mertie, Scott R. *Nashville Brewing*. Charleston, SC: Arcadia Publishing, 2006.
Nashville American, *Nashville Banner*, and *Nashville Tennessean*. Various issues (1863–1978).

Consistent with our mission to preserve history on a local level, this book was printed in South Carolina on American-made paper and manufactured entirely in the United States. Products carrying the accredited Forest Stewardship Council (FSC) label are printed on 100 percent FSC-certified paper.

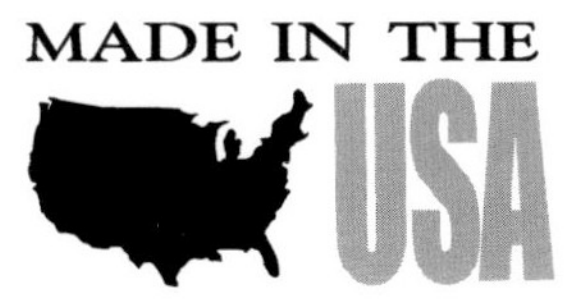